T0283278

Praise for *Book of Queens*

"In this magnificent story, Mahdavi unearths the tale of the feminist horsewomen warriors who from Persia to the contemporary Middle East overcame political tragedy and personal cruelty, creating a fighting force of their own and passing on their skills, defiant wisdom, and courage from generation to generation. Mahdavi weaves memoir, history, and recent events into an unforgettable narrative about East and West, the tragic costs of war, and the transformative power that bravery coupled with the bonds of sisterhood can unleash."

—KAREN J. GREENBERG, Center on
National Security, Fordham Law

"A fascinating story that follows Iranian women and their horses through generations of history. The window into their extraordinary bravery and resilience should serve as an inspiration to women everywhere. A must-read for those seeking stories of female empowerment and courage."

—JESSICA DONATI, author of *Eagle Down: The Last Special Forces
Fighting the Forever War*, a *Financial Times* Book of the Year

"An exciting, passionate story about a long bond of women and horses set against a backdrop of upheaval and war. Pardis Mahdavi's research is impeccable but even more, she is also a gifted storyteller who immerses us deeply into this world of courageous women and their incredible devotion to their horses. I loved this book!"

—ELIZABETH LETTS, #1 bestselling author of
The Perfect Horse and *The Ride of Her Life*

"*Book of Queens* is a riveting tale of intergenerational strength and the sheer power of cross-species bonds. A virtuoso storyteller, Pardis Mahdavi weaves together the voices and experiences of these fearless horsewomen and their fierce dedication to protecting each other, their horses, and the land they love. Inspiring and captivating from page to page, *Book of Queens* makes the mind and heart race—almost as if the reader is spirited along by a Caspian itself made out of words."

—CHRISTOPHER SCHABERG, author of
Adventure: An Argument for Limits

"A story worthy of Graham Greene . . . . Horse lovers will be fascinated, but with her focus on geopolitics and women's rights, Mahdavi reaches many audiences."

—*Kirkus Reviews*

BOOK *of*
QUEENS

ALSO BY PARDIS MAHDAVI

*Human Rights at the Intersections: Transformation through Local,
Global, and Cosmopolitan Challenges, co-editor*

Hyphen (Object Lessons)

Crossing the Gulf: Love and Family in Migrant Lives

*Migrant Encounters: Intimate Labor, the State, and Mobility
Across Asia, co-editor*

From Trafficking to Terror: Constructing a Global Social Problem

Gridlock: Labor, Migration, and Human Trafficking in Dubai

Passionate Uprisings: Iran's Sexual Revolution

BOOK *of* QUEENS

The True Story of the
Middle Eastern Horsewomen
Who Fought the War on Terror

PARDIS MAHDAVI

NEW YORK

Hachette Books
Hachette Book Group
1290 Avenue of the Americas
New York, NY 10104
HachetteBooks.com
Twitter.com/HachetteBooks
Instagram.com/HachetteBooks

First Edition: August 2023

Published by Hachette Books, an imprint of Hachette Book Group, Inc. The Hachette Books name and logo are trademarks of Hachette Book Group, Inc.

The Hachette Speakers Bureau provides a wide range of authors for speaking events. To find out more, go to hachettespeakersbureau.com or email HachetteSpeakers@hbgusa.com.

Books by Hachette Books may be purchased in bulk for business, educational, or promotional use. For information, please contact your local bookseller or Hachette Book Group Special Markets Department at special.markets@hbgusa.com.

The publisher is not responsible for websites (or their content) that are not owned by the publisher.

Print book interior design by Linda Mark.

Library of Congress Cataloging-in-Publication Data
Names: Mahdavi, Pardis, 1978- author.
Title: Book of queens : the true story of the Middle Eastern horsewomen who fought the War on Terror / Pardis Mahdavi.
Description: New York : Hachette Books, 2023. | Includes bibliographical references.
Identifiers: LCCN 2023018259 | ISBN 9780306832130 (hardcover) | ISBN 9780306832154 (ebook)
Subjects: LCSH: Horsemen and horsewomen—Middle East--History. | Caspian horse—Middle East—History. | Firouz, Louise | Women soldiers--Middle East—History. | War horses—Middle East. | War on Terrorism, 2001-2009—Cavalry operations.
Classification: LCC SF284.42.M628 M34 2023 | DDC 636.1/10956—dc23/eng/20230512
LC record available at https://lccn.loc.gov/2023018259.

ISBNs: 978-0-306-83213-0 (hardcover), 978-0-306-83215-4 (ebook)

Printed in the United States of America

LSC-C

Printing 1, 2023

For Maryam and Louise

The wind of heaven is that which blows
between a horse's ears.

—RUMI

Sometimes, women who aren't perfect are more interesting;
they've done more, or learned something.

—JEAN AUEL, *The Valley of Horses*

Author's Note

A FEW years ago, while sorting through old papers in my parents' storage unit, I discovered a diary written by an old friend. Louise Firouz was an American horsewoman and breeder who moved to Iran in the 1960s, married a Qajar prince, and became entranced by the Caspian horses of her adopted homeland. Her memories and the experiences she wrote about led me to unearth a story of survival—women saving a rare breed of horse, a way of life, the lives of US Green Berets, women saving each other and themselves. It is a remarkable story that is very close to my heart, because the female horse warriors Louise befriended and collaborated with for decades were members of my very own family, my aunts and my grandmother.

This book is a work of nonfiction based on the seven years I spent in Iran (2000–2007), the diaries and oral histories of my family, my field notes from riding horses in Iran and Afghanistan with Louise, and my own archival research. I conducted hours of in-depth interviews with members of my family and villagers from towns that dot the Caspian Sea in northern Iran. I also returned to interviews I recorded with young women for my first book, *Passionate Uprisings: Iran's Sexual Revolution* (Stanford University Press, 2008), and was fortunate enough to spend several months studying the archives at both the International Museum of the Horse in Kentucky and the International Caspian Horse Society in London.

The recollections, conversations, and personal details of the people presented here are based on my own impressions of the memories they shared with me. I also hired fact-checkers to ensure the accuracy of my representation of the events relating to the Caspian horses. I conducted and reviewed hundreds of interviews spanning the last two decades that are documented in transcripts, audio recordings, and stacks of ethnographic field notebooks, which fill the boxes in my family's storage unit. To vividly re-create scenes with accuracy, I tracked down photographs from my father's family and from Louise Firouz's children. For the military sourcing I relied on interviews with two former Green Berets as well as the recently declassified files about the American horse soldiers in Afghanistan.

I have used pseudonyms and, in some cases, combined characters to protect the identities of the individuals involved. In the rare case where I couldn't confirm exact details or dialogue, I have re-created them with help from my interviewees and, when possible, reviewed those scenes with those depicted.

Prologue

O N THE TWENTIETH ANNIVERSARY OF 9/11, I CLIMBED UP ON
my horse to ride, remember, and reflect. It was hard to believe it
had been twenty years since I'd watched the towers fall from my tiny
Manhattan apartment, no idea what might come next. What did happen,
of course, is American special forces invaded Afghanistan, determined
to defeat the Taliban. That's the story in an endless stream of headlines
and media, including the blockbuster movie *12 Strong*. But what Jerry
Bruckheimer and Chris Hemsworth and so many others missed is that
before those operatives could enter Afghanistan, they needed horses. And
they had to be taught how to fight on those horses. And so they were, by
an all-female Afghan army[1] made up of descendants of the region's storied horsewomen. And who helped to train those horsewomen in the first
place? My family members.

But it wasn't only the female riders who were legendary; their horses
were, too. They were Caspians, the oldest breed of horse on the planet
and one that would have disappeared forever if members of my family
hadn't bred it out of extinction.

The Taliban didn't disappear forever, either. By September 2021, they
were a threat again. On that twentieth anniversary, I was out riding my

own imported Caspian sorrel gelding, Ice (or Yakh in Persian), when the news broke that the Taliban had taken Kabul in Afghanistan. I knew it was likely that in a matter of days, they would also take Herat in Iran, where my friends were mobilizing a group of underground feminist freedom fighters. The extremists were also dangerously close to the border with Iran, less than one hundred miles from Mashad, where the Iranian branch of my family lived. I was cantering around a Scottsdale, Arizona, arena, my thoughts a world away, when the woman who owned the barn came running, shouting that Herat had also fallen.

"No! No, no, no, that can't be! That is just f—"

I didn't have a chance to complete the profanity. As soon as I started yelling, Ice pinned his ears, rolled his eyes into the back of his head, reared up, and bucked me off. In my shock, I didn't let go of the long leather reins, and they chafed my palms as Ice dragged me around the arena. Instinctively, I jackknifed my body so I could use my legs to slow us down. After years of being dragged around by horses, not to mention by life, I was finally learning to set aside trauma in favor of harnessing the strength my grandmother and aunts had passed down to me.

"Halt, boy," I said, in the calmest voice I could muster. Blowing hard, he stopped and shook out his dusty mane. I stood up, brushed the dirt from my battered body, and looped my arms around his neck. "They've taken your home," I whispered.

BOOK *of*
QUEENS

MARYAM, 1925

WITH HER MOTHER'S COOKING KNIFE, MARYAM CUT HER long, tangled ringlets and let the clumps of dark hair fall to the ground. Her newly shorn locks curled up and bounced around her shoulders, and Maryam exhaled; she felt a new sense of weightlessness. According to her next-door neighbor, shorter hair was in. Something called "the flapper look." She swung her head back and forth, her protruding chin leading the way.

That chin. The bone that pulled her face forward into the shape of a crescent moon. "It's a brave chin," her mother told her, when her brothers and the other village boys teased her. Maryam grabbed it between her index finger and thumb, pushing as hard as she could, willing her chin to conform. She didn't care about the boys teasing her; nor did she have any interest in being beautiful. What she wanted was to look more like her horse, Shokat, whose exquisite features were delicate but powerful. The chestnut mare's coat was the color of Maryam's favorite winter nuts, and her body was framed by a black mane and tail that matched Maryam's own hair. But where Maryam had an endless maze of curls, Shokat's long, silky mane hung perfectly straight, never tangling in the wind when they rode. As far as Maryam was concerned, there was no face as beautiful as Shokat's. Bulging, intelligent eyes met elegantly hollow cheeks and a firm

1

jaw. Her snout formed a perfect oval; no sharp edges. And she didn't need a protruding chin to prove her bravery.

Shokat had other admirers. Several of the men in the village stopped to stare at the little mare. Their horses, taller and thinner, with triangle ears and pointy noses, clopped up to Shokat, inhaling her scent just the way Maryam loved to do. "Turkoman or Arabian?" the men asked. Maryam knew that these were the types of horses they mounted. She also knew Shokat was unlike any horse that she—or most anyone in the village—had ever seen. Shokat was smaller but walked with longer strides and didn't tire in the summer heat or winter cold.

They had found each other two years earlier when Maryam was only eleven. After a particularly harrowing spat that ended with a large bruise on her forearm from her father's grip as he flung her across the room, the girl ran away from home. Her favorite spot was in the woods by the Caspian Sea. Ever since she could remember, her mother had taken her there to pick green olives in the summers and nuts in the winters. Maryam loved the quiet of these woods. She and Maman walked together, baskets in hand, and feasted on the fruits of their labors, away from everyone else. Sometimes, they played hide and seek; other times they spread out on a blanket, leaves rustling, staring up at the branches and the sky. It was their special time. But as her father's drinking and gambling increased their debts, Maman had less and less time for such mother-daughter adventures. So, Maryam took to going out on her own when she needed the peace only the woods and the sea gave her soul.

When her father hit her for the first time, Maryam felt shaken to her core. She ran as fast as her legs could carry her for what felt like an hour, until she reached the forest. But that day, Maryam found that she wasn't alone. When she entered the woods, she heard the sound of branches snapping and leaves rustling. Still struggling to catch her breath, she inhaled, searching for the familiar scent of the salty sea. Instead, a musky aroma reached her nostrils, and she realized there had to be horses nearby. She reached a clearing between the trees and stopped dead in her tracks.

Seven small, elegant horses in different shades of brown from light to dark grazed on the leaves and olives on her favorite trees. Their exquisite features, muscles rippling, were haloed by the sunlight pouring down through the branches. The horses looked like the mythical creatures her grandmother told her stories about. She had never seen such perfect creatures. They seemed to float rather than walk as they drifted from one tree to another, moving in perfect harmony, unfazed by her presence.

Maryam bit her lower lip, venturing into the middle of the clearing. She was keenly aware that she was outnumbered, but the gentility of the horses soothed her. Three of them drifted toward her, lowering their heads as they approached. Maryam never could explain why in that moment she placed her right foot behind her left and curtsied, but the majesty of the animals seemed to require it. One of the horses blew hard, then brought its head to touch Maryam's as she rose. When their foreheads touched, Maryam felt a wave of warmth throughout her body. As the horse nuzzled in close, resting its rounded cheek against Maryam's nose, she swore her heart skipped a beat before resettling in a new rhythm that matched the animal's. This was a connection she had never experienced before. The horse's kind eyes reminded Maryam of her favorite great-aunt, a woman named Shokat.

"I should call you Shokat," Maryam said to the horse. She folded at the waist to check the underbelly of her new friend, as she had watched other farmers do when trying to determine the sex of their animals. Reassured that this was indeed a mare, Maryam repeated the name. "Shokat!"

The horse swished her tail and licked her lips. Their fates were sealed. The horse gave her new friend the strength to go back and face her perpetually angry father. Shokat followed Maryam home that day and never left.

As soon as she could walk, Maryam began climbing onto the backs of the goats and the sheep that roamed the family farm. It wasn't until she was four years old that she first laid eyes on a horse, but when she did, she could think of nothing else, begging her parents for one. Her mother laughed, but Maryam refused to give up. She worked the neighbors' lands in exchange for the chance to climb up on the backs of their horses for an hour or two. But it wasn't until she met Shokat in the woods that the girl understood what it meant to feel complete. From the moment she swung her leg over Shokat's bare back, hiking up two layers of skirts to expose her wool trousers, and worked her long fingers into the thick black mane, Maryam was in love. The mare became the girl's solace as well as her escape from the suitors who, at her father's behest, began calling.

An experience with a particularly odious suitor compelled Maryam to cut her hair at age thirteen and gallop away into the woods. She hopped on Shokat's back, squeezed her thighs ever so slightly against the mare's belly, and with a click of her tongue, the two were off. It felt like flying, Maryam thought, her strong hands curling around the blue and white snaffle she'd woven. Her father didn't appreciate his daughter's sudden flight at the sight (and pungent body odor) of the latest gentleman caller. He came screaming out of their crumbling adobe house.

Maryam was so busy looking back at her father, trying to ensure he couldn't make out the direction she was headed, that she failed to notice her three brothers. The boys climbed one of the hundreds of olive trees lining their family's farm and began heaving palm-size balls of dirt at her. She instinctively dodged the first hit, but the next one smacked her hard in the shoulder, and the third landed right on top of her head. It felt like an egg cracking, drenching her scalp in dirt and causing her to bleed. She rubbed the soil from her eyes, her lashes nearly caked together.

"Take that, dirty girl!" her brother Asghar shouted. Less than two years Maryam's senior, Asghar's favorite pastime was torturing his younger sister. For as long as she could remember, his days had been spent insulting and playing pranks on her. Ever since Maryam returned home with Shokat in tow, Asghar had taken to calling her "dirty," which she could handle. After all, she did always have dirt caked on her boots and under her nails. Lately, however, Asghar had started in with a crueler word: "ruined." It was a gesture to the whispers in the village that girls who rode horses were seen as "damaged goods" by prospective suitors. Unfortunately, her brother's latest taunt had caught their father's attention, and he forbade her to ride.

"That's absurd." Her mother came to Maryam's defense.

"You're absurd," her father retorted. "I will not have my only daughter spoiled by that . . . that . . . that creature."

"Shokat isn't a *creature*, Baba. She's my best friend!"

This pronouncement sent Maryam's brothers into fits of laughter and a fresh round of insults claiming Maryam didn't have any human friends. She didn't care. She didn't need people. She far preferred the company of horses and other animals.

But now her father had seen her galloping across their property, hips swinging, hair billowing.

In a flash, her brothers descended the tree and landed on the ground in front of her. They lined up in formation, shoulder to shoulder, to make a human barricade that Maryam could not—or would not—cross. But Shokat had no respect for these boys. Her hooves pounded the ground, and she let out a snort.

Maryam's almond-shaped eyes widened. She pulled herself forward and grabbed a fistful of Shokat's mane. She gritted her teeth, which only made her chin protrude even more. Head held high, Shokat went straight for Asghar. At the last moment, Maryam's brothers dove out of the way. She pulled back gently on Shokat's mane and tightened her buttocks as they passed. Shokat slowed to a halt then turned around to face Asghar, who was rubbing his jaw and pouting. The horse reared up on her hind legs, and Maryam felt invincible. She felt her heart pounding throughout her entire body. The blood seemed to heat up as it beat through her veins.

"I hate you! I hate this whole family!" she cried.

"Then go live in the forest with your horses for all we care, dirty girl!" Asghar shot back. Amir, the eldest of the boys, rose slowly to stand in front of Asghar, second in birth order and just eighteen months Maryam's senior. His confused scowl contorted his entire face, wrinkling his leathered skin from forehead to chin.

Amir shared his brother's frustration with Maryam, but he didn't want to get in trouble with their father by acting without his permission. "Enough, brother. Enough. Leave her be."

"Maryam!" Baba's voice echoed across the freshly tilled soil. She saw something in his eyes she didn't recognize—was that fear? Shokat reared again, and Maryam held her father's shocked gaze a second longer before squeezing her left leg and clucking. They were off, galloping toward the safety of the forest. This time, Maryam didn't look back. She let the rhythm of the pounding hooves calm her trembling body.

When they had ridden for several miles and the throbbing of Maryam's head had lessened, Shokat slowed her gait to a gentle canter and then a trot. Maryam loved the trot. Her curls bounced in perfect rhythm with the beat of Shokat's hooves. It was almost enough to make her forget about the look in her father's eye—*almost*. She fought the shiver weaving down her spine, and the horse slowed to a walk.

"It's all right, my love," Maryam whispered. She looped her arms around Shokat's neck and stretched forward, resting her chin on the silky mane. This was her favorite position. She would sleep like this if she could. Once, her eldest brother, Amir, had caught her like this and grabbed her by the hair, yanking her to the ground.

"Don't ever let anyone see you lying down like that, abjee," Amir had said. "Legs spread open, ass in the air. It's a disgrace." When her brother finally walked away, Maryam started bawling. *Why was it that the thing she loved most in life was the greatest threat to everyone around her?*

Deep in the comfort of the forest, Maryam fell asleep on Shokat's back. When she opened her dirt-crusted eyes, it was dusk. They had been gone for at least eight hours. She took a deep breath, smelling saltwater. Shokat had led her back to the Caspian Sea. She gulped the salty air and guided Shokat toward the clearing at the edge of the woods. She heard the water then tasted it before she saw it.

When Shokat's hooves sank into the sand, Maryam dismounted and helped the mare find her footing. Then she took off her boots and tied up the fabric of her ill-fitting dress and rolled up her trouser legs. Together, they walked into the sea. Maryam basked in the peacefulness of the water. Not another soul to be found for miles. The sea stretched all the way across the horizon. It was calm, with only the gentlest waves lapping up to the shore. Maryam looked to the edge of the water to watch the last of the sun melting into the sea. Shokat rolled in the shallow water, spraying sand every which way. Maryam laughed and laughed, splashing cool water on them both.

"I'm never going back there," she told Shokat and the sea.

The sunset ignited the sky in shades of orange, yellow, and cherry red. *Why do sunsets always look like the fruits in our orchard?* Just imagining her favorite cherry tree made Maryam's mouth water. She hadn't eaten all day—her father had wanted her to look "perfectly thin" for the suitor. Maryam looked up at the darkening sky, seeing first one star and then another, and realized she was wet, caked in mud and sand, and starving. She tied Shokat in a grove of palm trees lining the edge of the beach and went to gather wood for a fire. Maryam knew she would have to walk deeper into the forest to find olive trees and branches, as her mother had taught her that the palms were no good for burning.

The girl was nothing if not resourceful. Within minutes, she also found olives, nuts, and several varieties of citrus fruit. She warmed herself by her crackling fire, listened to the waves, and savored every delicious bite of her feast.

By the time the moon was directly overhead, its round reflection mirrored in the ripples of the sea, Maryam was dry and satiated. But she felt a stabbing pain in her heart. She wanted her mother desperately. Wanted to hear her sweet voice reading a story or singing her and the sheep to sleep.

LOUISE, 1945

OUISE OPENED HER EYES. IT WASN'T YET DAWN, BUT SHE KNEW the cows were likely already up if she could detect the delectable scent of dew-fresh grass. She stretched and wrapped herself even more tightly in the quilt her mother had gifted her on her seventh birthday— five years ago, now. They had only just moved from Washington, DC, to Forestville, Virginia, then, and her mother had hoped the quilt would make the farm feel more like home. Forestville, which would be renamed Great Falls some years later when the big-city politicians moved in, was only a thirty-minute drive from the nation's capital, but might as well have been a world away. Their farm stretched for more than a hundred acres, and Louise still wasn't sure where it ended. Some days she looked up at the sky and wondered if their farm was as endless as the clouds. Each day, she and her brothers, John and David, rose beneath Virginia's early-morning mist to milk the cows and lay fresh hay for the horses, who swished their tails in greeting and, more than anything else, made Louise feel at home.

Climbing out of bed, the girl dragged the quilt with her, draping it around her bare arms. Summer was over. Soon, she'd be wearing the sweaters her grandmother had once knitted for her mother, which now fit Louise. Fall meant leaves bursting with brilliant hues of red, yellow, and orange, which she loved, but it also meant going back to school, which she did not.

She fought a shiver that wound its way along her spine as her bare feet shifted across the cold stone floor. Louise crept quietly through the redbrick home that reminded her of a schoolhouse, careful not to wake her father who was, yet again, sleeping on the living room couch. He was curled in a fetal position, his six-foot-two frame too big for the worn love-seat. Louise's heart ached for him, but it ached more for the horses waiting in the barn. The horses, at least, would be happy to see her. And she knew what to do for them.

As soon as she opened the front door, the smell of cool, damp soil filled her nostrils. She could almost taste the freshness of the dirt. It would be a good crop season for the root vegetables, after all. The chickens were clucking, the cows mooing, the horses neighing, and hearing them all, Louise couldn't help smiling, the last vestiges of sleep slipping away.

Her parents had purchased the run-down "pre–Civil War era house" and its red barn in 1939, just as the Second World War was intensifying. Moving to the farm taught young Louise that city life was not for her— she needed to live someplace where she could smell the changing of the seasons before she saw them. Where she could inhale the scent of the earth.

John, her elder brother, was pacing the length of the barn, ostensibly counting supplies, but he looked tired and distracted. He turned and greeted his younger sister. There were dark circles under his blue eyes again, and Louise felt another ache in her chest. John knit his brows and nodded, confirming what she already knew—that he had been up all night listening to their parents fight. The Laylin children understood that World War II was being fought overseas, but they couldn't help feeling as though they were at the front lines of another great war.

Louise pulled out a milking stool. She cracked her neck and knuckles as she had seen her mother do, before dropping into the squat that would strengthen her thighs and quads forever. David, the youngest child, was already hard at work on Misty, their most bountiful cow.

"I think I'm allergic to math," David announced. He stood from his squat to bring in a fresh bale of hay, then slid the dividing barn door tightly shut to ensure that the horses would not interrupt their milking chores.

"I think I'm allergic to hay," John quipped, blowing a raspberry for effect. David threw a fistful at him, and John tried unsuccessfully to dodge. A large chunk landed on his head. Louise grabbed onto a bale, and the three siblings erupted into a full-out hay fight. Louise wriggled and wormed as the rough hay clawed at her skin. The cows chewed their breakfast lazily, unfazed by the ruckus around them.

"Okay, stop it," John finally told them, winded. "We'll never get to school on time if we don't get these chores done."

"I think I'm allergic to school," Louise said, laughing. "Maybe we should skip today and go riding through the forest." Though she was the youngest of the Laylin children, she was already catching up to her brothers in height. Like John and David, her eyes sparkled a clear blue when she smiled. Unlike her brothers, however, she had long, unkempt blonde hair that she cut herself with her mother's sewing scissors. David teased that her hair was going to turn into string if she kept using those angled scissors.

"Mother will kill us. It's the *first* day," John protested. He ducked to avoid another barrage of hay his sister flung in his direction. But when he placed both of his hands up, they all stopped.

"Mother won't even notice," David sighed, as he began milking the third cow. "As long as the cows are milked, the horses fed, and the chores done, she won't know whether or not we even went to school."

Louise could hear the disappointment in her brother's voice. She blinked back a tear forming at the corner of her eye. In the years since they had moved to the farm, their parents had increasingly focused on supporting the war effort while arguing more and more with each other, leaving the children to fend for themselves. She shook her head, trying to shake off the heaviness they all felt, and a mischievous grin spread across her face. "You know, the chinquapin nuts are in season now. Can't you smell 'em? Let's go nut foraging!"

"Yes!" David agreed.

But John shook his head. "I'm going to school today to learn something. At least one of us is going to need a job when we're old."

"I *am* learning, John. I'm learning to lay hay, to train horses, and to live off chinquapin nuts, in case the world ends," Louise retorted, pursing her lips like the horses did when they wanted to challenge alpha members of the herd. She rolled her shoulders back to stand as tall as she could.

"That's reckless. You can't abandon school," her eldest brother shot back.

Louise shook her head. "What I can't abandon are the *horses*."

"Let's grab the Johnson kids and the Lawrences," David said. "We'll do a long ride through the forest to the river. And go swimming!"

"We can discuss what we want to do with our lives while we swim, too, so it'll almost be like we're in school with John."

"As Father would say, 'You are insolent children,'" John sighed.

"Father thinks everyone is insolent," Louise muttered. Her parents' shouting matches happened practically daily now, and they followed a pattern. Their mother would accuse their father of being overly obsessed with his career and of not being there for the family. He'd retort that his job as a prominent international lawyer demanded his full attention and that his contribution to the family was financial. It was, he argued, his income that allowed them to purchase and run a farm with all their horses and cows. The farm life was not his dream, he would point out. He had made the move to Virginia to appease his ungrateful wife.

Louise hated that the walls of their house were so thin that she could hear every painful word. At dusk, when the fighting began, she and her brothers scampered out to the barn, seeking refuge with the horses.

Her parents argued enough for everyone in the household, and the children made a pact to be kind to each other and do their best—however difficult—to keep their own bickering to a minimum.

Some nights, Louise and her brothers rode into the woods and made camp. The open sky, with the constellations her brother told stories about, was their solace. Louise let the brightness of the stars and the cool night air wrap her in the reassurance of the universe.

Their mother was so consumed with her crumbling marriage that she completely missed the fact that two of her children never learned physics, math, or how to write cursive. All she cared about was that they were doing their part to train the horses and help keep the farm running. They gave lessons to neighbor children and exercised other farmers' horses as a way to add to the family income.

Because they had moved away from their relatives in DC and because their own nuclear family was breaking apart before their eyes, Louise found herself and her brothers relied more and more on the horses for comfort and consistency. They found quiet solace in the companionship of the animals, whose love was unconditional. Louise adored how the horses bobbed their heads, licked their lips, and swished their tails in excitement whenever they saw her. When she brushed out their manes and picked their hooves, a sense of calm washed over her and the heavy burden she carried melted away. Louise never felt freer from the confines of a confusing world than when she galloped through the trees atop her horse.

"The more I get to know people, the more I love my horse." Some of her school friends had pillows or plaques stitched with this phrase, and Louise was certain truer words had never been spoken.

MARYAM, 1925

MARYAM MUST HAVE DRIFTED OFF AGAIN BECAUSE SHE AWOKE suddenly to the sound of hoofbeats cantering toward her. She scrambled to her feet and grabbed the sharpest stick in the woodpile. She put her body in front of Shokat's, but her horse seemed oddly calm.

The cracking of branches under hooves drew closer. Maryam looked out at the still, moonlit sea. Should they run? Terror rose in her throat, and she turned, vomiting up all the fruits and nuts she had eaten for dinner.

"So . . . not exactly a warrior . . . but pretty close?"

The phrase was familiar, and the voice too.

Maryam looked up. Was that really her mother perched atop a magnificent white horse? Had her mother always known how to ride? The girl's mouth fell open as she took in the sight of her mother, the horsewoman.

Maman slid expertly off the horse and began to rub her daughter's back. Maryam folded tearfully into her mother's arms. They sank into the sand, Maman stroking her hair.

"Why didn't I notice you had cut your hair?" Maman asked.

Maryam used the soft fabric of her mother's cotton dress to wipe her face. "Why didn't I know you can ride a horse?" she returned.

"You're not the only Gordafarid in this family, daughter," Maman said. Maryam's entire face brightened at the mention of her favorite character from her favorite bedtime story.

Maman gently released Maryam and unfurled a blanket that she had rolled up behind the makeshift saddle. Maryam helped Maman drape the blanket on the soft sand next to the fire and let herself fall back into her mother's arms. As she laid her head in her mother's lap, Maryam begged Maman to tell her the story of Gordafarid and the *Book of Kings*.

The *Shahnameh*, or *Book of Kings*, was not just a family favorite in the Mahdavi household, but a national treasure. Part history, part legend, part mythology, and penned by the Persian poet Ferdowsi. At more than fifty thousand two-line verses, the epic tells the story of the rise of the Persian Empire and how Greater Iran took shape. It was about bravery, family, culture, and love. And while most of the stories were about kings and heroes, Maryam always pointed out that the poem should have been called *ShahbanoNameh*, or "Book of Queens." The female characters, from the queens to the princesses to the brave warrior Gordafarid, were the linchpin of every story Ferdowsi crafted.

Maryam liked best the tales of women like Tahmineh, the cunning princess who gave birth in secret to the son of Rostam, who was lauded as the greatest Iranian Pahlevan, or warrior prince. She loved the power of Rudabe and Sudabe, women who inspired great kings like Zal and Siyavash to lead armies of men and horses into unknown lands. But Maryam's favorite character by far was the great warrior princess Gordafarid. The first time her mother read her the story, Maryam almost cried with joy. Here was a woman she could relate to.

Gordafarid was the daughter of Gazdaham, a brave Pahlevan from Persia. Before she could speak in complete sentences, her father trained her to ride, shoot, and fight atop their magnificent horses. One day, the rising warrior Sohrab, son of Princess Tahmineh and the greatest Pahlevan

Rostam, arrived at the famous White Fortress, the gateway protecting Greater Iran, and challenged the inhabitants to a duel. Sohrab was on a mission: he wanted to conquer all of Greater Iran, both to make his father proud and to show him that he—Sohrab—was worthy of the family name. He was also trying to find his father, whom he wanted to install as the ruler of all Persia. But first, he had to get through the White Fortress.

Hojar, the commander of the White Fortress, reluctantly agreed to a duel with the young warrior. During hand-to-hand combat, Sohrab quickly defeated Hojar by lassoing him with a rope and then hanging him on the fortification's wall for all to see. The other warriors in Hojar's army panicked. Who was this fearless challenger who had bested their leader in seconds?

"Who is next?" Sohrab boomed for all to hear. "Come out and fight, or surrender the fortress and be gone."

Gordafarid watched this scene with a mixture of anger and disgust. Why was no one standing up to this Turanian warrior who had come to take their land? This would not do. Ferdowsi explained in painstaking detail what Gordafarid did next:

> But one of those within the fortress was a woman, daughter of the warrior Gazdaham, named Gordafarid. When she learned that their leader had allowed himself to be taken, she found his behavior so shameful that her rosy cheeks became as black as pitch with rage. With not a moment's delay she dressed herself in a knight's armor, gathered her hair beneath a Rumi helmet, and rode out from the fortress, a lion eager for battle. She roared at the enemy ranks, "Where are your heroes, your warriors, your tried and tested chieftains?"

Atop her buckskin horse, Gordafarid pounded toward Sohrab and his men, riding fearlessly. The young warrior flashed a wicked smile and climbed up onto his black stallion. Gordafarid drew her bow and arrow, narrowing her left eye and taking careful aim at her opponent—straight for his heart. But he blocked her arrow with his oblong red and gold shield.

Sohrab guided his horse to gallop in a circle while he drew his lance. Charging toward Gordafarid, he leaned forward to launch his weapon with the full weight of his body, and the princess sensed an opening. Sohrab was off-balance. He may have been larger and faster than she was, but his riding skills were no match for hers. Gordafarid caught him off guard by riding toward his side and slicing the lance in half. His weapon splintered in his hands. Sohrab was shocked. Gordafarid took advantage of his confusion to lay her back on the horse so she could use her full weight to kick his ribs, knocking him off his stallion. The horse reared and ran for the woods. Gordafarid followed the enemy horse, determined to bring him home as evidence of her besting this supposed great soldier.

Sohrab's army watched in wonder as Gordafarid galloped away. Sohrab saw their faces and pulled himself to stand. He pushed one of his men off the nearest horse and leaped on, giving the animal as strong a kick as he could muster.

"Catch me if you can!" Gordafarid called over her shoulder, the mane of her buckskin mare flying in the wind.

Was that the voice of a woman? Sohrab nearly fell out of the saddle. *No, it couldn't be. He, the great Sohrab, couldn't possibly have been bested by a woman.* He beat on the horse's rib cage, standing in the saddle as he charged for Gordafarid. When he was close enough, he reached his hand out and yanked her helmet off, sending her long velvety-black hair whipping out behind her. She turned and winked at him as she raced ahead.

Sohrab threw the helmet to the ground with a loud grunt and smacked the hind legs of the horse. She would *not* outride him. When he finally pulled his horse in front of hers, he threw his lasso around the one kink in her armor—her tiny waist. He pulled her off the mare, and she rolled several feet on the ground before managing to push herself upright, dirt caught in her armor and blood streaking her cheek. The princess stood fearlessly in the tall grass, holding the usurper's gaze.

"You win, great man. Now take me back to the fortress," Gordafarid said, with a mischievous smile.

Sohrab dismounted. "Why are you smiling?" he growled.

"I can't wait to see the faces of your men when they realize that the warrior who knocked you off your horse, broke your weapon, and humiliated you is a woman."

Sohrab was silent. He slowly encircled Gordafarid, taking in every detail of her face and eyes. Black hair. Pale skin. Full, pink lips. Dark, terrifying eyes, the same color as his stallion's. This could be the greatest warrior in Greater Iran. But she was a woman.

Gordafarid sensed an opening. "If you let me go, great warrior, I'll return quietly back to the fortress and open the gates."

Sohrab narrowed his hazel eyes. He knew his options were limited. Reluctantly, he untied Gordafarid, who hopped back on her horse, moving more quickly and elegantly than any Pahlevan Sohrab had ever seen. She waved at Sohrab's army as she galloped back to the fortress, and the men stood shocked, their mouths agape, staring at the long black hair cascading down her back.

"Open the gates!" Gordafarid called to the top of the tower. The gates creaked open, and she could hear her attacker following closely. She counted hoofbeats as he drew dangerously close. Sohrab was only moments behind her, but it was enough time for her to slip inside the gates and shut them.

Sohrab threw down his sword in anger. "You said you would open the gates!" he snarled. He didn't care anymore that everyone had witnessed his loss to a woman. All he wanted was the fortress. All he wanted was the power.

Gordafarid climbed to the top of the wall. She looked down at the man, made small. "I said I would open the gates, and I did. I never said I would let you in!"

Laughter rippled through the rows of Sohrab's army. Applause thundered from the Iranian soldiers inside the fortress. And Greater Iran was once again safe from the Turanians. Gordafarid was the true heroine.

"GORDAFARID IS everything that is right with the world, Maman." Maryam tilted her powerful chin up as she looked into her mother's kind eyes.

"You know, daughter, it always surprises me that your favorite character is Gordafarid and not the horses. Book of Queens, yes," Maman said, almost whispering now. "But Book of Horses, too."

She stood to check on Shokat and the white horse she had ridden into the forest. The mares nuzzled her face, and she stroked their manes. Maryam's eyes widened as she watched Maman at such ease with the animals. She had never seen this side of her.

"Maman, how long? How long have you been a horse whisperer? A horse warrior?"

"I'm a horsewoman, not a whisperer or warrior." Her mother smiled, not taking her eyes from the horses who were now nuzzling her shoulders.

"How long, Mamanee?" Maryam was growing impatient. She had a million questions, but her mother seemed a million miles away. She knew that look, that feeling. Once her own gaze was locked in with Shokat, the rest of the world faded.

"Thousands of years, child, thousands of years."

Maryam rose and gently tugged her mother's wrist. Maman shook her head. She took Maryam's hand and wove her own delicate fingers between her daughter's. She placed their hands together on the neck of the white horse, where they could hear her heartbeat.

"The history of our people, Maryam, is intertwined with these horses. The Persian Empire. Greater Iran. All that you love about the *Shahnameh* and Gordafarid. It is the horses who have given us this rich history. The horses gave us empires. They kept us safe in Greater Iran when first the Greeks, then the Turks, and then the Arabs wanted to invade. Think about the *Shahnameh*. When was it written?"

Maryam paused to think about the first few hundred verses of the epic. "It was written exactly one thousand years ago."

"Right. And what language was it written in?"

"Persian, of course."

"Not just Persian, and not of course. It was written in the same Persian that we speak today. The unchanged Persian. The Persian that has no Arabic in it. Many people say that the reason our language survived is the *Shahnameh*. The reason our language survived is because of the history that the *Book of Kings* documented. And that history—our history—our successes and greatness as a people, Maryam joon, is because of the horses."

Maryam nodded, acutely aware of her mother's dark eyes on her face. How much could she see in the flickering firelight?

"Daughter, think about Gordafarid. She couldn't have bested Sohrab without her horse. And she wouldn't have had the advantage if she wasn't a horsewoman, right?"

"Yes, Maman. That's true. I guess I always thought about her as a horse warrior, not a horsewoman."

"She was a warrior because she was a horsewoman. Because she knew, like so many of us women born and raised on the powerful soil of Persia, how to ride *with* her horse, not just atop her horse. Something that Sohrab and all the other men didn't. She was a true horsewoman. Part of her lives on inside each of us."

Maryam's entire body ignited. She felt her insides filling with light, with history, with joy. *A part of Gordafarid inside of me.* She looked at her mother in awe.

"So, when you ask me how long I've been a horsewoman, well, I say at least a thousand years. Because for as long as Persia and Greater Iran have existed, as long as our horses have made us who we are and taught us how to live with the land, to protect the land, that protecting the land is protecting our culture, well, that's how long I've been a horsewoman." Maman braided the manes and tails of the two mares as she spoke. Next, she retrieved a small, curved knife from her pocket and quietly picked each hoof, removing small rocks that had worked their way into the crevices.

"But Mamanee, when did you learn . . . when did your spirit become *one* with the horses?" Maryam was still struggling to wrap her mind around the woman who stood before her, the same one who allowed her father to chastise her every time she touched a horse, permitted him to forbid her from riding, watched as he chased Maryam to the edge of the forest. How could her mother sit by and watch all these years?

"He is my husband," Maman said, as if reading her daughter's mind. "You'll learn one day soon that you must use Gordafarid's cunning when you are in a marriage. You must pick your battles. Know the right time to push and the right time to retreat. That's what it's like with your father."

"Has there ever been a time when you didn't know how to be a horsewoman?"

Maman arched a perfectly plucked eyebrow. The question hung in the air between them.

Maryam chewed her bottom lip—a habit she had developed in trying to make her chin smaller. She couldn't remember not knowing how to talk with horses, how to walk with them, how to gently, steadily, climb up onto their backs, squeeze her legs, and take off.

"It lives in us. Horsewomanship comes from Gordafarid and the powerful female riders before her," Maman explained, shaking sand, stones, and dirt from the folds of her skirt. She tucked the knife back in her pocket and stood to smooth the unruly curls that had escaped her braid. Maryam suddenly realized her mother's ability to exact a perfect braid was likely the result of all the horse manes she had twisted throughout her life.

"It's getting late, Maryam joon. We need to go home. Your father will be sending a search party soon."

Maryam recoiled at the mention of her father. She shook her head so hard, the horses startled. "I'm never going back there."

"Don't be ridiculous, daughter. What kind of Gordafarid are you that you are afraid of your own father?"

"Maman, I can't go back there. Baba, he . . . he . . . and the boys . . ." Maryam's voice trailed off, and she was crying again. She sank down to the sand.

Her mother folded in half and grabbed Maryam by the elbow, pulling her back upright. "Is that what we do? Cower because of men? Is it?" A sudden edge in her voice. Later, Maryam would learn that this was what bravery sounded like when she heard the sounds emanating from her own throat.

"He is going to make me marry that . . . that . . . that monster!" Maryam spat. She shook her head again and writhed free of her mother's grip.

"First of all, that *monster* could buy you two farms and help you feed as many horses as your heart desires—"

"I don't care! He disgusts me! How can you not see that, Maman?"

"Let me finish. If you don't want to marry him—fine. I can help, but you must trust me."

Maryam looked at her mother and then at the horses. Shokat looked different with her mane and tail braided. Horse and girl locked eyes, their gazes steady, their connection clear. Maman climbed up onto the white horse.

"Enough with your tantrum, Maryam. Let's go home."

She was disoriented. The day had started out so badly; she'd felt desperate and afraid. But her mother's revelation had filled her spirit in ways she never could have imagined. Maryam was reluctant to return home to her angry father and cruel brothers, but she was curious about this new horsewoman who carried her history. It was this love and curiosity that gave Maryam the strength to straddle Shokat and follow her mother through the forest and fields.

Baba was waiting at the edge of their farm, smoking hookah by a fire, when the two mares brought the women home. Maryam could see his anger in the swirls of smoke he exhaled through his mouth and nose. She and Maman had deftly slowed their horses' gait from a gallop to a walk a kilometer before their property. They hoped to slip back and quietly put the entire day behind them. No such luck.

Maman brought her horse to a halt, and Shokat followed. Baba stood and threw the glass hookah into the lettuce patch, where it shattered. Neither Shokat nor the white horse flinched. Maryam knew that later she would be the one ordered to pick up every last shard.

"Get off those *things*," Baba snarled. It was then Maryam realized that, instinctively, both she and her mother had stayed atop their horses. It gave them height and an escape.

"Amir, we are not dismounting until you calm down," Maman said, in the sweetest melody Maryam had ever heard tumble off her mother's tongue.

"Calm down? How am I supposed to calm down? *You* and . . . and . . . *that girl*"—Baba couldn't even speak her name—"you have made a fool of me in front of the whole village!"

"That's enough, Amir jaan," Maman soothed. "No one has made a fool of anyone. Your daughter thought she was trying to make a point, but we've settled that, and she has learned her lesson."

"The boys are right: She is a *dirty* girl. She is *ruined*," Baba growled.

"Husband, please—"

"Don't talk to me like that, *woman*! And look at you, back on a horse. You *promised*, wife. You promised that when you became my wife, you—"

"Bastah, Amir! Enough. I promised you I would save my body for you only. And I have kept my promise. But our daughter needed me, and I need to honor the promises I made to my mother, her mother, and her mother before that."

"Shut up!" Baba barked. "I've had enough of this! What do you have to say for yourself?" Baba now directed the full weight of his rage at Maryam. She was grateful to be looking down at his face rather than up, and stroked Shokat's neck to calm herself.

The last several hours played like a slideshow in her mind. The repellant suitor smiling with his yellow teeth and sour breath. Maman handing her a tray of tea to serve their guest. Maryam dropping the tray and running for Shokat. Her father's angry face as he chased her. Asghar, Amir, and Asif hurling dirtballs at her head. And then . . . the forest, the clearing of the trees, the Caspian Sea, and her mother's thundering arrival with her own secret to share. Her mother the horsewoman. The warrior princess who doled out tenderness but donned her sword when necessary. The magnificence of Gordafarid coursing through their veins.

This last image made Maryam smile.

"What are you smiling at, you wicked child?" her father bellowed. He kicked Shokat's leg, and the horse reared up angrily. Maryam hadn't seen the buck coming and fell to the ground. In an instant her father was on her, grabbing her by the collar. She could smell apple tobacco and whiskey on his breath. His hypocrisy disgusted her. He claimed that Maryam shouldn't ride a horse because it was "un-Islamic," but he himself had no problem violating one of the five pillars of their faith.

"Maman is Gordafarid," Maryam spat at her father. "You're just angry because she's making you into Sohrab, humiliating you." Maryam shoved her father and wrenched herself free of his grip. She took two steps toward her mother and the white horse, but her father grabbed her hair and yanked her to the ground, raking her across the carrot and beetroot patches.

"Bastah, Amir! Stop this!" Maman slid off her horse and reached for her husband's hand.

Baba let go of Maryam's scalp, but not before driving his foot into her ribs. "Get her out of my sight!" he yelled.

Maman pulled Maryam up, but the girl fell back to her knees in pain.

"Amir, no. This is unacceptable. Don't be this monster who is taking you over," Maman said, her voice quiet but simmering.

"You think *this* is a monster? I'll show you a monster worthy of the *Book of Kings!*" Amir barked. The two women watched him storm back toward the house, disappearing into the darkness of night.

"I'm sorry, my child. I'm so, so sorry," Maman whispered. She knelt beside her daughter in the vegetable beds. Maryam inhaled the scent of freshly tilled soil. Her mother stroked her hair. Tears slid down her cheeks. As she drifted off into a wounded sleep, the girl wondered if this year's carrot crop would taste of her salty tears.

MARYAM AWOKE to the piercing sound of Shokat whinnying. She tried to sit up but was in too much pain. A loud thud shook the ground. Maman jolted to her feet and pulled her daughter up. Together, they limped toward Shokat's makeshift wooden stable. The purple and navy of night were fading fast, overtaken by the rising morning light, and the girl stared across the field in horror.

Shokat lay on the ground, and Maryam's father stood panting over her, glimmering knife in hand. A pool of red seeped into the black soil beneath the chestnut mare's lifeless body.

Even as the last of Shokat's final cry faded from the air, Maryam's voice took up the call as she screamed.

LOUISE, 1945

AFTER THE SECOND WORLD WAR ENDED AND JUST AS LOUISE was about to start high school in 1945, her parents finally announced they were getting divorced.

Each of the Laylin children coped with this news in their own way. Louise turned to the horses—riding, training, and breeding them to bring in income. David busied himself with taking care of the land. The farm was the children's sanctuary, and it was the one thing they could control. John, meanwhile, threw himself ever more into his studies. He also researched top boarding schools and managed to secure scholarships for both his brother and himself at an academy nearby. John reasoned that boarding school would not be desirable for his little sister, who preferred to run wild with horses than be in a classroom. She deserved a few more years of life on the farm, he told her.

Louise's father had long worried that his children were not scholastically driven. During the inevitable custody battle, he used this concern as ammunition against his ex-wife, arguing that he should get sole custody of the children because their mother was unfit to oversee their education. He succeeded in getting the boys, and John and David were sent to boarding school. To Louise's great relief, however, he lost the argument for his daughter. Instead, she moved with her mother to a farm in New

Hampshire and was able to continue riding her beloved horse, Rhoda, every day.

Louise missed her brothers terribly. In a letter she wrote from New Hampshire to one of her best friends and fellow riders back in Great Falls, she explained, "My brothers were sent off to boarding school, but I stayed with my mom. Our farm is ten miles down a dirt road, and our only neighbors are deer. At first, my mother drove me to the local grammar school every morning. But when it started snowing heavily and our car got stuck, we bought a small Morgan mare, a sleigh, and a buggy. Every day I get up in the dark to hitch up the mare and drive to school, and I hate every minute of it." Louise continued writing to her brothers as well, but tried to create some distance with her father.

As far as Louise was concerned, horses were meant to be ridden freely through the woods and up into the mountains. The only thing she hated more than the long, dark New Hampshire winters was the fact that she couldn't ride her horse, couldn't feel the mare's muscles tighten and ripple beneath her thighs. Instead, she had to sit atop the buggy, doing what little she could to shield herself from the wind and cold, curling in on herself as her father had done all those nights sleeping on the worn loveseat in Virginia.

Slowly, Louise's mother began to emerge from her decade-long depression. Her parents' separation had been painful on many levels, but the newfound peace that developed between her and her mother in New Hampshire gave Louise hope. Her mom was newly invested not only in the farm and the animals, but in her daughter. She listened when Louise complained of her frustrations with the school and the long commute and eventually agreed to enroll her in private school. Mother and daughter cooked together, ate together, worked the land together, and, best of all, rode together.

To get to her new school, Louise rode Rhoda to Hancock, left the mare in a church stable, and took a taxi another twelve miles to reach campus before the bell rang. But this was infinitely better than the buggy. Riding home to her mother's smiling face at the end of the day was worth it. Several times a week her mother rode to the church to meet her, and the two would take the long route home, their horses quickening their hooves in excitement as they rode toward the hills.

But this renewed kinship between mother and daughter was short-lived. When Louise was in her final year of high school, her maternal grandmother died. Now an orphan and struggling with a hip injury that prevented her from riding, Louise's mother closed in on herself.

When John and David visited at Christmas and grasped the situation, they were concerned about not only their mother but also their sister. John invited Louise to stay with him in New York, but she refused, reasoning that she should stick it out these last few months, just until graduation.

Her brothers understood. They told her that she had grown and matured quickly.

"I didn't have a choice," Louise told them. The heaviness of her mother's condition weighed on her. She longed for the days, only months earlier, when she and her mother had ridden in the hills, free of worry and care.

"What will you do after graduation?" John asked. Louise had assumed she would go to college, as her brothers had. But where she would go and what she would study, she had no idea.

"I think I want to be a veterinarian," she blurted out, to her own great surprise.

"That might be tough; your science grades are abysmal," David said, laughing.

"I'll figure it out. I always do," Louise shrugged.

"*We* will figure it out, Lou," John said. "*We* always do."

MARYAM, 1926

B AHAR NARENJ, THE SPRING ORANGE BLOSSOM, BLEW A PER-
fect jasmine-like fragrance from the Caspian Sea across the country, announcing the arrival of the season of rebirth. It was Nowruz, the
Persian New Year, and Iranians were celebrating the arrival of the year
1305 by the Jalali Solar calendar,[1] which marks the passage of time on the
spring equinox. Meanwhile, three months earlier, the rest of the world
had welcomed the dawn of 1926.

Maryam held a shimmering bahar narenj petal in her palm. It was
her favorite flower. Inhaling its strong, comforting scent, she closed her
eyes. She remembered that repugnant suitor and fleeing with Shokat
to the Caspian Sea, where girl and horse feasted on the fruit of the
orange-blossom tree. A tear slid down her cheek. It was the last time she
and Shokat had been together. The last time she had felt alive.

The passage of time was a strange thing. That single day had given her
a year's worth of memories—good and bad. The six months that followed
had evaporated from her mind. Had the sun really set, the moon really
risen, followed by dawn, over and over again? Maryam felt dead inside.
And as if mirroring her soul, the very same day her father had murdered
Shokat, a harsh winter had set in, casting a blanket of frost over their
lands and hardening the soil. Most of the crops were killed before they

even reached the surface, and the few that did manage to burst through died before they could be harvested.

That winter, Maryam mostly stayed in a bed of blankets and straw on the floor of her mother's bedroom. Their house was really a series of five small houses, rooms with gray clay walls and thatched roofs that leaked at the first drop of rain. During the summer months, they often slept outside in woven hammocks or on sheets near the crops. But in winter, they gathered in the warmest rooms. It was often the case that the women slept in Maman's bedroom and the men in the kitchen.

That first week after her father killed Shokat, Maryam had refused to get out of bed and did not eat. She alternated between daylong sleep and sleepless nights. Eventually, she began to take meandering walks through the forest. She willed her feet to carry her farther each time, determined to make it to the sea, but she grew weary and weak and had to lie down beneath the bare winter trees. Maryam watched the citrus fruits she had savored just weeks earlier rot and fall.

On the day the last orange fell, her mother came to her in the forest. This time she rode a gray speckled horse who appeared lame.

"He is the only horse the neighbors would let me borrow," Maman said, her marvelous pink lips curling into a smile.

Maryam wanted to force a smile for her mother's sake. After all, it wasn't her mother who had destroyed her life. If anything, she was the only person in the world who had ever tried to help her. But all she could muster for her dear Maman was a shrug and two raised eyebrows. Maryam had all but stopped speaking, except when she and Maman were alone, and to the neighbor's son, Ali, who brought over his uncle's horses so that she could braid their manes and tails.

Ali, who was the same age as Maryam, didn't speak much either, but he loved to watch his neighbor with their horses. He adored the way the animals knelt before her, relaxing their ears and lowering their heavy heads, and how Maryam took such care massaging their shoulders, knees, and ankles. He marveled that the horses, so jittery around the men in his family, surrendered to his friend.

"How do you do it?" he finally asked, after weeks of observation.

"Do what?" She had forgotten the sound of her own voice and cleared her throat to wring the high pitch out of it.

"The horses. You're magic with them."

Maryam tilted her head, considering. "I surrender to them."

The next day, Ali brought her five shades of yarn and fabric, and they sat together weaving bridles for the horses. When they finished, he sold them at the Friday market and split the proceeds with her. It became their ritual and was the one bright spot in her life.

But today was Friday and Ali was at the market, so Maryam had decided to spend the day in the woods. She had taken to carrying a knife after watching her mother with hers, and she now began using it to carve objects out of the fallen branches. When her mother found her, she was making a tiny wooden horse. She felt the carving coming alive under her hands, the wood warming like when she pressed her palms to Shokat's neck.

"Come now, daughter, I have news. Please, stand up and talk to me."

Maryam stood and tucked the small wooden figurine into the folds of her waistband. She had stopped wearing skirts and dresses, preferring the freedom loose pants afforded her.

"Maman, I don't want to come home. Please leave me here today," Maryam begged.

"I think you'll like this news, child. I really do." Maman slid off the horse. She interlaced their fingers and kissed the top of Maryam's trembling hand. Maryam arched a curious eyebrow.

"It's Ali!" Maman said. She was brimming with excitement.

"*My* Ali?" Maryam puzzled.

"Well, he's about to be your Ali, yes!"

"What?"

"I convinced your father to give your hand to his in marriage!" Maman beamed.

Maryam was stunned. She and Ali had grown close, yes, but marriage? How were two thirteen-year-olds supposed to figure out how to raise a family? Her head spun, and her chest grew tight. Maryam thought she could see a hint of despair in her mother's face, too. Was Maman begging? She was terrified of what her mother was asking her to do, but knew she could proceed gracefully or rage all the way through her vows, but there was no real acceptance involved. She and Ali would wed.

Maryam followed Maman home in a daze. Ali was her friend. Maybe this could work. It would certainly free her from her tyrannical father. She looked at her feet as she walked and couldn't help but notice a softening of the ground beneath her.

Their entire village of Gonbad-i-Kavoos was invited to the wedding, and the next six months passed in a blur of matrimonial preparations. Maryam couldn't face Ali during those months. She shut herself in, emerging only to walk to the woods and back.

As the bahar narenj began yielding its petals to fruits, the wedding day arrived. That morning, Maryam held an orange blossom, tracing the golden edges of its petals. The oranges had fallen, and the flowers had opened. Spring was here. The passage of time, the supple softening of the earth. And now she was supposed to blossom into a woman overnight. Would she be trimmed in gold, too?

The warm sound of Maman's laughter gently interrupted Maryam's reverie. Here was her mother and Maryam's aunt, her mother's only sister, along with several of the other women from the village. As soon as they saw Maryam, they broke out into the guttural nuptial chant.

"Hi, li, li, li, li, li," they trilled, cupping their hands over their lips lest any lusty men catch a glimpse of their luscious mouths curling. "Aroos khanoum! The bride is here! Picking her flowers!"

Maryam blushed. She knew what came next. Her mother, aunt, and the aunties from the village would bathe her, cover her hands in henna, and begin the process of readying her body for her husband.

She followed the women into the hammam.

"Wherever did you get the idea to marry her off to Ali? I mean, he is so young, a child almost," Auntie Parvin said. She began pulling Maryam's hair taut over a series of heated metal rods to create perfect ringlets out of her tangled, wild mane. Meanwhile, her mom's closest friend, Auntie Manijeh, picked her nails clean. Maryam never understood why her aunt and aunties talked as if she wasn't in the room, despite holding parts of her body in their hands.

"Well, he isn't a child, sister. No more than our bride here," Maman said confidently.

"He does come from a wealthier family," Auntie Manijeh said. "I heard his grandfather has twelve servants! And his uncle owns so many horses." Maryam had heard from various relatives that Ali's family was wealthier than theirs, but she did not know what this meant for her as his wife.

Maryam turned her head at the mention of her betrothed and his horses. She imagined Ali, whose deep-set eyes reminded her of Shokat's, riding atop a beautiful black horse with a shiny mane the same color as his thick hair. Maryam loved the way Ali's straight hair flopped over his eyes when the two of them went riding together. She smiled as she remembered the afternoon when Ali asked her to weave him a headband out of the same yarn they used for the horses' bridles. She had chuckled then refused, telling him she loved his floppy hair, using her own delicate fingers to sweep it from his forehead. It was the first time she had touched him. She was surprised at the jolt of energy it sent through her. Now, remembering, she let out an audible sigh.

"Oh, the blushing bride! She must be thinking about her groom!" Aunt Parvin clapped. "So, sister, is our girl marrying for love then?"

"Khaleh Parvin, I'm not—" Maryam stopped. She wasn't sure how to finish that sentence. An awkward silence filled the room.

"Ladies, when I was pregnant with aroos khanoum over here, Ali's mother was pregnant with him as well," Maman said, brushing her daughter's hair from her face. Maryam's whole body relaxed at her mother's touch.

"We worked the land side by side, our bellies bumping, Ruqaya and I," Maman continued. "We joked that the two lives growing inside us were destined to be intertwined. But I had forgotten all about that until I saw Maryam and Ali together, almost grown, lost in their own world."

Maryam couldn't believe it. She looked up through her curling lashes and pulled in her lower lip. "Is that true, Maman?"

"Every word."

"I didn't know."

"There is much you do not know, little bride," Auntie Parvin interjected. "So maybe it's time we tell you about how your body will bloom soon."

"Please, Parvin, she grew up on a farm. She knows how babies are made," Auntie Manijeh commented.

"Well, dear, just remember the orange-blossom tree." Auntie Parvin plucked a gold-trimmed flower out of the basket at Maryam's feet and tucked it behind her ear. "Just like the tree blossoms in the spring and makes the summer soil fertile, so must your body."

"And then will come the citrus fruit!" Auntie Manijeh laughed. Her giggle was contagious. Soon all the ladies were roaring with laughter. Maryam forced a smile but shifted uncomfortably in her seat.

THE NEXT time the orange-blossom tree announced the arrival of spring, it was with an especially lush burst of white petals. Overnight, the entire village was awash with the fresh scent of the bahar narenj wafting through

34

the air. Some of the villagers speculated it would be a particularly good crop if the yield of orange blossoms—double that of the year prior—was any indication.

Like her favorite tree, Maryam's body had blossomed and was yielding new fruit. After a few weeks of bungled attempts following their wedding, Ali and Maryam had figured out what all the farm animals seemed to do so naturally. She was surprised at the way her body unfolded and sang for her husband. And then she had noticed the tiny bump, almost like a nascent navel orange, which had appeared just below her belly button. When she showed it to her mother, Maman had fallen to her knees and kissed the ground. She and Baba, with whom Maryam was still not speaking, sacrificed a goat to share the news with the entire village. They prayed for a boy.

"I don't care if it's a boy or a girl," Ali told Maryam. He gently cupped her stomach as they lay in bed, just a few feet from the olive trees they had climbed as children.

Marrying the next-door neighbor meant Maryam could stay close to her mother and continue to work the family land, which quickly became a necessity. Amir, her eldest brother, had moved to a village near the border with Turkey, where he was training as a carpenter; Asif joined him a few months later. Their father was also spending more time on the road, trading. Then her brother Asghar fell ill. So it was Maryam who took over the farming duties, plowing the land and sowing seeds.

Her father-in-law and his family were prominent merchants. They sold textiles all over Iran and owned land that reached to the Caspian Sea. Envious of such success and distraught over a brutal winter that had destroyed most of their crops, Baba had made business partnership a condition of his daughter's marriage. Now he had all but abandoned the farm in favor of learning merchantry from his in-laws.

Only a few weeks after the wedding, Maryam and her father had had a tense encounter in the forest. She and Ali were riding to where the woods met the sea when she caught sight of her father wielding a large axe. This time his victim wasn't her beloved horse, but one of her favorite trees.

A primal scream escaped her throat, causing her horse to rear. Ali's mount startled, and her husband slipped from the saddle with a sickening crack. Baba froze, and dropped his axe. He turned to see his son-in-law writhing in pain, having fallen on his wrist. Then he saw Maryam. She stared back at him, jutting her chin forward and grinding her teeth. They were in a deadlocked silence that was broken only when Ali pulled himself up and stood between father and daughter. He cradled his left wrist gingerly.

"Not today, Maryam joonam," he whispered to his young wife.

"If you are a real man, you'll forbid her from allowing an animal between her legs," Baba snarled. Ali and Maryam both glared at him. Baba spat on the ground, just inches from Ali's feet. Maryam pursed her lips and raised her chin, a silent indication to Ali to get back on his horse. He nodded then moved to mount the buckskin mare.

"I'm serious, Ali agha," Baba called after them. "That daughter of mine will bring you nothing but misery if she is allowed to be around horses."

"I hate you!" Maryam screamed as she galloped away. "You're a murderous monster. You murdered my horse, and now you are killing this forest. All for your selfishness!"

In the months that followed, her father spent most of his time on the road, riding in a horse-drawn carriage packed with the goods he traded on behalf of Ali's father and uncles. Maryam saw less and less of him, which suited her fine.

As her body expanded with new life, her brother's shrank. Asghar's stomach was nearly concave by the time a doctor finally arrived to announce his diagnosis of peech khordegi-i-roodeh, or twisted intestines. Much as she had felt disdain for her brother throughout their childhood, Maryam was terrified at the thought that he might die.

Given Asghar's diagnosis and that Maryam's belly and feet were swelling, a sign, the elders said, that the baby would be coming any minute, Maman asked the doctor to stay on at the farm. Baba was on another of his extended trips to Tehran with Ali's grandfather. It could be weeks if not months before his return.

Fortunately, Ali and Maryam had already moved back to her parents' house. Maryam worked the land as long as the baby inside her allowed. But when the kicks became too much for her narrow ribs and her fatigue overwhelmed her, even Maryam could not be of much help anymore.

If she was tired caring for her family and their farm, Maman never let on. She rose before anyone else in the household and was on her feet long after her children had gone to bed. She harvested the crops, tended to the flock of sheep, and fed the chickens, only breaking to make sure her children were also fed.

The baby was kicking so much now, Maryam thought it was trying to claw its way out of her belly. It became increasingly difficult to sleep, and Asghar's moans in the middle of the night were no help.

One night, she rose from her bed to check on her brother, but when she entered his room, she dropped the candle she was holding. No sound escaped her throat. Her eyes fell to his, those once-shining emeralds. He lay motionless, eyes and mouth open.

Asghar died three days shy of fifteen. On the morning of his birthday, in her stricken state, Maryam rose before sunrise and wandered to a neighbor's farm, where her mother's favorite horses were stabled. Belly nearly bursting, Maryam couldn't contain the wave of emotions storming inside her. She was determined to ride; it would calm her. But before she could find a way to heave herself up onto the same white horse her mother had ridden into the forest in search of Maryam all those nights ago, she felt a wave surge between her legs. It was as if the Caspian was pouring out of her.

Terrified, Maryam stumbled home. She found Maman asleep at the table, her kohl-lined eyes crusted shut. She put her hand on her mother's bony shoulder, realizing in that moment just how much weight her mother had lost in recent months, a testament to the grief and exhaustion she was carrying, which worked her body to the bone.

"Maman. Maman, please wake up. Something is wrong."

Maman used her calloused fingers to pry her eyelids apart and immediately began to cry. "Everything is wrong, daughter. My child was taken from me. It is unnatural."

Maryam nodded. But it would be years before she understood the hell her mother was living through, that no one should have to survive.

"I know, Mamanee, I know."

Her mother's gaze sharpened. "Oh, Maryam. Why didn't you tell me it's time?"

"Time?"

"Your face . . . your eyes are on fire. Your belly has dropped!"

Instinctively, Maryam reached for her stomach. "Should we . . . should we tell Ali?" The girl's voice trembled. All these months, she'd been dreading the moment when the baby would tear its way out of her body. Every fiber in her being told her she wasn't ready. She was only fourteen.

"Ali? Yes, we will tell Ali, but first the doctor." Maman sprang into action. She rang the bell to summon the doctor, scurried to light the fire, and filled a large pot with water from the barrels in the kitchen near the stacks of coal and wood. She was glad she'd had the foresight to fill the barrels from the well some months ago.

"Maryam, we need more water. Boiled water. You'll have to—" She stopped midsentence. Her mother had forgotten Maryam was the one in labor. Maman dug her fingers into her hair. She paced the kitchen, choking back tears.

"And of course, your father isn't here, off gallivanting with those in-laws of yours. They call it 'tejarat.' It's not trade. It's one long festival of debauchery."

"I'm sorry, Maman." A wave of pressure came over her belly, and Maryam winced. Her mother ran to her.

"You're having a contraction." Maman interlaced her fingers over her daughter's and placed both of their hands on the girl's belly. She took a deep breath in, then exhaled, and motioned for Maryam to do the same. The women melted into one another. There was a fleeting moment of peace between them—Maman transitioning to Maman bozorg (or "big mother/grandmother"), daughter transitioning to Maman, baby transitioning from womb to world—before Maryam's strong legs gave out and she could no longer carry the weight of all three of them.

At that instant, Ali and the doctor appeared in the doorway. Maman looked up to the ceiling, sending a silent prayer of thanks that help had arrived.

"Oh, oh, it—is the baby—is this the . . ." Ali trailed off. He was woefully unprepared for this moment, and everyone in the room knew it.

"Fetch some blankets. Or pillows. Even a carpet would do," the doctor interjected.

The boy nodded, relieved to be given a task, but Maman was already out in the yard, searching the clotheslines for clean linens.

"What you need is a midwife." This from Maryam's mother-in-law, Ruqaya, who had suddenly appeared behind her son. With her blonde hair and blue eyes, she had once been considered the most beautiful woman in the village. Ruqaya had tried to insist that Maryam refer to her as Mamanee, as her other daughters-in-law did. But that would never happen. Maryam had little respect for Ruqaya, who paid little attention to Ali. He wasn't the eldest or the youngest. Wasn't the only boy. Just the third son and fifth child, with three more following close behind.

Occasionally, though, her mother-in-law remembered him, and by extension Maryam—usually when she needed something. When Maryam's
pregnancy was announced, she and Ruqaya found a détente of sorts—her
mother-in-law would stay out of Maryam's way just so long as she produced a son.

"Khanoum, I am a doctor," the physician protested.

Ruqaya tsked and shook out her graying curls. "I delivered eight perfect children—never needed a doctor. My sister is the best midwife in
the village."

"Madam, I assure you, she'll—" But the doctor was interrupted by
Maman, who had dumped the pile of linens on the floor and now wrapped
her long, thin arm around Ruqaya's waist to gently lead her out into the
courtyard. Maman agreed with Ruqaya, but she also wanted to get her
out of Maryam's sight before her blood pressure rose.

"Ruqi joon, so nice of you to come see how Maryam is doing. Thank
you, but we'll handle it from here."

"What Maryam needs is a midwife. How dare you allow a man to be
doing that work!" Ruqaya had long perfected her signature tone of disap-
proval. It was usually one of her most effective weapons, but Maman was
impervious. She flashed Ruqaya a winning smile and tilted her head.

"You are so kind, my dear. But the doctor is here, and I know you can
appreciate that my daughter needs me to help deliver our grandchild—"

"Grandson," Ruqaya interrupted.

"Inshallah. For now, I must devote all my attention to her. I will bring
the baby over to see you before nightfall." Maman escorted Maryam's
mother-in-law out of the courtyard. She smiled and waved, watching to
make sure the woman really left.

The doctor examined the girl. It hadn't occurred to Maryam until she
heard Ruqaya that she should be ashamed that a doctor was seeing her
private areas. A wave of embarrassment suddenly came over her, and she
resisted the urge to squeeze her legs together.

"The baby is upside down, Khanoum Mahdavi," he announced.

Maryam looked anxiously between the two adults crouched at her feet. "What does that mean, Mamanee? Is the baby okay?"

"Ssshhh, don't you worry. The baby will be fine." Maman helped Maryam sit up, propping a pillow behind the girl's back. She stood and turned to the doctor. "I think you've done enough here. You can go."

The man looked at her, stunned. Maman quickly packed his medical kit and handed him the large leather bag.

"I'm going to call on the midwife. Her skills delivered each of my children. I don't know why I let my brother talk me into using a doctor for you. Ali can go and get the midwife now," Maman said, as she ushered the doctor out into the courtyard and rang the bell for Ali. Maryam caught a glimpse of the terrified face of her young husband, then passed out from the pain.

When she came to, the kitchen was filled with people. Maman cradled her head and waved smelling salts under her nose. Auntie Manijeh, the midwife, had waded her hands, wrists, and forearms into Maryam's insides. She could feel every movement and tried to distract herself, searching for the eyes of her beloved. Behind Manijeh were Ali and his sister.

Auntie Manijeh began singing. "The baby turned nicely," she crooned.

Maman clapped, and Ali let out an audible sigh of relief.

"Okay, Maryam joon. I'm going to need you to start pushing."

Maryam nodded. She had been dreading this moment ever since Ali's sister had described her own horrifying experience of childbirth. But she looked at Ali, and he softened when their eyes met, offering his wife his smile. She winked back at him and found the strength to push.

Maman couldn't make good on her promise to bring the baby to Ruqaya by nightfall. The labor was long, slow, and painful. Maryam felt her narrow hips expanding, her ribs shifting, her body changing, adapting, moment by moment. Maman and Ali never left her side. Ali's sister came and went, bringing food, water, fresh blankets, and towels. But it wasn't until sunrise that they finally heard the magical sound of new life howling into the world.

The labor had taken more than twenty-four hours, but in the end, Maryam held an angel of a baby girl, and didn't know whether to laugh or cry. The baby had warm, almond-shaped eyes. Maryam smiled as she recalled the last time she had seen such perfect eyes, and the baby's name came to her.

"I'm going to call her Shokat," Maryam announced. Ali smiled and wrapped his arms around his wife and daughter.

"What a lovely name," Auntie Manijeh said. She was busy cleaning her hands and rinsing the blood from the blankets and sheets, but she nodded from across the room.

Maman hung her head. "Oh, daughter, your father will never approve."

As if the mere mention of his name could conjure him, they heard the bells of the horse-drawn carriage chiming. Maman and the others ran out to greet the returning men.

Ali's father pulled the horses to a halt. Moving slowly, ever so slowly, he descended from the carriage and tied the reins to an olive tree. Ali's grandfather stepped down from the back of the carriage, trembling. Baba-bozorg was fighting back tears. Then Ali's uncle emerged. In his arms was a body, and he held it the same way as only moments before Ali had cradled his newborn child. But this body was limp, lifeless.

Maman was the first to understand. She sank to the ground, pounding the soil beneath her.

"No, God, no!" Maman grabbed fistfuls of soil and flung it as she screamed.

Maryam passed Shokat to Ali and vaulted toward the earth-splitting sound of her mother's cries. She pulled Maman into her lap, and her mother clung to her, burying her face in her daughter's shirt. Beside them, Manijeh and Afra prayed. They screamed and pounded their chests and looked to the sky, their arms raised, palms open, beseeching. They begged the universe for mercy.

But tears didn't come for Maryam. She felt a wave of sadness, one of many feelings threatening to undo her at that moment, but her sorrow was more for her mother than for herself. As she tried to sort through her emotions—rage, grief, emptiness, relief, worry—there came the magical sound of her daughter gurgling. Ali had brought Shokat out to the court-yard, and now all eyes were on the baby.

"Is that? Is it . . . ," Ali's father choked out. Maryam had forgotten that he was the baby's grandfather, too. And then it hit her that Shokat would never know two of the most important men on her side of the family. This realization knocked the wind out of her, and she crumpled over her mother's sobbing body.

"What happened?" Maryam managed to ask. She was surprised at the rasp in her voice. She took her mother's hands in her own. She knew she had to be strong, and part of that strength was understanding what had brought this tragedy down upon the patriarch of her family.

"B—b—bandits," Ali's uncle stammered. "It was terrible. They attacked us and our carriage. Your father was very br—brave. He wanted to protect the carriage."

"They were on horseback, encircling us. We were outnumbered," came the deep, authoritative voice of Ali's grandfather. Even with his spine curled from age, he was still the tallest among them. His voice, stature, and presence commanded respect. Maryam watched him intently as he spoke. "The thieves—there were probably ten of them—surrounded us. Your father put his body between the carriage and the men. He didn't even flinch when they took a knife to his throat."

A shiver slid down Maryam's spine.

"We didn't stand a chance," Ali's father said, though it was clear his thoughts were elsewhere—he couldn't take his eyes off his son and grandchild.

The men took Baba's body inside. When they returned, Ali introduced Shokat to her grandfather, her great-grandfather, and her great-uncle. "A life taken, a life given," Ali's father said somberly.

"It was two lives taken," Auntie Manijeh whispered, meaning Asghar. The losses were too much. What had befallen Maryam and Maman was so horrifying, the other villagers dared not speak of it too loudly, lest they suffer the same fate.

LOUISE, 1955

"NEXT STOP: PARIS, GARE DE LYON." THE TRAIN CONDUCTOR'S voice jolted Louise awake. She winced as she pulled herself upright in her seat. A few months earlier, she'd fallen from a young horse, and her back had yet to fully heal.

"Is this your destination, Mademoiselle? Paris?" the passenger sitting beside her asked, his tone pleasant. Louise stared back at him. *Was she truly going to Paris to meet—and possibly marry—a man she had met only a handful of times? Was she really going to move halfway around the world to start a new life with him?*

Louise thought of herself as strong, adventurous, and free. But the events of the past two years surprised even her. Breaking in a bucking horse—that, she knew she could handle. But swashbuckling around the globe was something else. Yet here she was, about to marry a Persian prince and move to Iran.

JOHN AND David had made good on their promise to Louise during her senior year of high school. Despite dropping out to care for their ailing mother, Louise, now fully grown at nearly six feet tall, with long blonde

locks, kept up her studies, reading the books John sent and working dili-
gently on her math and science assignments. John and David had also grown
in height and stature. Framed by blond curls, their faces now looked more
like each other and even more closely resembled their father. Growing up on
a farm, both young men had always been strong, but now their bodies had
filled out.

"My Sisyphus is incline planes, and no matter how much I puzzle
over rates of acceleration and deceleration, I just don't get it," Louise
bemoaned to her brothers. She tried but didn't pass the entrance exam for
veterinary college.

"I talked to Father," John told his sister. It was the summer of 1951,
and her eldest brother was on his way to Yale. But first, he came to visit
Louise and their mother in New Hampshire.

"Let me guess; he doesn't want to help me."

"You don't give him enough credit, Lou. And in this case, you'll want
to thank him."

John had convinced their father to use his connections to secure a
spot at Cornell for his daughter. Louise was to enroll for the fall semester.

Despite the miraculous opportunity for which she worried she was
unqualified, Louise bemoaned the news. "Cornell? Why can't I go to Yale
with you or to Harvard with Fereydoun?" For several years, their father
had been working on a high-profile legal case involving Iran and the Soviet
Union, representing Iran. He had grown close to the Iranian ambassador
to the United States, Hussein Ala, and the ambassador once accompanied him when he visited Louise and her mother in New Hampshire.
Though Louise's parents never fully made amends, living apart allowed
the couple to regrow a friendship and appreciate their shared passions
around international justice.

Ambassador Ala brought along his son, Fereydoun, on these trips.
Fereydoun became quite close with the Laylin siblings, as he was just a

year younger than Louise, joining them for skiing, rock climbing, and, of course, horseback riding.

Louise loved Fereydoun and the ambassador's stories about Iran. Everything she heard intrigued her. At night, she dreamed of wild white stallions, bazaars, and opulent palaces where princes and princesses roamed the halls. She imagined Fereydoun and his friends pounding across a sparse landscape atop Arabian horses, wielding swords. By comparison, her life in the United States felt tame. Fereydoun became an honorary brother to Louise.

"David is going to Cornell, too," John reassured her. "You'll only be a couple hours' train ride from both Fereydoun and me."

"Where even *is* Cornell?"

"New York; Ithaca. They have horses there. You might not be able to study veterinary medicine, but you can certainly join a riding club."

Louise softened at these magic words. While she would miss her mother and their horses desperately, Louise could not wait for a new adventure, a new home, and new lands and horses to discover.

When she arrived at Cornell, however, Louise found herself failing class after class. She had wanted to study physics, hoping to excel in the sciences and to try again to enter veterinary school. But by her sophomore year, she relinquished the dream. Science was clearly not in her future. She decided to give in to the other dream that had come to fill her imagination: the Orient, as it then was known. She wrote to tell John that she had declared herself an Arabic major.

To Louise's shock, John responded with a letter declaring his own love of Arabic. He had been studying economics and history, intending to take over his father's legal practice, but his sister's note stirred something in him. John never let himself indulge in fantasies, but every part of him was telling him to leave Yale and go to the Middle East. To let himself explore a world that occupied his—and he now realized his sister's—dreams ever since the Ala family entered their lives.

Lou, your letter touched me. Learning of your change in studies inspired me. I have decided to follow my heart to the Orient.
I'll be studying at the American University of Beirut. You should join me. It might even be good for your studies.

Louise's heart leaped into her throat. Letter still in hand, she ran to the registrar's office to request a year's leave of absence. Once granted, she and John made plans to leave together from New York City. They would board a ship headed to Naples, then transfer to a smaller boat that would sail to Alexandria and then on to Beirut.

David was dumbfounded when he learned of his siblings' sudden change in plans. *Wasn't his sister pursuing veterinary medicine, while his brother was supposed to focus on becoming just like their father, a serious lawyer with a strong business sensibility?* Instead, he found himself encouraging his siblings' adventure.

On the day of their departure the siblings hugged each other tightly. There were tears sliding down Louise's cheeks. She was going to miss her brother and mother. She made a note to herself to convince them both to join her in Lebanon by year's end.

When they changed ships in Alexandria, Louise and John beheld a world they'd only read about in books. King Faroukh's palace on the Mediterranean Sea glistened gold, the ornate carvings on the building shimmering with ancient hieroglyphics. They sailed on to Beirut, which sat on a promontory protruding powerfully into the Mediterranean at the foot of a mountain range. This juxtaposition of mountain and sea stirred something inside Louise. She could hardly wait to be mounted on an Arabian stallion, pounding down the precipitous trails toward the water.

Beirut's streets in the 1950s were the opposite of what she'd imagined. Congested lanes, pollution and smog, and drivers who swerved within an inch of their lives all clogged the roadways. Honking horns, blaring rock and roll, and the most up-to-date cars revving their engines overwhelmed

Louise's senses. It was only when they arrived at the American University that Louise felt her soul stir.

"Compared to Cornell, the student body appeared much more mature," she wrote in her diary that year. "This observation was supported by the black beards and sweeping moustaches of students from Aleppo, Damascus, Amman, and various towns of Lebanon. The first day in Political Science class, our professor, Cecil Hourani, asked the students to park their sidearms on his desk or leave the class. A rattle of guns hit the desk from half the students and the other half left class firmly wedded to their weapons and their right to bear arms."

Louise was entranced by her Middle Eastern peers. They were "more interested in toppling governments than resorting to 'panty raids' to burn off high spirits," she wrote in a letter to her mother. Louise and John, two of only five Americans, learned quickly that the university was in and of itself a political proving ground. "Pitched battles between students and the army resulted in the university being closed as often as it was open," she continued. Louise made many friends who shared her love of horses, poetry, and living life through adventure.

While John dove headfirst into studies of Islamic Marxism and heady political theory, Louise was seduced by the student body. "Their long history in an area famous for internecine battles and invasions left them with a kind of quiet dignity and quick temper," she mused in her diary. "This salad of radical genes was spiced with wealthy Arabs from Saudi Arabia and other Muslim countries who came to Beirut to wallow in the bars and discotheques."

Beirut was entering its Golden Age. Men and women dressed in haute couture gathered at any number of hip cafés or restaurants. New forms of experimental art brought Arabic creators together with artists from around the world. An explosion of luxury hotels, chic nightclubs, and high-end watering holes sprang up, drawing crowds of the rich and famous from around the world.

But in a foreshadowing of the fate that would befall Iran in the 1970s and lead to a revolution, the 1950s were also a time of increasing political tensions. Similar to the critiques that would be leveled against the shah of Iran two decades later, some underground activist groups—ranging from Islamists to Marxists to an emerging student faction of Islamic Marxists at American University of Beirut—accused the mainstream Lebanese population of becoming "Westoxicated," or overly infatuated with the West. They criticized the government and local businesses for turning Lebanon into a playground for the rich and famous. Worried that they were losing their "Lebanese" identity by becoming enamored with Western brands, lines, and luxury, they began staging protests.

Louise followed her new classmates into underground bookstores, parties, raves, and political gatherings, infatuated with the thrill of such passionate uprisings. But this seduction ended up being costly for her.

After being caught at a campus protest by a school administrator, Louise and two other young women (but, to Louise's chagrin, none of the men) were expelled. This particular protest focused on the recent controversy over the Suez Canal. Egyptian president Abdel Nasser called on Lebanese president Camille Chamoun to cut ties with the West over the conflict regarding control of the canal. Lebanon refused, causing great turmoil internally and externally. This was further exacerbated when Chamoun declared support for the "Baghdad Pact," a military alliance formed by Iran, Iraq, Pakistan, Turkey, and the United Kingdom, which Nasser deemed a threat to Arab nationalism. When Lebanese prime minister Rashid Karami took a stance of support with the Egyptian president, Lebanon was divided. The students sided with Karami, protesting Chamoun's deference to the West. Despite being an obvious Westerner, Louise found herself drawn into the protesters' cause.

Louise was unable to face the prospect of returning home after her expulsion and deflated by a stern, reprimanding letter from her father.

"You're not coming home, then?" her mother asked, during one of their weekly phone calls.

Louise had to take a deep breath to steady herself each time she heard her mother's voice. Most of the time she was so enamored by her new home that she didn't have time to be homesick, but those weekly calls when she walked a mile from her apartment at eight at night to stand in line to use the telephone always pulled at her heart. On that particular night she was both looking forward to and dreading the sound of her mother's melodious tone.

"I, uh, I . . . am not coming home. I'm sorry, Mother." Louise exhaled audibly.

A long silence ensued.

"Mother, are you still there?" Louise's deep voice rose several octaves when she spoke with her family members, and now she sounded childlike.

"How are you going to tell your father?" her mother said, after several moments had passed.

Now it was Louise's turn to be silent.

"Lou, I know this is hard, but you are going to tell him. And it is going to break you a bit to do so."

"I know," Louise sobbed.

"Take a breath. Pull yourself together. We're going to plan."

Louise wiped her face with the sleeve of her torn sweater, the one her mother had knitted as a gift last Christmas. She was grateful for the shroud of darkness that kept her fellow students and others in line from seeing her unraveling.

"Thank you, Mother. But I'm afraid I'm coming apart."

"And what do you do when you come apart, my girl?"

"I don't know!" Louise blew her nose in the collar of her sweater.

"You turn to horses. They'll give you the answer. And as soon as the snow melts, I'll be over there to join you. We'll find a way."

MARYAM, 1926

MAMAN FELL INTO A STUPOR. MOST DAYS SHE DIDN'T EVEN get out of bed. Maryam and Ali worked tirelessly to keep the crops alive, but the farm soon fell into disarray. Without Maman to guide them, and without Asghar and the villagers, it was simply too many acres.

Then Maryam had an idea. With her father gone, she no longer had to worry about being caught on horseback. And now that she was a wife and mother, no one could accuse her of risking her virginity when she rode. Maryam had been horrified when her sister-in-law told her the real reason Asghar had called her "ruined." Though it also struck Maryam as absurd when she recalled the pain of her wedding night.

So, at last, she was free to ride and could cover more acreage on horseback, too. Maryam took a couple of scarves and slung them across her body, wrapping them—and Shokat—into a tight X. With the baby secure on her abdomen, she'd be able to climb up onto a horse safely. Only, first she had to find a horse.

Maryam walked with Shokat on her back to her neighbor's farm, determined to buy the white horse her mother had borrowed to ride into the forest that fateful night nearly two years ago. The rancher was hesitant. Maryam stroked the glistening white horse's mane, feeling the same peace that had settled her soul when she met her first horse, Shokat, in

PARDIS MAHDAVI

the woods. She knew that this horse had to become part of the family. The rancher remained staunchly opposed. But when Maryam offered him the gold-coin earrings Ali's grandfather had given her as a wedding present, he couldn't refuse.

"What's her name?" Maryam asked, as she and Shokat mounted their new horse.

"Shokoufeh," he said. Maryam smiled. The horse's name referred to the white flowers that bloomed in spring. As a girl, Maryam believed that riding made her whole; she had felt more complete atop her horse than anywhere else. But now, as a mother, riding with her baby daughter cocooned against her chest, she felt a new depth of wholeness; she was complete, because she understood that she was part of a whole far greater than just herself.

With Shokoufeh's speed and agility, Maryam was able to survey the entire farm and fully assess the damage from both the prior winter and the now deceased bounty of spring. As hot summer days began to over-take Gonbad-i-Kavoos, the crops shriveled. Worse still, the soil was dry-ing too fast, changing from black to a graying brown set by a hardened crust that she'd have to break through to reap. Maryam knew her family's survival depended on the fertility of the land. She also knew that they would not be able to make a living on lettuce, beets, olives, and carrots. They needed a new crop, one that required less care and water. She would have to look to neighboring farms to better understand her options.

Like her mother, her mother's mother, and her mother's mother's mother before her, Shokat loved being atop a horse. She squealed in excitement as Shokoufeh took them careening around to other plots so Maryam could do research. In the afternoons, when their work was done for the day, they rode out to the Caspian Sea.

By the time autumn rolled in, Maryam had visited more than a dozen farms, invoking her father's memory to persuade the farmers to speak to her. She spent many of these trips at the edge of the sea, and it was at the

53

farms nearest the Caspian that Maryam found the answers she needed. As she galloped back through the forest one afternoon, a plan crystallized in her mind.

For his part, Ali had become less invested in the family farm and was spending more time with his father, learning the trade and textile business. She saw less and less of her husband, but this suited Maryam just fine. She was back with the true love of her life: horses. And her main task was caring for her mother and her little girl.

"MAMAN, WAKE up!" Maryam called out, breathless from her ride. Half a year had passed since Maman had fallen into her grief-stricken silence, but Maryam continued to talk to her every day and brought Shokat to her grandmother's bed every night. Maman didn't speak but smiled gratefully each time Maryam placed the baby in her arms. Maryam knew it was up to her to bring her mother back to life, just as she would have to be the one to rejuvenate the weak earth of their farm.

"I have a plan, Maman. A good plan. But I need your help."

Her mother rubbed her eyes and squinted at the light pouring in through the window. Maryam had returned earlier than usual, and Maman had taken to sleeping all day, waking only at nightfall when her daughter and granddaughter returned. She would wait for them to fall asleep and then roam the courtyard in her nightgown. A ghost in her own home.

Maman sat up and stretched out her arms for Shokat. She bestowed a delicate kiss on her granddaughter's forehead.

"I know what we must do now. We can't keep living like this, trying to keep this dying farm alive. Even though I have Shokoufeh, it's still too much land and too many different crops for me to work alone. No one wants to help us because they think we bring bad luck. We need a new plan for some new luck."

Maman sat up straighter in bed. She was in awe of her daughter, who seemed to have aged decades while she was buried in her own grief. She nodded for Maryam to continue.

"We need to plant saffron. Saffron doesn't require much water or even much work most of the year. The hardest is when we first plant the seeds. But here's the thing, Maman: saffron needs washed-out, sandy soil. We're going to have to sell our land. I want us to buy nine acres I found at the edge of the forest, close to the sea." Maryam wanted to rush on, excited to share her plan. Instead, she hesitated, biting her lip and wringing her hands, because Maman was shaking her head, scowling. Her mother's curls were now almost completely white, her skin translucent, but her expression was stern and forceful; she could still summon something of her old fierceness.

Maryam took her mother's wrist and interlaced their fingers. "Listen to me, please. I need you. *We* need you. We can't go on like this."

A tear rolled down Maman's cheek, and Maryam wiped it with her thumb.

"It's a good idea, Maman. It is. Saffron commands the highest price of any crop in town, and the farmers tell me it commands even more in the capital. We can plant it, and then Ali and his family can trade it when they go to the cities. It will keep us comfortable; I promise. I already have Shokoufeh. We'll get you a horse, too. We'll be able to work the land that much faster and harder."

Several pregnant moments passed. Maman looked from her daughter to her cooing granddaughter. She pushed herself to stand and enveloped her daughter in a deep embrace. The two women held each other for a long time.

"Let's do it, Maryam joonam," her mother whispered, the first words she had uttered in six months. Shokat gurgled and waved her hands and feet.

LOUISE, 1955

LOUISE HUNG UP AND FOUND A NEW RESOLVE. TAKING HER mother's advice, she managed to land a job training the racehorses of wealthy Arabs. She rose in the dark, accustomed to early-morning farm chores and work with the horses in the hours before dawn. She got a second job cataloging at Khayat's Bookstore, which was located across the street from the university, and even took on writing assignments for the school alumni magazine, continuing to indulge her fascination with the student body. She profiled graduates as well as older alumni, voraciously consuming each of their stories. Her meager earnings were sufficient to scrape by, but she was weary and deeply relieved when her mother arrived for an extended three-month stay that spring, providing both maternal nurture and financial support.

Now, Louise and John could join their new friends on the ski slopes amid the cedar pines of Lebanon, explore the souks of Damascus, and ride for days into the mountains and along the sea. It was during this respite that Louise discovered a kind of horse she'd never seen or read about before: shorter and stockier, with a wide neck, oval face, and bulging eyes. Despite their—in Louise's opinion—awkward appearance, these horses seemed to glide rather than gallop. They held their heads high and rotated their shoulders forward, swishing their tails in the wind.

It seemed they were dancing or prancing, Louise thought, and she could not wait to mount one, to wrap her long legs around their rounded bodies, to fly through the air bareback. Decades later, Louise wrote in her diary, "This was when I discovered the Oriental horse. And although I did not realize it at the time, this was the major turning point in my life."

Their old friend Fereydoun wrote, saying that he had completed his studies at Harvard and would be spending the summer in Tehran. He implored both John and Louise to visit.

News of Fereydoun's graduation snapped John back to his ambitions. Their year in Beirut had been the best time of John's life, but it was time to return to Yale, mend fences with disagreeable professors, complete his legal and economic training, and get himself to law school. Beirut had been a brief fantasy, and he had to concede to the reality of being the eldest son, finally reminded of David at home, caring for their way of life.

For Louise, on the other hand, there was no way she was going to pass up the opportunity to see Iran. This was the country she had been hearing about for decades. She persuaded her mother to travel with her, and so mother and daughter bid farewell to John in Beirut and headed for Persia.

When they arrived in Tehran, Fereydoun brought them to his family's garden home in an area known as Shemran, just north of the city. Many of Fereydoun's friends turned out to greet the American guests. "That first night, in a garden scented with jasmine and moonlight sliding in the shadows of giant plane trees, with the Alborz Mountains looming black against them and jackals howling faintly in the distance, I met Narcy," Louise wrote in her diary.

Narcy Firouz was the descendant of a long line of royalty known as the Qajar dynasty. The Qajars, descended from a mixture of Ottoman and Persian lineage, ruled Iran from 1789 until 1925. They were credited with bringing Iran into modernity, taking the country from a series of feuding tribal confederations to a centralized monarchy and then constitutional parliament. It was the Qajars who were in power during the Constitutional Revolution of 1905–1910 when Iranians paved the way for a burgeoning press, free speech, and a constitution that upheld their rights as citizens. Notably, the Constitutional Revolution, or Mashrouteh, was put into motion by women elevating the importance of women's rights, all with the full support of their rulers.

The Qajar dynasty was overthrown by the Pahlavi family in 1925, but many Iranians continued to feel a strong allegiance to the Qajars, whose rule was seen by some as more democratic, progressive, and transformative.

That first night, Louise knew nothing of his lineage, family prominence, or wealth. "We had stumbled over a small, white stray dog in the garden; discovered we both liked dogs and stoutly defended this one against Madame Ala (Fereydoun's mother) and her outraged protests. We lost the argument, and the dog was ushered out of the garden by the head gardener. But it was the start of friendship and when Narcy returned to Shiraz, where he was Chief Engineer for the Nemazee Hospital, he invited my mother, Fereydoun, and me to visit," Louise recorded in her diary.

She was smitten with Narcy from the start. He had black curls that framed his round, golden-brown face and dark-brown eyes that brightened when he looked at her. There was his height, too—he was one of the few men she had met in the region who was taller than she. And his voice: deep and raspy; she loved the way he said her name, *"Lou-eease."* When he recited poetry, his words reverberated in her bones.

Narcy, too, was quite taken with the tall blonde woman who loved animals as much as he did. When he learned of her keen equestrian skills, he arranged for a wild boar hunt, reasoning it would be best to court Louise from atop a horse.

As soon as Louise, her mother, and Fereydoun arrived in Shiraz, they were whisked off to a village called Dasht-e-Arjan, or "the valley of lions." As they bumped along during the three-hour drive to the village, Louise took in her first glimpses of the Iranian countryside: open sewers, children playing as their mothers washed clothes, olive and barberry trees, rolling green hills that gave way to lakes and rivers. And in the background, always, a soothing call to prayer from every mosque and minaret they passed. Louise's dreams were coming to life before her very eyes. There were wild horses running through the fields and bazaars that tickled every one of her five senses.

"What an exotic place," her mother said.

"But, Mother," Louise contradicted, a smile enveloping every fiber of her being, "it feels more like home than anywhere else in the world."

MARYAM, 1930

B Y THE TIME THE ORANGE-BLOSSOM TREE UNDER WHICH HER father and brother were buried ushered in the next several springs, Maryam's plan was in full effect. They sold the farm, leaving behind the painful memories and haunting deaths that hung in the air. The land Maryam purchased straddled sea and forest, and its soil was indeed hungry for the saffron seeds Ali procured. Maman sold her wedding ring and bought a new horse named Kayvan, a black gelding. Within just a few short months of the big move, three horses—each reminding Maryam of her first love, Shokat, because of their large heads, protruding eyes, and slender but shorter legs—found their way to the farm. Shokoufeh and Kayvan didn't seem to mind these new friends. Before long, they became members of the growing family.

The new horses were smaller but smarter, faster, and more agile than Shokoufeh and Kayvan, who were, Maryam learned from the local villagers, Turkoman horses called Akhal-Tehke breeds. The new horses moved like Shokat had, in a gentle rocking motion. And they loved being ridden by Maryam. At first, Maman didn't trust the smaller horses to carry the load of the farm labor, but she came around when she saw how much more work Maryam was able to accomplish when she rode them. They were able to bend and curve their paths, making it easier for Maryam to plant, reap, and sow. And they helped identify threats to the crop like mice and spiders because of their heightened sense of smell. They would freeze when they scented vermin near. Most important, they weren't spooked by the sand. Whenever they got close to the sea, Kayvan and Shokoufeh hesitated, nervous and uncertain, but the sure-footed new horses galloped confidently through the sand and even carried their riders right into the water. Shokat clapped her hands in delight whenever they trotted into the waves.

Before long, as she honed her skills, the muscles in Maryam's arms began to bulge like those of her horses. Her body memorized the torso twists that helped her hurl a four-foot spear into the water to skewer fish. And she felt the thrill of the kill when her archery skills helped her successfully take down her first deer as she rode atop her horse hands-free, so she could focus on drawing the arrows back, pulling tension with her tightened biceps on the tense string, and then the adrenaline rush of letting go and watching the arrow fly. Ali brought his wife weapons that the metalworkers in his father's business crafted. By summer, Maryam was providing food for the entire household and then some.

The success of the Mahdavi women caught the attention of the villagers. Stories spread faster than the scent of jasmine across Iran. The family that had suffered unspeakable tragedy was now coming back to life. Slowly, their old friends returned to them, lured by their strength and resolve, and Maryam and Maman embraced them. A farm, a family, can survive without community, but it is much harder. Maryam knew the presence and spirit of their friends would help Maman heal.

News of their successful saffron business also spread. In a single season, they made more money than any other farm within a hundred miles. Everyone wanted to know their secret, propelled by jealous curiosity. But Maryam would never disclose that the secret was the horses. They were the reason she was able to tend the crops so efficiently. Maryam and Maman treated the horses like children. They all ate together, played together, and slept in the same wide-open room that Ali and his father had built. Maman slept near Kayvan and Shokoufeh, her attachment growing every day. The three new horses, whom Maryam had named Khosrow, Majid, and Asghar, slept with her and Shokat. When Ali was not traveling, he joined them.

The buzz about the Mahdavi women also brought unwanted attention. Farmers demanded to know how their saffron crops yielded such robust harvests during an otherwise bleak year. Saffron was a lucrative but challenging crop. The delicate seeds had to be sowed and watered—but not too much—at just the right angles during planting season. Many of the yields were crushed and destroyed by gruff hands during the harvest. By contrast, Maryam and Maman gently plucked the purple flowers, taking great care not to damage the yellow stamens or the three-part orange-red stigma that yielded the saffron strands. Using the horses to cut down on time between acres, they were able to take the necessary extra moment with each bloom to ensure its health and safety.

As their success grew, so too did people's jealousy. Other saffron farmers were not happy, and a bounty was placed on the Mahdavi women's heads; they had to be taken care of, once and for all. Only then could their lands—and their crops—be divvyed up.

One night, Maryam awoke suddenly. As usual, she and Shokat were sleeping with what they had started calling the "sea horses." Maryam's favorite horse, Asghar, was neighing loudly, and Maryam sprang to her feet. She wouldn't make the same mistake she had as a child. She knew this sound signaled danger.

Asghar shook out his black mane and pounded the ground with his heavy hoof. Like the brother after which he was named, the horse was a spirited soul who did not suffer fools. He would only ever let Maryam near him, biting any other hand that tried to feed him. Now, she could sense his heartbeat quickening. She grabbed her knife and dug out the bow and quiver of arrows set that Ali had given her. She tucked Shokat next to Khosrow, who was clearly her daughter's favorite horse.

"Watch over her, mighty Khosrow," Maryam whispered into the horse's twitching, velvety ear. "Take care of my little girl."

For a moment Maryam considered seeking out her mother, who had fallen asleep at the kitchen table. But the kitchen was on the other side of the field. There wasn't time.

Maryam climbed up on Asghar's back, and the horse tracked the unfamiliar scent and heartbeat of a stranger. Through the clearing in the courtyard, Maryam spotted two men carrying lamps. Suddenly, one of the men blew out his candle. Without a second thought, Maryam released her arrow, aimed at the fresh darkness. It was a perfect hit. The man screamed and crumpled to the ground.

The other man now came running toward Maryam. Asghar galloped in the other direction, giving her more time to nock the next arrow. This one she aimed at her attacker's leg. She squinted her right eye, pulled back the bowstring until it was tight, and then exhaled as she let it loose.

The arrow punctured the man's flesh a few inches above his knee and to the left of his groin. That did the trick. The man fell in agony. As Asghar ferried Maryam close to him, she saw that he was still holding a knife in his right hand. She swiftly let fly another arrow. It landed in the center of his palm.

Maryam rode over and, from her position atop the horse, loomed over the bleeding man. He was trembling, alternating between clutching his leg and his hand.

"You bitch!" he growled between set teeth. "You'll pay for this."

Maryam tsked and shook her head, just as she'd seen her mother do her whole life.

Suddenly, Maryam looked up and saw the other man—the first one she had knocked off his horse—limping away, clutching his bleeding quad. She thought about following him, but then she got a better idea.

"You better run, coward!" Maryam called after him. "Tell your friends that Gordafarid lives here!"

Filled with the power of saying her idol's name, Maryam took a deep breath. She looked down at the writhing man, pitying his pain. Her heart sank when she saw the bloodthirsty look in his eyes. He had come to murder her and her mother and daughter. Like Gordafarid, Maryam would have to send a message for all to understand.

She slid off Asghar and pulled out her knife. The man's angry expression immediately turned to fear, and he started scrambling backward on his elbows, begging for mercy. Maryam felt age-old rage overcome her, and her mind went quiet. Elegantly and swiftly, like she had seen her mother do hundreds of times with deer and sheep on the farm, she stalked the man, pinned him with one knee, and grabbed his jaw. He bucked and bleated as she pulled her knife across his throat. Blood splattered her face, but Maryam didn't react. She watched the man's body go limp and blood carve rivulets through the soil. When he finally stilled, she stood and went to get the ropes she and Ali had woven. She bound the corpse with his right arm and leg. With the end of the rope in her hand, she climbed onto Asghar's back. Together, they dragged the body to the edge of their property and tied it up high on the wooden fence.

A sign for all to see. A lesson for all to learn.

LOUISE, 1955

NARCY HAD ARRANGED FOR A GROUP OF TURKOMAN HORSES to be waiting when they arrived in Dasht-e-Arjan, and as soon as they were all mounted, he led them on a ride through swamps and forests, finally reaching an open field where they could hunt. Louise had been riding her entire life, but she had never felt the smooth suppleness of a gait like the horse she had been given. The mounts she had ridden in Lebanon were smoother than her quarter horses back home, that was certain, but here was a purebred Turkoman horse and the experience was unlike any other.

The Laylin family were farmers and could stretch to ranching, but hunting was new to Louise. She expected to feel more conflicted about it, but after Fereydoun explained how hunting helped create a healthy ecosystem, Louise found herself enjoying it more than she could have imagined.

When the hunt was over, Fereydoun set up camp, and Narcy cooked dinner. After a feast of wild boar and wine, Fereydoun and Louise's mother wanted to tuck into their sleeping bags near the crackling embers of the fire. But Narcy suggested they go on a leopard hunt. Midnight was the perfect time to spot a leopard, he insisted.

"I'll go!" Louise heard herself say. Her mother shook her head and slunk deeper into her sleeping bag. By now she knew better than to question her daughter's endless thirst for thrills. Little did she know that it was something more than an adventurous spirit tugging at her daughter's heart.

"I'll stay here with your mother," Fereydoun chuckled. "You two kids enjoy yourselves."

Narcy led the way, his rifle cradled professionally in his arm. His grace contrasted sharply with Louise, who followed behind as closely as she could, tripping over rocks and scratching herself on thorn bushes.

After walking for about thirty minutes, the pair settled on a large rock that looked out onto the village of Dasht-e-Arjan, which glimmered in the moonlight. Louise squinted in search of leopards, but Narcy lowered his rifle and knelt in the soft dirt. He took her hand in his.

"Marry me," he asked. Louise nearly fell off the rock. This was only the second time they'd met. But Narcy's gaze steadied her. There in the moonlight, looking out at the hills and village nearby, Louise knew in her heart that Narcy was her future. Before she could reply, she began crying.

"Is that a 'yes' crying or a 'no' crying?" Narcy asked nervously.

Louise choked on a laughing sob. Her heart and soul wanted to say yes and disappear into the mountains with the handsome prince. But she remembered that her mother had always regretted rushing to marry her father without finishing college. Unwilling to let her future go the way of her parents, Louise asked Narcy to wait for her.

"I need to return to Cornell to complete my degree. But I will marry you, Narcy Firouz, and I will make you and Iran my home. I just need a year."

Narcy reluctantly agreed, on one condition.

"Meet me under the Marble Arch in London exactly one year from today," he said. "There I'll make you my wife, and we'll come back to Shiraz together."

Louise returned to Ithaca and finished her courses with renewed fervor. She spent every waking hour taking extra classes and studying, in order to be sure she'd graduate in the spring. As soon as she did, she boarded a ship bound for England. Fereydoun was pursuing graduate work in Edinburgh and came to London to meet her. The two set off for the Marble Arch to await her groom.

But Narcy didn't show.

Apparently, he had forgotten the agreed-upon date and time and was out hunting with his cousins near the Caspian Sea. But it was not until Fereydoun got hold of Narcy's cousin in Tehran, who had stayed behind with a cold, that they learned of Narcy's whereabouts. When Fereydoun hung up the phone on that rainy London evening in the red booth they had both squeezed into and translated the news of her fiancé's location, Louise burst out laughing. For most women, this would have been reason enough to call the whole thing off. But for Louise, this was further evidence that Narcy was indeed the man for her, a man whose love of adventure and animals trumped all. Louise was undeterred in her love for him, and rather than feel slighted, she laughed, reasoning that she would have likely done the same if she'd had the opportunity to go for a week's ride along the sea.

Deeply apologetic, Narcy begged Louise to wait for him in London.

"It's not going to be that easy, Narcy. You're going to have to hunt *me*!" she told him.

Louise's mother, whose depression had slowly lifted, was embracing her own adventure. That spring, she was in Paris. Fereydoun suggested Louise go see her. "If Narcy Firouz wants to marry you, he's going to do it the right way," Fereydoun quipped. "He will come to Paris, the most romantic city in the world, and then the two of you will marry at a place of *your* choosing, Lou. After you're married, then, and only then, will you run off to Shiraz with him."

Which was how she ended up on the overnight train, sore back and all, hesitating to answer her fellow passenger's innocent question. *Was Paris her destination?* Not exactly. But it was an important stop along the way. A smile spread across her face. Hunting her fiancé was proving as tricky as the leopard under whose pretenses Narcy lured her to the moon-lit rock. The glow of that memory renewed her faith, and she quickly collected her things and prepared to depart. *Yes, Paris was her destination.* As her brother John would say, "How hard is it to find your way in Paris after you've found your way in Beirut and Tehran?"

Louise chuckled and slid out of her seat. Overstuffed backpack hoisted and energy revived, she stepped off the train to find her beloved.

Narcy was waiting for her on the banks of the Seine near the Pont Royal Bridge. When he saw her, he fell to his knees, but Louise pulled him back up for a kiss, their bodies entwined. He wanted to marry the very next day, but she had her own plan. Hoping to mend her relationship with her father, she insisted they be married on the first farm she had ever loved—her childhood home in Great Falls, Virginia. Her father, who had returned to Great Falls after retiring from his legal practice in Washington, DC, would preside over their ceremony.

They journeyed together to America, and Narcy was introduced to the entire Laylin clan. Louise's father was about as happy with his daughter's choice of husband as he had been at the news of her expulsion from the American University of Beirut. He had expected Louise to marry one of the bright young lawyers at his firm. When it was made clear that she was going to marry Narcy with or without his blessing, her father relented and submitted a notice to the *New York Times* that his daughter was marrying a Persian prince and moving to Iran, where she would continue to pursue her love of horses. "I was glad to be enlightened on the subject," Louise wrote in her diary some years later. "I hadn't known until then that Narcy was a Qajar prince, nor had I cared!"

The wedding took place with little fanfare. As soon as it was over, Louise bid farewell to her father, her mother, and her country of origin, setting off on what would be the greatest adventure of her lifetime.

MARYAM, 1933

THREE YEARS AFTER MARYAM AND MAMAN STARTED THE saffron farm, a pair of visitors came to them in need. It was evening, and the sun had just started to set. Maryam was sorting the feed for the horses with her firstborn son and third child, Atta, tied to her back, when an older woman appeared with a younger woman in tow. As they drew close, Maryam saw that the younger one's face was covered in bruises and one of her eyes was swollen shut. She untied Atta and gently set him down. As soon as his chubby little feet met the earth, he took off at a wobbling run. Maryam then ushered the women inside and made them tea, stirring strands of saffron into the younger woman's cup. When mixed with liquid, especially hot tea, saffron dulled pain and was known to calm nerves and lift the spirits.

"Perhaps you don't remember me, my child," the older woman said, muffled. She was missing several teeth, and those that remained were yellow and black. She held the end of her headscarf in her mouth, wrapping and unwrapping the fabric around her tiny, curved torso. "My name is Soudi. I'm an old friend of your grandmother's."

Maryam nodded politely. She didn't recall the woman at all.

"Your tea smells delicious, Khanoum. Tales of your beauty, strength, and hospitality have traveled far and wide throughout Shomal," Soudi said. She had a slight lisp. "All of the North now talks of the Mahdavi women."

"They are kind," Maryam replied, smiling awkwardly. She was all too aware that villagers talked about her, though she wasn't sure how generous the words were. Three years had passed since Maryam slit the throat of a jealous farmer and strapped his body to her fence for all to see. Three years since they had earned a reputation as the toughest women in the North. The family had caught the attention not only of jealous farmers, but also of their wives. For many months, no one dared visit their home, not even Maryam's in-laws. But the curiosity of the northerners could not be quelled forever. Slowly, friends drifted back into their lives, and farmers asked to come pay their respects. They wanted to taste the saffron and see for themselves this marvel. But these two visitors were different.

"Please. Have some tea. It will calm you," Maryam said to the younger woman.

"How rude of me, Khanoum Mahdavi. I should have introduced my granddaughter, Soheila." Soudi stroked her granddaughter's back, as the girl began to cry.

Maryam pressed the cup of tea against the girl's palms. She couldn't have been more than fourteen, but her gaze held many more years.

"It's nice to meet you, Soheila. Thank you for coming to pay us a visit." Soheila nodded through her tears.

"Khanoum Mahdavi . . . ," the elderly woman began.

"Please call me Maryam," she interjected. Whenever people called her khanoum, she wanted to turn and search for her mother or grandmother. She knew the elderly woman was trying to be polite, but Maryam had never learned to embrace the hierarchies that came with success. Such reverence was the honor of age and wisdom.

"Maryam khanoum," Soudi continued. Maryam smiled as the old woman found a middle ground. "Forgive me for coming to you. I'm here because of Soheila. We're desperate. Please." Her voice trembled.

Maryam nodded for her to continue. While she listened to the grandmother, she kept a close eye on Soheila, who was hardly breathing. She hoped the tea would help soon.

"Well, Khanoum, ah, Maryam jaan, I know I don't have to tell you what scoundrels men are . . ."

Maryam arched an eyebrow, rested her heavy chin on her arms, and thought for a moment. "Actually, Khanoum, my husband is a kind and wonderful man."

"Oh, yes, of course. Everyone knows of his gentility! That wasn't what I meant. I just meant, just that . . ." Soudi's voice trailed off, shifting uncomfortably.

But then Maryam understood. "Ah, you mean the farmer."

"That was such bravery," Soudi said exhaling, composing herself.

"I had to protect my family," Maryam said stiffly.

"So, you understand—the need to protect your family. I'm trying to protect mine." There was no confidence in Soudi's words, and her hands shook. "But I need your help. Your . . . your brave *ways*."

"I don't understand," Maryam said, though she did. But she needed to hear Soudi say it.

"Please. Look at my granddaughter's face." Both grandmother and granddaughter were crying now. "I implore you. We need to get rid of him."

"I'm sorry, are you asking me to *murder* your son-in-law?"

"Grandson-in-law . . . I . . . that is why I'm here," Soudi stammered.

"Khanoum, you can't, I can't . . ." Maryam stood and poured a glass of tea, stirring in several extra strands of saffron for herself now.

At that moment, Shokat, her younger sister, Ezzhat, and littlest Atta came running into the kitchen. When Shokat saw that her mother had guests, she stopped short. "Oh, Maman, I'm sorry. We didn't mean to interrupt."

Ezzhat wordlessly grabbed a handful of cookies and began to tear around the kitchen, until Shokat managed to corral her siblings back out into the courtyard.

Maryam watched the children run toward the horses, her heart swelling.

"Khanoum Mahdavi, Maryam jaan. You have daughters, I see. One day they will be married. And God forbid"—Soudi opened her hands and looked up, whispering in prayer before finishing her sentence—"God forbid one of your daughters should suffer the same cruelty as my Soheila. What would you do?"

Maryam looked out the window at her playing children and then back again at the old woman before she spoke. "I would do anything."

Soudi stood up slowly and placed a gold coin in Maryam's palm. "I know I'm asking a lot. Believe me, I do. I don't know where else to go. Your grandmother was such a good friend. She was one of the bravest women I have ever known . . . and the tales of your courage, our very own Gordafarid in the North . . . forgive me."

A heavy silence gripped the room. The calming aroma of saffron swirled in the air, but the grief, worry, and pain were etched across the faces of both visitors who sat opposite Maryam. She gulped back the lump that was forming in her throat, looking at Soheila's battered face and trying to imagine what she would do if it were Ezzhat or Shokat.

Maryam set the gold coin down on the table in front of Soudi and stepped out into the courtyard. Her head was buzzing. She had to help these women; of that she was certain. But she wasn't an assassin. That's not what Gordafarid would have done.

Eventually, she went back inside. The women hadn't moved. Soheila stared into the dregs of her tea while her grandmother stroked her hair.

"I have an idea," Maryam said.

The older woman fell to her knees in grateful prayer, but Soheila looked uncertain.

"Don't give me your money now, Khanoum. This will take some time. Soheila, I'm not going to kill your husband. But I am going to get you away from him. You understand?"

The girl nodded tentatively.

"Can you ride?" Maryam asked.

Soheila's undamaged eye darted to her grandmother and then back to Maryam. She shook her head.

Maryam bit her lip. This was going to be even trickier than she'd thought.

Earlier that year Maryam had accompanied Ali on a trip to Mashad, the largest city in the North and believed to be one of the holiest cities in the country. He was trading fruits of their harvest for gold and jewelry that they would store up as dowry for their daughters.

When they arrived in Mashad, a merchant friend invited them to his home for dinner, insisting they stay the night.

Maryam had inherited her mother's tenacity about trade and merchants. After all, it was these trade routes where members of their family had been swindled, taken for unsuspecting farmers, and it was on a trade mission to Mashad that her father had been killed. Maryam fought a shiver that she could only assume was the ghost of her father. Still, this man was going to be an important trade partner for her husband, so she accepted. As soon as she met his wife, she was glad she had.

The merchant's wife, a woman aptly named Ghazal, for she was tall with long, thin legs and had sun-lightened hair that gave her the appearance of a gazelle's stripes, welcomed Maryam with open arms. She, too, had heard of Maryam's bravery and found her inspiring. Ghazal invited Maryam to join her and her sisters for a bath at the local hamam, where they could speak in private.

"Maryam joon, we aren't so different," Ghazal said, referring to her three sisters who were gathered around a gurgling marble fountain, sponging dirt from their faces and hands. "We've killed, like you. But, like you, we only did it when we had to."

Maryam was puzzled. She bit her lip to pull in her chin, but also leaned closer, breathless with anticipation.

As Ghazal continued her story, Maryam relaxed into her new friend's voice, entranced.

Three of Ghazal's sisters lived in Afghanistan—north of the city of Herat, just across the border from where they were bathing in Mashad. There, in the hills between Herat and Mazar-i-Sharif, these sisters along with roughly two dozen other women had made their homes in a series of mountain caves. Some had children; others did not. No men were allowed. The women were raising an all-female army trained on horse-back to protect themselves against the various rounds of invaders that threatened their country and families.

If Afghanistan was the graveyard of empires, the corridor connecting Mashad to Herat and Mazar-i-Sharif was the bridge between the living and the dead. Along the route, a vestige of the Silk Road, warlords still traded opium and weapons. Women, if unarmed and untrained, could be raped by the warlords and illicit traders who caught them there. It was also an entry point for the invasions of the Mongols, then the Brits, and then the Soviets. When each successive round of soldiers arrived, the women warriors were ready for them, guarding their lands as fiercely as they could when so underresourced.

Once or twice a year, the sisters in Iran—Ghazal included—traveled to Afghanistan to bring in new recruits. Ghazal invited Maryam to join as a recruit. Though she knew Maryam was happily married, rumors of her bravery and skill had reached them, and she hoped Maryam would stay and train to become one of their generals.

"That is inspiring in every sense of the word," Maryam smiled. "And please do not misunderstand me, sister. I am in support of what you are doing. I do believe that all women should learn to fight for their rights and to protect our families and our lands—we can't just leave it up to the men. But I can't join you. I have a family, a farm, a herd to care for."

"We need you in the fight, Maryam," Ghazal pleaded. She took Maryam's hand in hers, green eyes bright. Ghazal squeezed Maryam's hand tighter, leaning in closer so that their foreheads touched. "Men in Iran and Afghanistan—they are raping and murdering our mothers, sisters, daughters, and friends."

Maryam leaned away from Ghazal so she could wipe a tear sliding down her cheek. "My heart hurts for them. It does, my friend. And I am glad you are part of the fight. Perhaps someday I will join you."

Maryam was silent for the duration of the trip home from Mashad. She contemplated Ghazal's words, her invitation, her story. A part of Maryam wanted to follow these sisters to Afghanistan, to meet the women of the caves. To run, ride, and revolt with them. But her family and her farm needed her.

Now, many months later, as a grandmother and her daughter sat pleadingly in Maryam's living room, she realized that the merchant's wife was going to be a part of her story after all. A plan began to form. She could take this trembling young woman across the border to Afghanistan and turn her into a fighter. This would also give her the excuse she had been looking for to reconnect with Ghazal. She could ride into Afghanistan and join the fight by bringing a new recruit. It wasn't the same as living there herself, but at least she could get a window into this intriguing group of women.

When Ali returned home from Tehran the next day, Maryam was waiting for him.

"I need you to stay home for a bit with Maman and the children," Maryam ventured. Ali shot her a puzzled look. "I need to go for a long ride. Could be many days. I'm not sure."

"Why, my dear? Are you feeling restless?"

Maryam shook her head and told her husband about the old woman and her granddaughter. His eyes grew wide. And then she told him her plan, and she watched as his lungs stopped filling with air. They were both only twenty years old, but as she looked at her husband, Maryam marveled how his face grew more handsome with each passing year. He had finally lost the roundness of his cheeks that Maryam now saw in her children, and his hair had grown over his ears, curling at the temples she loved to kiss at night. His eyes, like hers, she imagined, looked much older than their years. They watered with pain when Ali thought she wasn't looking. He felt like a constant disappointment to his family because he hated trading on the road, preferring to be home with his wife and children.

"I'll go to Mashad first and connect with the merchant's wife I met last time, the one who has sisters across the border. Then I'll ride to Afghanistan, to the hills and the cave women there."

Ali's mouth fell open. Maryam hadn't previously shared with him the story Ghazal told her of the women in the caves. He studied his wife's face for clues. She never ceased to surprise him. As she told him about Ghazal and her sisters, Ali nodded, but an anxious frown began to turn his mouth downward.

"That's a dangerous journey, and an even more dangerous place to cross the border." Maryam thought she could detect a slight tremble in his voice, his face drained of color.

"Dangerous for someone who can't ride, but I'll take two horses, Asghar and Khosrow. I need to find a safe place for the girl, Ali. I have to get her far away from her husband."

"So you're going to smuggle her into Afghanistan?" he asked, incredulous, his voice rising three octaves.

"Azzizam, I'm not a murderer. But . . . a smuggler? Well . . ." Maryam didn't meet her husband's eye. "The merchant's wife says that up in those caves they train women to be strong, to be fighters."

Ghazal had talked about how these cave dwellers were forming an all-female army to fight the invading Soviets; imagining these modern-day Gordafarids lifted Maryam's heart.

Ali drew in a deep breath and dug his hands into his hair. "Does the girl even know how to ride? That's not easy terrain."

Maryam softened at his words. Her perfect husband. She could see him trying to find it in his heart to support this terrifying plan.

"She doesn't, but I have an idea for that too. We'll use a batch of Maman's home brew, either the dog vodka or the whiskey."

"For the girl? Didn't you say the family was devout?"

"Not for the girl, for the horse."

Ali stared at his wife. "You're going to get the horses *drunk*?"

"Only to calm them at the border. Not my horse, of course, but whichever one I put Soheila on. For her, a bit of opium." Maryam held her breath, searching Ali's face.

Ali took his wife's calloused hand in his. "I'm terrified of losing you, my love. But I also know you, and once you put your mind to something, God himself couldn't stop you."

Maryam exhaled audibly. She hadn't realized she'd been holding her breath. She had decided that she would go with or without his blessing, but knowing that he supported her gave her a sense of tranquillity and reassurance that this was indeed the right thing to do.

Maryam instructed Soudi to bring Soheila to the saffron farm under the cover of nightfall. They would set out at the first light of dawn, at which point Soudi would have to bid her granddaughter good-bye. That part of the plan had been hard for Soudi—she might not ever see her granddaughter again—but Maryam assured her that she would be in good hands. Most important, she would be safe. It would have to be worth the trade-off. Grandmother and granddaughter agreed.

Maryam readied the horses before the sun kissed the sky. She chose her favorite horse, Asghar, a sturdy and sure-footed horse who was among the most forward and brave in the herd. Even if Asghar was a bit too eager to race, his fearlessness signaled to the other horses that they could follow with confidence. Maryam hoped to inspire the same feeling in Soheila. For the young girl, Maryam chose an older sorrel red gelding named Zereshk, meaning "barberry" in Persian. At twenty-one years old, Zereshk was one of the older horses on the farm. He was known for his even temperament and good nature. No matter how hard any of the kids pulled on his mane or how much they twisted the hand-woven reins Maryam and Ali gave them, Zereshk never stirred or bucked. As long as another horse was in front of him, he just kept trotting along, licking his lips and grabbing the occasional bite of grass or leaves when unsuspecting riders loosened their grip. Maryam also decided to bring along two other horses—one to carry their belongings and a second to have as backup in case anything were to go wrong. If all went according to plan, Maryam decided to offer one of the horses as a gift to the women of the caves as a sign of good faith. With Shokat's help, Maryam chose two twelve-year-old chestnut mares, sired by a stallion who had passed the previous winter. The mares were not as reliable as the gelding and stallion, but Maryam knew they did well on longer rides, not tiring or losing their footing on difficult terrain.

As nautical twilight gave way to dawn, Maryam, her four horses, and a saffron-settled Soheila were ready for the journey. It took them five days to cover the 448 miles from the village of Gonbad-i-Kavoos to Mashad. If Soheila didn't know how to ride on the first day, by the third day she had definitely learned. They made camp in the evenings, stopping to rest the horses, and then rose with the sun each morning.

The first night, Soheila couldn't sleep from the pain in her legs and buttocks. Then Maryam showed her how to ride with the horses by letting go of her muscles and letting her hips rock forward and back, swiveling along with the shoulder movements of the animals. A still traumatized Soheila listened intently to every word Maryam said and, by the third night, slept pain-free through until morning.

Ghazal was waiting on the outskirts of Mashad to accompany them across the border for the first introduction. Maryam had insisted that it was not necessary, recognizing that Ghazal would be in danger by including her in the smuggling effort. But Ghazal was adamant that she wanted to be part of the journey.

Ghazal had her own horse, a larger spotted gray and white stallion who caught the attention of the twelve-year-old mares, causing them to rear up as they went into heat. Maryam smiled and shook her head as the mares tossed their manes and encircled Ghazal's horse. It allowed for a moment of laughter between the three women that eased the tension each carried as they drew closer to the border.

After three days of riding, they finally reached the part of the Iran-Afghan border that Ghazal and her sister Ghashang, who was the commanding general of the women of the caves, had deemed safest for an illicit crossing. Other parts of the border were closer to Mashad but were littered with land mines. Ghazal told Maryam and Soheila that she had seen dozens of horse carcasses along that path.

"They use the horses as land-mine clearance," Ghazal said as they sat around the fire on their last night before the crossing. Maryam closed her eyes against the image. Soheila, whose nerves were no longer calmed by the saffron candy Maryam plied her with throughout the journey, turned away from the fire and vomited.

They rode to the top of a jagged hill where they could look across the border to assess the landscape. Maryam could feel her heart pounding in her throat. She wanted to look at Soheila, to see how the young girl was faring, but knew that if their eyes met it would only deter their resolve to make the crossing. Out of the corner of her vision she spotted Soheila glancing back over her shoulder. Maryam knew that she was taking in her last glimpse of her homeland before looking across to Afghanistan and a life in exile.

"Afghanistan and Iran are not so different, my girl," Ghazal said, as if she could read Maryam's and Soheila's minds. "In fact, I love both countries as my own, and you will too, Soheila jaan."

Soheila burst into tears. Maryam watched her grip loosen, then drop the reins, and instinctively she dismounted to run to the gelding. Before the reins hit the rocky soil, Maryam caught them in one hand. She pulled the leather bag she had been wearing across her body forward, so she could retrieve the bottle of homemade whiskey.

Maryam looked from Zereshk to Soheila, both of whom were on the verge of losing their nerve. She had planned to feed the drink only to the horse but in that moment decided Soheila needed it as well. She uncorked the glass bottle and tipped it first into Zereshk's mouth. He shook his head instinctively, and his skull would have collided with Soheila's face had Maryam not been holding the reins to pull him forward. Maryam reached again into her bag to retrieve an apple and fed it to Zereshk to change the taste in his mouth. Within seconds as bits of apple chunks spilled out of his mouth, he had forgotten the bitter taste of the home brew. His entire body relaxed as the whiskey worked its magic.

Soheila was next. "You need to drink this, my girl," Maryam insisted, lifting the bottle up to her lips. She had to stand on a rock and on her tiptoes to reach Soheila, who was still, thanks to Maryam, mounted on Zereshk.

Soheila's eyes widened. She shook her head. "I'm sorry, Khanoum. I don't drink. It's not proper."

"This is not about being proper; it's about survival," Maryam responded, her voice dropping almost to a whisper.

"Go on, girl, drink it," Ghazal intervened. "We don't have much time before a group of men—either Soviets or Afghan warlords—inevitably turns up at the border. We need to reach my sister's caves by nightfall. So just drink."

Soheila looked from Ghazal to Maryam to the horses and then back to the bottle in Maryam's hand. She had come this far. And she did not want to let down these two women whose strength inspired her and to whom she had grown attached during the journey. Mustering up all her courage, Soheila grabbed the bottle from Maryam and tipped it back into her mouth.

She instinctively spit out the first sip. Maryam and Ghazal laughed.

"It's not for the taste. Think of it like medicine."

"Drink or don't drink, but make up your mind fast; we only have minutes to get through this crossing, ladies," Ghazal insisted. She rode around the other horses to bring them into formation so that they were all facing the same way, ready to ride into the valley, across the border, and then up a steep hill.

In a flash, Maryam tipped the bottle back into Soheila's mouth. After she gulped it down, Maryam took a swig herself, before offering some to Ghazal. Ghazal shook her head.

"I don't need it to cross; we will drink the rest tonight in celebration of the successful journey," she quipped. "Now, let's ride."

Five horses and three riders pounded down the jagged face of the hill toward a clearing. Ten minutes later, Ghazal, who was leading the group on her gray stallion, turned over her shoulder and winked. This was Maryam's signal that they had crossed the border. Maryam nodded and smiled.

After three more hours, they finally reached the base of a series of mountains that rose into the air like smokestacks. Small rectangular doorways and oval windows were carved into the hillside. Maryam and Soheila stared up in wonder at the formations. How had these women created homes built into the stone?

Ghazal dismounted slowly. Maryam followed and then instructed Soheila to do the same.

Before they could speak, Ghazal began to sing. Her melodious voice echoed across the mountains. It was a familiar song that Maman used to sing whenever family members returned from a trip.

I went with you; I came without you. From the top of the mountains, my heart grew crazy with desire. It was a desire for my friend. It was a desire to be—home . . .

As Ghazal sung out the last word, a chorus joined her. Suddenly, there were at least a dozen women pouring out of the windows and doorways of the smokestacks, singing. They synced their voices in unison, completing the words of the song as they drew closer. By the time they had all reached the bottom of the hills where Maryam, Soheila, and Ghazal were standing, the song finished, and a tall woman with Ghazal's sparkling green eyes but whose hair was black like the color of Rostam's mane ran to embrace her sister.

"Ah, you must be Maryam Mahdavi. I have heard much about you, as tales of you have reached us here from traders who bring us goods and weapons," Ghazal's sister said. She reached for Maryam, bending at the waist given their height difference, and pulled her in close so that she could kiss each cheek three times.

"And you must be Ghashang." Maryam smiled. "What a pleasure to meet you. Thank you for hosting us."

"And who is this?" Ghashang asked, walking up to Soheila. The general towered over the young girl, who trembled from head to toe.

Maryam looped her arm around Soheila's waist to reassure her. "This, General Ghashang, is Soheila Mohseni, your newest recruit."

Soheila's eyes widened as they drifted to Ghashang's waist. She had multiple rounds of artillery slung across one shoulder and a belt of knives.

Though Maryam had explained to Soheila on the journey that she would be joining an all-female army, it hadn't actually sunk in until this exact moment.

"Worry not, my child. You are welcome here," Ghashang said. A warm smile softened her weather-worn face.

Soheila's body remained stiff even when the general pulled her into an embrace and kissed her once on the cheek. She stood looking up at Ghashang's eyes, unable to speak.

A moment of silence passed between the women. It was broken by Ghashang turning back to the women who had followed her down the hill.

"Where is my daughter, Mina? Bring her so that she might meet our new friend. I imagine they are close to the same in age."

"I'm here, Mother," came a soft but deep voice from the back of the crowd. A young girl who couldn't have been any older than twelve, it seemed to Maryam, began making her way to where she, Soheila, Ghazal, and Ghashang stood. Though the girl was tall like her mother, it was clear by their smooth, rounded faces that neither Soheila nor Mina had yet been through puberty, and thus the general's assessment of their close ages was likely correct. It was also clear to Maryam as she observed Soheila watching this young girl float through the crowd that her presence, and the confidence with which she moved toward them, immediately put Soheila at ease.

"It's good to see you, Auntie," Mina said. She kissed Ghazal on both cheeks and then stepped back to her mother's side. Maryam studied their faces. Mina had the same emerald eyes that had entranced Maryam the first time she met Ghazal at her home in Mashad. She carried herself with the same grace as her aunt and mother, shoulders back and chins high despite their height. A halo of calm around them. Mina's hair was black, but unlike her mother who let her locks fall long and wild about her shoulders, Mina cropped hers at chin length, the way Maryam did when she was her age.

Ghashang whispered something in her daughter's ear, and Mina nodded. She reached out and took Soheila's hand in hers. Gently, she led her new friend away from the crowd and began skipping toward the smokestacks.

A wave of relief washed over Maryam as she watched the two, their friendship already cemented. Soheila would never again get to hug her beloved grandmother. But this new life would offer her strength, safety, and friendship—things her old life with her abusive husband would never have afforded her.

AND SO it was that Maryam became a smuggler. She told herself that helping women was a calling for her and the horses. The story of Soheila's escape spread, and it wasn't long before a mother arrived with her daughter, followed by another, then another. Some paid Maryam in gold, others in crops and goods. Some brought gifts for the horses. A few even brought horses as gifts. Maryam began seasonal trips planned around the weather and the crop cycles. Soon she was smuggling up to a dozen women across the border at once. The family began training more horses for border crossings and brewing more whiskey to meet the increased demand. Maman hired more farmhands and taught the children how to perform their mother's chores in her absence.

Ali rode with them sometimes, but always stopped at the border. Occasionally, a woman would change her mind just before crossing and choose to go back to her husband, however harmful. For these women, the pain of being away from home and their families, even for a few years, was too high a price to pay. But mostly, the women crossed and didn't look back.

When Maryam met Ghashang, Mina, and the women of the caves, every fiber of her being ignited with inspiration. Their strength gave her the courage to return year after year with ever more women for their army. And on every trip, Maryam saw how the women she had brought were growing stronger and more confident, until they were unrecognizable as the terrified girls they had been. Soheila grew strong, doubling in musculature within only a year. And just as Mina took Soheila under her wing, Soheila in turn took others under hers, and they similarly paid the sisterhood and mentorship forward. In time they learned combat, and a few, like Soheila, became lieutenants, choosing to remain in Afghanistan and embrace a whole new kind of life.

And Afghanistan in the 1930s, as the country entered its Golden Age, was the perfect place for reinvention. The year 1933, when Soheila arrived at the caves, was a turning point. On November 8 of that year, Mohammed Nadir Shah, a king known for his brutality and raising armies to rape and pillage the lands, was shot by a seventeen-year-old named Abdul Khaliq at a soccer game. King Nadir was succeeded by his son, Mohammed Zahir Shah. Zahir, only nineteen at the time, was the opposite of his father. Named the "Father of the Nation," he ushered in a new era of peace for the country that calmed the land for the next few decades.

For five years, Maryam managed to shepherd these women to safety without the knowledge of their husbands. Ali brought home stories from the trade bazaar of men who claimed a "wife killer" was on the loose. Some did believe their wives had been murdered, others thought they'd committed suicide, and a few assumed they'd run away only to meet an untimely death by accident—bad luck. Most didn't care. But as Maryam smuggled more and more women across the border, stories of her success, which had been kept within the realm of women, began to spill over to angry men who beat the truth out of reluctant wives, sisters, and daughters.

By the time Shokat was ten years old, Maryam had developed a reputation. Drunk or high or just plain furious husbands began appearing at the farm, slurring insults and taking out their fury on the crops. Occasionally, an angry—usually older—woman would arrive. These women screamed into the night, calling curses to rain down on Maryam. They accused her of being a ruined woman who broke apart families and damned her children to have broken lives. One man arrived in the middle of the night and slaughtered one of their horses. By this time, Maryam and Ali both had shotguns. They chased the horse murderer into the forest and shot him in the leg. They didn't kill him; he was a message. For a couple of years after that, no one else came.

MINA, 1950

MINA COULDN'T REMEMBER NOT KNOWING HOW TO RIDE. Horses were her life. She depended on them, and they never let her down.

When Soheila asked her how she had learned to ride, Mina could only shrug. She could no more answer that question than explain how she had learned to walk. Her body was made to ride. Mina trusted the horses, and she trusted the women of the caves, those who trained her and those who became her friends, her compatriots like Soheila. Her solace was in these two loves.

When Mina was seven years old, her mother, Ghashang, had left her at home in Kabul with her father and brothers and traveled to Iran with Mina's aunties Ghazal and Ghesmat. One afternoon while her mother was still away, Mina's friend Hiba invited her over for lunch.

After feasting on lamb and rice pilaf, Hiba suggested they play dress-up. This was Mina's least favorite activity. If she couldn't be on a horse, she at least wanted to be outside climbing rocks and trees. But her mother was gone, her brothers and father were out hunting, and she had nothing better to do, so she agreed.

"Let's stage a wedding," Hiba said, sorting through the dresses in her mother's modest clothing trunk. Mina was to play the bride, her most hated role. Hiba helped her into a white dress and twisted her long black hair into a bun. She even had a tiara for Mina to wear. Her grandfather, Hiba explained, would be Mina's groom while Hiba officiated. The girls spread out a cloth on the floor and anchored it with teacups and a few dolls as the wedding guests.

As soon as Hiba pronounced the bride and groom to be husband and wife, Hiba's grandfather asked his granddaughter to leave the room. It was only when the other little girl had gone, shutting the heavy door behind her, that it occurred to Mina to be afraid.

The old man ordered her to lie down on a small mattress in the corner of the room. "It's our wedding night," he told her. Mina, frozen in fear, didn't move, so he picked her up and put her on the bed himself. Sunlight poured in from the window above the mattress, and the brightness blinded her. The old man placed something cold and hard in the palm of her hand. She traced the shape and realized it was a perfume bottle.

"Put some on."

Her fingers trembled. She rolled over, out of the sun's glare, and saw the old man taking off his clothes. Something deep inside her jerked her out of the state of suspension, and she leaped off the bed and raced for the door—only to find it locked. She ran around the room, but Hiba's grandfather grabbed her and threw her down. The back of her head hit the bed frame, and she screamed.

Later, Mina pulled the wedding dress back over her body but could not find her underwear. She walked to the door and peered through the keyhole. What she saw was not a key, but Hiba's eye staring back at her.

Her friend unlocked the door, and the two girls stood face-to-face.

"I'm sorry," Hiba said, her voice flat.

For months, Mina did not dare speak about that afternoon. Her mother was still in Iran helping her sisters, and Mina knew she could only wait. But when Ghashang finally returned, Mina told her parents what had happened. Her father became enraged.

"How dare you make such an accusation! Hiba's grandfather is a prominent man in our village. Why would you say such a thing?" her father roared.

Tears rolled down Mina's face, and her mother rushed to envelop her little girl in her arms.

"Don't blame her, husband. It happened to me, too, and to my sisters. You know it's true."

Her father shook his head. "Your daughter brings shame upon this family!"

"No, it is you who brings shame, Ahmed."

Mina's father raised his hand. She knew what was coming but could not bring herself to look away. She felt the pain of the slap across her mother's face as sharply as if it were her own cheek stinging. Her father raised his hand again, but this time Ghashang reached for the steaming pot on the stove and flung it at him.

"You disgusting whore!" he shouted, hot stew dripping down his shirt. He lunged for his wife, but Mina wedged her body between her parents and kicked her father in the shin. In one swift motion, he picked her up and threw her across the room. Ghashang grabbed a knife, and just as her husband turned to bring the full force of his rage back on her, she drove the blade into his stomach. Dazed, Mina watched as her father crumpled and blood began to seep across the tiles.

Ghashang dropped the knife and grabbed her daughter. "Mina, we don't have much time. Go get Ruba." At the mention of her favorite horse, the girl ran to the yard. Ruba and her mother's horse, Farah, seemed to sense something awful had happened. They and the three stallions the family owned formed a circle around her, protecting her. In that moment, Mina would have given anything to be a horse rather than a girl.

"We need to ride north, far north, to the caves. Do you understand?" Her mother came into the yard carrying two large bags and several blankets.

At seven, the girl was already stronger than most boys in the village, and she helped her mother distribute the weight of the bags on one of the stallions. Then she used the blankets and some rope to make sitting pads first on Ruba and then on Farah. Ghashang tied a rope to the packed stallion, and mother and daughter mounted, riding away from the house. Mina could feel Ruba's heart beating, and she focused on its steady rhythm, reassured by its consistency and power.

Mina and Ghashang never saw their home village again, never confirmed Ahmed's death, though they knew, and never again saw either of Mina's two brothers. But they had their lives, which were finally their own.

Ghashang had known to go north, to the caves, because of the lore of the women there, the ones who had escaped abusive husbands and fathers and brothers. The legend was shared like an amulet among wives and daughters and sisters. Whispers in the wind ensured that their stories reached those who needed to hear them. Ghashang first learned of the cave women when she was pregnant with Mina. Her husband had beaten her, again, and she had sought solitude and refuge in the mosque. While she was praying, an older woman approached her.

"I know you, Ghashang jaan, because I knew your mother," she said, taking the young woman's bruised hands in her own. "Your mother was strong, and so are you. Stronger and better than this man. Go north. Join the women of the caves."

From then on, Ghashang carried the woman's story with her and sought out more knowledge. But all those years later when she and Mina fled, she still didn't know how much, if any, of the stories was really true. When after five long days of riding they reached the caves and were greeted only by eerie quiet, Ghashang wondered if maybe it was all myth. Mother and daughter were exhausted and had no place else to go. That night, they made camp at the base of the caves.

And then, there they were: a dozen women emerging from the darkness. They scooped up the weary travelers and took them into the caves and a new way of life. Ghashang and Mina never looked back. They rose with the sun, fed the horses, and mended the clothes and linens. When all that was done, they turned to their other work, sharpening their swords, cleaning their guns, and polishing their armor. Each woman was given her own woven silver metal chest plate to mold to her body. Mina learned to heat metal to shape her sword into jagged points that favored the movement of her hands. She was trained in the delicate art of metallurgy and found she had a knack for it.

The girl loved their new life. She loved that she was constantly surrounded by women who looked out for her and guided her and rushed to soothe her when she woke screaming in the middle of the night, her memories having found her in sleep. She watched her mother relax, flourish, and grow stronger. Mina, too, marveled at how her own body was changing day to day. The muscles in her calves, biceps, and trapezoids swelled.

Fighting came naturally to both mother and daughter. Within only a few years, Ghashang was promoted to general, and Mina became a confident hunter, soldier, markswoman, and killer. She shot her first leopard when she was ten, rode brazenly into her first battle against a group of drug lords at barely eleven, and on the night of her twelfth birthday, she dreamed of killing Hiba's grandfather. The dream was so vivid that when Mina woke up, she knew her rapist must surely be dead. He never bothered her dreams again.

When Mina met Soheila, she recognized the way the girl carried herself, the look of terror and panic writ large across her face, because she had arrived at the caves in the same state. But she wasn't that scared little girl anymore, and she had known that Soheila didn't have to be either. If she could heal, so could her new friend.

Most nights, Soheila cried so hard in her sleep that she woke herself up, and Mina, too. The two girls sat in the dark, holding hands and whispering until morning. Mina told the story of her rape, and Soheila described being raped every night of her marriage.

"The horses can help heal you," Mina promised.

"They are beautiful, but they frighten me," Soheila sobbed.

"I was frightened of many things when I arrived here, too. Not horses, though; never horses. They are the gentlest beings on this earth, I swear it. The best of God's creations. Trust me, my sister, they *will* heal you, if you let them. If you trust them."

Slowly, hour by hour, Mina helped Soheila remember who she was. Learning to ride was the first and most significant step. When Soheila learned to mount the horse that the great Iranian woman Maryam had left behind for her, her eyes danced with joy.

The girls practiced riding up and down the jagged peaks of the mountains surrounding their caves, and Mina told Soheila that not only were the horses healing her, but they would also enable continued survival.

"*You* are my survival, Mina," Soheila said, smiling at her friend as they bounced along the sandstone landscape, their hair blowing free and wild. "You, the women of the caves, and our horses, too. You are power, joy, and healing. I am lucky to be among you."

"No man will ever hurt us again," Mina replied, as much to herself as to Soheila.

MARYAM, 1940

THE LAND WHERE THE FOREST KISSED THE SEA WAS WHERE Mother Earth presented her best gifts, it seemed to Maryam. A dozen spring plantings had brought a bounty of fall harvests, each year richer than the last. The fertility of the soil was matched only by Maryam's own body, which had birthed a dozen more children between 1927 and 1940. One, who would have been her fourth child and second son, died during childbirth. And while she was devastated, her other children needed her, so she summoned her warrior strength to bury her son and carry on. Maryam could no longer remember a time when she wasn't pregnant or nursing, and Shokat, who was nearly the age Maryam had been when she married Ali, now had eleven siblings. Twelve children to help care for and pluck the delicate saffron crop. Twelve children to tend to the growing herd, which now numbered twenty-two horses. Their bounty was indeed overflowing.

Despite her loud giggles as a baby, Shokat was a quiet young woman. She preferred the company of horses and other farm animals to people, and she loved working the land. Next in line, Ezzhat was everything Shokat was not: boisterous, with a contagious laugh that seemed to echo through the forest and bounce off the sea, Ezzhat was everywhere at once, indefatigable. She reminded Maryam of her mother in her glory days.

Maman still lived with them and still worked the earth, but the vigor that had ignited her when Baba and Asghar were alive was only a memory. Her initial enthusiasm for work on the new farm had also faded, replaced by a deep, unrelenting, grief-induced exhaustion. While Maman continued to rise before the sun and tend to the horses, many of her daily chores were taken over by her grandchildren. Ezzhat, in particular, took great pains to care for her grandmother. The two slept side by side, talking late into the night.

Ezzhat even looked like Maman, sharing her thick black curls, deep-set dark eyes that danced with mischievous fire, luminous skin, and sharp cheekbones. But she had Maryam's ruby-red lips—and they were permanently curled into a smile. Shokat, by contrast, looked more like her paternal grandmother. Her eyes were a soft hazel, but in the mornings when she first woke up, they were green. Her hair was light brown, almost blonde, and fell in gentle waves like the Caspian Sea at low tide. Where Ezzhat was all sharp angles, Shokat was softness embodied. She didn't speak unless spoken to. Ezzhat wanted to know everything—and wasn't afraid to ask and ask again. The two were less than eighteen months apart, and they were inseparable.

In between caring for her growing family and tending to the growing farm and herd, Maryam still found time to travel to the mountain caves in Afghanistan twice a year to smuggle women who sought freedom from abusive husbands. But the crossings were getting more difficult. The border was more heavily policed now, and conflicts over who controlled the poppy fields and by extension the opium trade between Afghan warlords and Soviet soldiers were on the rise. Ghazal, the merchant's wife in Mashad and her original contact with the horsewomen, had died as well. Maryam never knew if she died of natural causes, if she'd been murdered by soldiers during a crossing she undertook by herself, or if a jealous husband had been so enraged that Ghazal had helped his wife escape that he'd taken revenge.

And then the war in Europe crept closer to their border. By 1940, Afghan drug lords had started routing opium through the North to Europe. Enchanted by the poppy, the Soviets also had their eye on Iran as a faster trade route to selling heroin and opium to the masses in Europe. But the Afghan and Iranian kings clamped down on the drug trade, wanting to send a message to the Soviets: stay out. All borders were tightened, but especially those in the North.

"I won't be able to pass the usual way," Maryam told Ali one morning. They were forking out bales of hay for the horses when Maryam received a telegram from Ghashang. Ali asked her to read it aloud. Maryam unfurled the paper, cleared her throat, and began reading:

BORDERS BAD. DRUGLORDS EVERYWHERE. DO NOT KNOW
WHO FIGHTING WHO. FIND A DIFFERENT PATH.

"You'll have to swing north, my dear," Ali advised. "Straight up and over the mountains instead of around."

Maryam shook her head. She wanted to do anything but change her entry route. The road Ali was advising was a rockier, stormier, more challenging path, impassible in winter. The horses had a hard-enough time finding their footing in snow that froze to ice underneath. To ask them to travel uphill and then downhill, when the risk of slipping would result in certain death, was not something Maryam wanted to entertain. And the snow would not melt until late spring. Best-case scenario: if the horses did make it up and then down the steep, jagged cliffs in snow, they might still be met with violence on the other side if the opium routes shifted.

"I can't get in that way; it's a march to death," Maryam told her husband.

"I've said all along that these rides into Afghanistan are suicide, Maryam jan. Can't you find somewhere else to go?"

Maryam began contemplating Ali's advice. Perhaps Afghanistan was not the place to ride into in the midst of winter and a drug war. She had heard that Turkey was determined to avoid any involvement in the drug trade. Kemal Attaturk had turned the country inward, focusing on economic prosperity. The border crossings from northern Iran into Turkey were also less strenuous. Maryam could ride across the steppe plains where the snow fell only like powdered sugar, an easy ride for her sure-footed horses, around the Caspian, and into Turkey via the Kurdish-occupied town of Van. The terrain was softer and the weather much gentler. Ali had business contacts in Van, so they decided to travel there in search of women who might be willing to create a safe house.

As they rode into Van for the first time, a crowd gathered around them. They were less interested in Maryam and Ali than in their horses, who held their heads high even when mounted. One of the local children held up her schoolbook, pointing to a copy of a horse painting. The horses were smaller than Arabians, Turkomans, or Akhal-Tehkes, but larger than ponies. No one in Van had ever seen such delicate but powerful animals. They could gallop at high speeds but just as easily stop and turn about-face. These horses were friendly, yet guarded, loyal first and foremost to their riders.

One night as Maryam made camp, three Kurdish women approached. They wore their brightly colored floral headscarves tied under their hair rather than their chins, as the Afghan militant women did, their tempestuous curls springing out of the fabric. They wore layers of coin-patterned jewelry around their necks like jingling scarves. Coins hung from the fabric of their dresses, skirts, and even the cuffs of their shirts. They were shorter than Maryam, about the height of her daughters, but much more curvaceous. When they spoke to her, they looked at her out of the corner of their eyes, turning their heads in profile, which made Maryam instinctively lower her chin.

The women were interested in the horses. They loved the size of their bodies, that they were closer to the ground, their rib cages narrower. One of the women asked if she could climb up on Khosrow, and Maryam agreed. The woman clapped her hands in delight and then laid her torso along the horse's long neck and mane when mounted. She closed her eyes as she stroked his hollowed-out jaw. Khosrow, ever the lover of attention, closed his eyes in relaxation.

The Kurdish women told Maryam that they were training to play an old Turkish sport that was used as combat training, called cirit, or javelin. It consisted of riders throwing spears at their opponents to knock them off. It was a brutal, bloody sport, but the women were determined to incorporate it into their combat training. Being good at cirit brought a level of respect, they told Maryam, one that would allow them to keep their husbands—who were just as inclined to abuse their wives as the men in Iran—and the other men of Van in check. But they needed horses.

"You need horses. I need a safe place for women running away from bad men. This is a good match," Maryam told them. And with that, Maryam had found her partners in Turkey—an unlikely group of javelin-throwing Kurdish women who took in the women Maryam smuggled away from abusive husbands in Iran, kept them safe, and trained them in the art of a combative sport.

While her mother was away setting up the second safe house in Turkey, Ezzhat, at twelve years old, continued to grow more beautiful and outgoing. She spent her days riding to different farms, meeting potential suitors, and setting hearts aflame.

"She's growing wilder and more beautiful," Maman said to Maryam and Ali one evening after she returned from Turkey, "while your reputation isn't exactly improving."

"She's right, my dearest," Ali agreed. Maryam wondered if they had choreographed this conversation. "We need to think about a good match for Ezzhat. Especially with us gone so often."

Feeling cornered, Maryam started to shout. "I won't hear of it! No, no, no!"

"Then darling, would you consider a break from the crossings?" Ali pleaded. "It might help with our reputation. And you could spend more time at home with the children."

At this, Maryam leaped up and began hurling dishes to the floor, shattering one after the other. She stormed out to the courtyard, mounted Khosrow, and rode off. She was gone all night, returning only after Ali had left on another trading trip.

One evening, as Shokat and Ezzhat prepared dinner for their nine brothers, Maryam heard unfamiliar hoofbeats. She followed the sound into the courtyard. There was Ali atop the largest horse she'd ever seen. The stallion's coat was a dark, dappled gray that rippled with shades of black, purple, and even blue. His neck was long, longer than any of the other horses in the herd, and it was punctuated with a narrow face and deep-set gray eyes. As she studied the newcomer, her husband slid off the horse's back and stepped around to enfold her in an embrace from behind.

"Don't even think about it, Ali," she warned playfully. He marveled at her slender, delicate waist and how she had retained her girlish figure. Maryam leaned her head back, resting on his chest, and felt something cool against her skin. Ali had draped a silvery chain around her neck. She felt its weight and looked down to see a smooth turquoise stone at the end of the chain. Ali spun her around and kissed her, but Maryam pulled back quickly.

"Wait, what is this about? What do you want?" she asked, arching a single black eyebrow.

"What are you talking about, azzizam? I saw this in Mashad and thought of you. I saw you eyeing Auntie Manijeh's daughter's turquoise rings. And I wanted you to have some turquoise, too." Ali bent to plant a kiss on the side of her protruding chin. Maryam felt her entire body flush.

Her body awakened for his, but she shook her head and took another step back. She let her eyes linger on his as she fingered her new necklace.

"Okay, Maryam jooni, if you don't like the necklace, at least tell me you like the horse?" Ali's voice cracked with uncertainty.

Maryam narrowed her eyes and drifted toward the magnificent creature. He was taller than any horse she had ever seen, his body narrower, his conformation more pronounced.

"He's a purebred Arabian stallion," Ali whispered in her ear.

"An Arab?" Maryam gasped. She clapped her hands and smiled with her whole body. "He is a dream."

Her husband exhaled audibly.

"Ali, where did you get him? I've heard about the Arabians, but they are so expensive . . . How? Where?" Maryam was overcome with excitement.

Their children shuffled into the courtyard, stopping dead in their tracks when they saw the horse.

"Oh, he is magnificent," Shokat purred. She leaned her face into the gray speckles of his fur and kissed his nose.

"Move, sister. I wanna see," Ezzhat ordered. But when she went to put a hand on the horse, he jerked his head away and backed up onto his hind legs.

"Mmhmm, an Arabian, all right," Maryam smiled. "Hot-blooded. Just like you, Ezzi." The other children laughed.

While Maryam, Shokat, and Ezzhat were fawning over the horse, Ali scooped up one son and then another, curling them tight against his chest.

"Baba, you were gone so long this time!" Parviz, the second son, pouted.

"What did you bring from Mashad?" asked little Mahmood.

"I brought spices, herbs, and lots of stories," Ali told him. "But first . . . what is that delicious smell?"

"Abji made olive tapenade from the olives we picked," Mahmood said with pride.

"And older abji made a lamb stew. But dadash ate all the tahdig," Parviz lamented.

"Your sisters are amazing cooks, you know that? And as the eldest brother, your dadash will always get first service; that's just the way it goes, boys. That's how it was for me growing up, too."

Parviz and Mahmood shrugged, wriggled to be let down, then rushed off to finish their chores before nightfall, when the late autumn air would turn bitter cold.

"My dearest, let's leave the girls here with the Arabian. I want to talk to you for a bit. I've been away so long." Ali gently took Maryam by the hand and led her to their favorite spot in the forest, the same spot where they had played as children. The same soil on which they had lain to make their children.

"Ali, I've missed you, azzizam, but I don't have the energy. We have too many children as it is. They are a gift from God, I know. As are you. But please."

"Darling, I actually want to *talk* to you," Ali said. He unlatched a blanket that he had rolled up and attached to his messenger bag during his journey and spread it on the ground in their usual ritual. Ali pulled Maryam into his arms, and they laid together, looking up at the stars through the forest canopy.

Maryam nestled into him and rested her pointy chin on his chest. Ali stroked her hair and inhaled her scent, a heady mixture of dirt, breast milk, and the orange-blossom petals she tucked into her brassiere and nightgowns.

"Azzizam, it's time," he said, taking a deep breath, willing himself to be calm.

"Time for what?" Maryam asked, sitting up, instantly on high alert. She sat on her knees so she could scrutinize her husband's face, but all she could discern was that he was more uncomfortable than she'd ever seen.

"It's time, for Ezzhat. And I guess Shokat, too." Ali braced himself. Knuckles white, he gripped the blanket, digging his nails into both the fabric and the soil.

"What are you . . . oh. No. You can't be serious. You mean . . . ?" Maryam pushed herself to stand and began pacing. She inhaled deeply, taking in the sea and the mist. Now she understood why he had come bearing such lavish gifts. Instinctively, she curled her fingers around the turquoise stone, yanked the necklace off, breaking the chain, and threw it at her husband.

"Azzizam, don't be like this. You know it needs to happen."

"She's a child, Ali! They both are. Just girls. We can't do that to them," Maryam snapped.

"Shokat is the same age you were—we were—when we married." Ali sat cross-legged now, watching his wife pace back and forth, chewing on her generous lips.

"Exactly, she is thirteen! And Ezzhat is only twelve!"

"It worked out for us, my darling. I couldn't be happier," Ali said softly. "And . . . and Ezzhat is the one they all want. They say she's our wild beauty."

Maryam shot Ali an icy stare. She shook her head and continued to pace. She concentrated on her breathing, the salty smell of the sea, the pine scent of the forest. She closed her eyes as she tried to wrap her mind around what was happening. "We can't marry Ezzhat off before Shokat. We just can't."

"Of course not. That's why I've been saying no to all the suitors who come for Ezzhat."

Slowly, the pieces began to fall into place. "Something has changed then, hasn't it? Someone has come for Shokat?"

Ali nodded. "Someone important. Someone our family—you—needs."

Maryam turned to her husband, eyebrows raised. He stretched his hand out to her, and she knelt beside him.

"He's a prominent lawyer and a judge. Think about it. He could protect us, protect you, given your . . . well, you've increased your . . . *operations* . . . and not just to Afghanistan but also Turkey."

It took Maryam a moment to understand the compromise Ali was suggesting, but when she did, she settled back into his arms and recalled Soheila, her first smuggle. Maryam remembered how Ali had supported her and her dangerous plan; not many men would have done the same. Year after year, Ali helped her get the women to safety, first to Afghanistan, then to Turkey. He had put his opinions and fears aside to stand by her. Now he was asking her for something. It was the first time he'd ever asked her for anything. She could see from his uneasiness, from the pleading look in his eyes, how desperately he wanted her to agree, how much he wanted to settle their daughters. Her shoulders slumped.

And so, it was decided. They would marry off both of their daughters— Maryam had given birth only to sons since Ezzhat and wouldn't birth another daughter for another two decades—in a double wedding in just one month's time.

The next four weeks passed in a chaotic and emotional blur. Predictably, Ezzhat was over the moon that she was to be married. Shokat was not. When they met their grooms, Ezzhat talked and laughed gaily with Mehdi, her betrothed, while Shokat could not even bring herself to make eye contact with the tall, slender man who sat before her. She had glanced at the shoes he left by the door—pointed and suspiciously shiny. This was a man who did not walk in dirt, who had almost certainly never worked the land.

Maman shoved a tea tray into her hands, and Shokat remembered her duty. Inside, Maryam could see her daughter was crumbling, but she did what was expected and bravely rose to serve her groom his tea.

Shokat still carried that brave face when the big day arrived, but Maryam could see she was also still struggling to contain the deep well of fear and dread she felt.

"You come from a long line of warrior women," Maryam counseled her brooding daughter. "Summon our strength, and you will see it will all work out."

Shokat didn't respond, but instead dug her fingers into her eyelids to will the tears away. Maryam recognized the tactic as one she had employed when she didn't want her father to see her pain. She kissed the top of her daughter's head. The aunties fussed over her hair and hennaed hands, and Shokat let them, while doing her best to hide her tears.

Maryam sighed. She wished Shokat was as easy as her other daughter when it came to matters of the heart. Ezzhat had fallen in love with Mehdi at first sight, or so she claimed. She'd also helped to sew her own wedding gown, dyed her hair with beetroot, and gone along with Maman and Maryam to invite the entire village. Everyone knew Ezzhat made the perfect bride. She was born for the part.

MINA, 1940

B Y THE TIME MINA AND SOHEILA WERE EIGHTEEN, THEY WERE
two of the best fighters in the eighty-eight-woman army. One morning just a few months before the Soviets would crash through the Afghan
border, the women patrolled to ensure no warlords stole their horses or
weapons. Mina and Soheila were out riding at sunrise. Their beautiful
morning was cut short, however, by a group of Russian and Afghan soldiers, supporters of General Mohammed Daoud Khan, the cousin of the
king, and self-proclaimed prime minister of Afghanistan. The men were
riding the hills in an effort to disrupt the drug trade that had taken over
the country.

"You girls look lost," one of the men called. He gestured to the six
others riding alongside him, and they quickly encircled the young women.

"You know, General Daoud has proclaimed that women are allowed
to attend university now," one of the men said. "You should be in school,
not out here playing ponies."

"Though you are quite beautiful," another of the men said, in heavily
accented Dari.

Soheila had learned Dari in less than two months; it was so similar
to Persian, her native tongue. But this man was clearly not from Iran,

Afghanistan, or Pakistan. His tongue was harsher. Later, she would learn to identify his as a Russian accent.

"But perhaps they are too beautiful for school," another chimed in.

The men moved closer. Soheila and Mina exchanged knowing glances.

Mina let out a trilling scream. Soheila's horse, Zereshk, the very same she had shared a flask of whiskey and crossed the border with, reared on his hind legs. Mina's horse, Ruba the Second, or Ruba II, who had arrived like a gift the same day Soheila was brought to the caves, did the same. In an instant, the women drew their bows and began firing off arrows. Two blond men drew their guns, but Mina's arrows pierced their hands before they could even take aim.

One of the Afghan men rode furiously at Soheila, a rope in one hand and a gun in the other. He twirled the rope and hurled it toward her, aiming to pull her off her horse and drag her behind. But Soheila ducked expertly, and Zereshk, who had proved to be even more precocious than his rider, tucked his head and moved swiftly out of reach with a grapevine-like motion.

The Afghan man had never seen a horse move in this way. Shocked, he lost his balance. As he fell to the ground, his gun went off, which spooked his horse to rear high. Soheila watched as the horse brought his front hooves back down on the man's chest with a sickening crack. His body jerked three times, he wheezed, and then he fell still.

This was all the other men needed to see. With one of their soldiers dead and three wounded, they rode back in the direction they'd come, leaving their dead brother and his horse behind.

Wordlessly, Mina dismounted and tied the dead soldier to his horse using his own rope. She then used the other end to tie both horse and rider to Ruba. In silence, the two young women rode home to the caves.

When they arrived, the girls were celebrated. Not only had they bested the soldiers, but they had brought a new horse for the herd. Ghashang, who was by then the commanding general, the highest rank of the three generals in the group, beamed with pride.

"It's time, daughter," she whispered in Mina's ear.

"Time for what, Mother?"

"Time for you to start the next level of your training. You will be the next commanding general of our army."

SHOKAT, 1942

T HE WEDDING HAD BEEN ANYTHING BUT JOYFUL FOR SHOKAT, and things went downhill from there.

In the weeks leading up to that fateful night, she had focused all her attention on the horses, desperate to savor every last moment with them. Her intended, Arsalan, who was thirty years her senior, had announced that when they were married, they would live in Mashad. He had just been promoted to superior court judge and had no intention of spending a second longer than necessary in the rural North. In her new city life, she would be far from home, from her mother, grandmother, and siblings. From her horses. Despair overwhelmed Shokat, and during the ceremony, she held not Arsalan's hand but her sister's, praying that some of Ezzhat's joy would rub off on her.

At the reception, Mehdi and Ezzhat were inseparable. They danced and danced, staring into each other's eyes. Arsalan disappeared right after dinner, and Shokat, on the verge of tears, slipped away to the stables to say good-bye to her horses. She pinned up her wedding dress and climbed atop her favorite, Shokoufeh, the daughter of her grandmother's first white horse. She wanted one last ride, but no sooner was she up on the mare's back than Arsalan appeared, his pupils dilated, his mouth twisted into a scowl.

"What are you doing? Get down this instant!" he commanded his young bride.

Shokat felt the blood in her veins run cold. Her lungs seized.

"Please, please, Arsalan jaan, I just want to go for one more ride," she sobbed, tears running down her cheeks and dripping into Shokoufeh's white mane.

"Did you say one *more* ride? Good God, girl, you've been *riding* these creatures? Have you no shame? No faith?" His green eyes darkened. "Disgusting. Your hymen is probably broken. You're damaged goods. I should give you back."

"Please, Arsalan, please don't do that. You would be dishonoring my parents and—"

"Did you just use my first name? Did you think you could call me Arsalan, you silly girl? You will address me as *Mister* Sadr!" he growled. "You've probably been having sex with these animals, too, haven't you?" He yanked Shokat off the white mare and slapped her across the face. The force of the blow sent her to her knees, coating her white gown in dirt and mud.

"Get up, you filthy girl. Clean your face. You're a *disgrace*."

Legs shaking, Shokat rose and buried her face in Shokoufeh's neck. She sobbed into the mare's perfect white coat, clutching her best friend. Shokoufeh curled her head around to pull Shokat closer. The mare licked Shokat's face, wiping her tears. Mr. Sadr sneered and then stalked back out into the night.

Things only got worse for Shokat in Mashad. Maryam had promised to visit her daughter on the way home from her Afghan border crossings, only she was taking many more trips to Turkey instead. Afghanistan was being ravaged by feuds between opium lords, their battle for territory threatening to spill into Iran. After all, Iran was the most direct route from Afghanistan to Europe. Going through Iran would bring the opium trade global and make more money quickly. If it did, Mashad would be hit hard and fast.

When the beatings started, Shokat found herself wishing that the skirmish of the drug lords of Afghanistan would spill over into Iran. Maybe the guerrilla soldiers seeking a path for their poppies could burn down the city. Then she would be released from this hell she was trapped in. *Let us burn to death. What difference would it make?* Shokat thought. There was already a war raging inside the lavish apartment she shared with Arsalan. She prayed for a quick death. Anything to save her from her husband who, when night fell, met her not with tenderness but with a belt and a fist. They still hadn't had sex. Shokat would lie in bed praying that they'd finally make love, that then maybe the abuse would stop, but Arsalan never reached for her in desire, only anger. Without her family or her horses, Shokat felt lost. She turned to the mosque, becoming more fervent with her prayers and hoping God would save her.

One night while Arsalan had turned their apartment into an opium den, Shokat slipped quietly out to spend some time at her favorite mosque, the Imam Reza shrine. It was the largest mosque in the country, and was the only place Shokat could find peace. She would lose herself in walking meditations and prayer, the softly lit walls soothing her pain as she opened her heart to let God in.

After walking for hours around the inner courtyard of the mosque, Shokat wandered into the ladies' prayer hall to take some seated meditation. As she slipped her shoes off and gathered her headscarf around her head, she bumped into a woman about her mother's age who looked familiar.

"Shokat jaan, is that you?" the woman asked. "It's Laleh, your father's cousin. I was at your and Ezzhat's wedding."

Shokat rubbed her eyes. The woman had a trace of resemblance to her father—she had his crooked nose and kind smile. Shokat heard herself exhale audibly. Somehow being around family in the sanctity of the mosque finally allowed her to relax. As she did, the tears that she had been holding back for months overflowed, and she began sobbing, collapsing to the carpeted floor in a puddle of tears.

Laleh knelt next to her second cousin. She tried to pull her into an embrace, but when Shokat winced in pain, Laleh pulled back.

"Oh no, you too?" she asked. She knew instinctively the hell in which Shokat had been living. "Mine hit me too. Until he died of an overdose, I lived in a state of terror at all times."

Shokat looked up at Laleh, wiping the tears from her face. "I'm so sorry to hear that, Laleh khanoum." Her voice was barely a whisper.

"Why are you sorry? It is the men who should be sorry," Laleh replied. She stroked Shokat's covered head gingerly. "But how it is that Maryam Mahdavi's daughter is living this way? She who saves so many women. Does she know?"

Shokat shook her head. She was too embarrassed to tell her parents, worried that they might see it as a failure on her part.

"This won't do, my child," Laleh said. She carefully rolled up Shokat's sleeves to assess the bruises on her arms. Shokat was grateful in that moment that it was just after midnight and the mosque was relatively empty, save for a few women who had dozed off in the prayer hall. "There are far too many bruises, Shokat jaan. You'll not survive this much longer. I need to alert your mother."

Shokat's body trembled from head to toe. Fear and hope simultaneously gripped her. But then she heard her mother's voice in her head and the echoes of those words her mother whispered in her ear on her wedding day: "You come from a long line of women warriors, my child." Shokat took a deep breath and nodded in agreement.

Laleh pulled the young woman in close. "Your warrior mother will be here soon."

MARYAM, 1943

LALEH SENT AN URGENT BUT VAGUE TELEGRAM TO MARYAM, begging her to come to Mashad as quickly as possible but to be discreet about her travel plans.

Six weeks later, Maryam tied her horses up outside the apartment where Laleh had told her Shokat lived. Maryam didn't know how long she would stay or how deep the trouble was that her daughter was in, but she had brought two horses and a carriage with enough supplies for months. She had brought not just her own horse, but her daughter's favorite, Shokoufeh, too.

Upon opening the front door and seeing Maryam, Shokat collapsed into her mother's arms, both of them consumed by grief. They clung to each other under a wave of tears for hours as Shokat told her mother the whole story, beginning from the intimidation she had faced during her wedding night up through the ongoing beatings. Maryam didn't know where her shaking ended and her daughter's began, but she knew she never wanted them to be separated ever again.

At the sound of the keys in the door, Shokat startled and pulled herself away from her mother: Arsalan was home. Terrified of how her husband might react to her mother's unexpected visit, she rushed to the kitchen to prepare him a calming saffron tea.

But the saffron wasn't needed. As soon as Arsalan laid eyes on Maryam, he became a different person. Almost reverent, he bowed before her, telling her that he assumed hers were tears of joy at seeing her daughter flourish with her prominent husband in a prominent city. Maryam, too stricken to respond, silently followed him to the guest room, where he set her bags down. After he left and she was alone, she fell across the bed and pounded the cushions. How could she have let this happen? How had she missed the signs when this suitor came calling? How could her own daughter have met the fate of the women she had dedicated her life to helping?

She knew what she had to do.

Maryam emerged from her room, drank the warm saffron tea her daughter had made, and then helped Shokat prepare an opulent dinner of lamb and coriander stew. They dined to the uncomfortable crackle of the judge's monologues as he regaled them with stories of his triumphs in court. Maryam steadied herself by focusing on the plan forming in her mind.

For dessert, Maryam had made a saffron rice pudding and laced Arsalan's serving with opium. As soon as the drug began to work its magic, she and Shokat packed the barest of the girl's belongings. They wrote a note explaining that Maryam wanted to see the mosque at night, to visit Imam Reza's shrine. This way, even if he were to awaken sooner than expected, Arsalan wouldn't come searching for them.

The two women crept out under the cover of darkness, and Shokat gasped when she spotted Shokoufeh. The horse almost blew their cover when she started neighing loudly at the sight of her former rider. She shook out her entire body, tossing her gleaming white mane. Maryam felt a pang of relief that her maternal instincts had kicked in before she left. She had intended to bring a second stallion to pull the carriage, but changed her mind at the last minute. Something told her that her daughter needed her best friend—and there was no substitute for the love of a horse. Shokat needed all the help she could get. The little white mare could give her the confidence she now needed to flee.

Maryam untied the horses from the carriage and tethered the wagon to a nearby tree. She swapped the driving reins for blankets. Then she handed her daughter a set of blue and white woven ropes she had made a few years earlier.

In one fluid motion, Shokat pulled herself onto Shokoufeh's withers, but her heart sank as she recalled the last time she had sat atop her best friend: her wedding night, when Arsalan revealed himself for who and what he really was. Shokat wished she had had the courage to run away then.

Maryam had made the five-day three-hundred-mile ride from Mashad to Afghanistan many times over the years. She knew the rhythms, knew the terrain and surroundings changed dramatically sixty miles outside of town.

The temperature dropped and the wind rose as they rode north and east toward the Afghan border. Maryam wrapped one of the blankets she'd strapped to the stallion around her shoulders and instructed Shokat to do the same. Shokat wore her headscarf tied under her chin rather than more securely behind her head, because Arsalan had worried that the exposure of his teenage wife's neck would draw too much unwanted attention. But the northern winds had no respect for such arbitrary rules, and her headscarf soon flew off. Shokat shook her head with an initial thrill of excitement—she felt free. In the next moment, however, the wind blew her hair across her face and obscured her vision. She let out a guttural scream, releasing all the anger, frustration, and fear she'd been holding inside for the long, terrifying months of her marriage.

Maryam halted her stallion, Khosrow, and Shokoufeh followed suit. "Tie your hair back properly," she said. Shokat pulled out a floral headscarf that her mother had given her and that Arsalan had not allowed her to wear ("Too eye-catching," he had sniffed). She tied it under her hair to match her mother's.

Maryam slid off the stallion and opened the pouch tied under his belly. Despite the ominous weather, she moved with the ease of experience. The border crossing never got easier, but Maryam grew more confident.

Shokat knew what was about to happen; she had heard her mother describe each step of the passage to countless young women over the years. The crossing was the hardest part of the whole journey. Gunshots or land mines could erupt any moment, spooking the horses into bucking off their riders. Shokat knew all the stories about the horses who didn't make it and why her mother usually rode with at least three if not four extra members of the herd. She shuddered, thinking of the horses and their riders, all plied with whiskey.

Now she watched as her mother gently eased the carafe into Khosrow's mouth. He fought her at the first taste, rearing up onto his hind legs and backing away. Maryam tugged on the reins to pull his body back toward hers. She looked him squarely in the eye and pulled on his mouth two more times. The horse bobbed his head. Maryam pushed his mouth open and poured in the bitter brew. He swallowed hard, then dropped his head. Shokoufeh would be next.

Shokat dismounted at Maryam's insistence. Shokoufeh had never made the crossing into Afghanistan, only Turkey, and Maryam didn't know how the horse would respond. She had brought Shokoufeh to comfort her daughter and give her confidence, but now Maryam began to doubt that decision. The terrain was difficult, and the wind was whipping hard; the mare was nervous. As soon as Shokat's feet touched the ground, Shokoufeh took off running. The girl was still holding the reins, and her bruised body dragged across the earth as the horse thrashed through the rocky field.

"Tell her to halt!" Maryam screamed into the wind. "Push your feet down and make her stop!"

Shokat obeyed. She sunk all the weight of her battered, shaking body into her buttocks and heels and bellowed the command at

Shokoufeh. The horse stopped instantly. Shokat fell forward onto her face and, because her hands were still gripping the reins, couldn't break her fall. She felt a warm liquid and realized it was blood. Maryam ran to her, bandages in hand. She cleaned and taped her daughter's face and, within minutes, was pulling Shokat and the white mare back to the stallion at the top of the hill. There they could watch the border and time their crossing.

Maryam handed the flask to Shokat, who had never tasted alcohol. She started to take a sip but pulled away at its strong scent.

"Drink it, daughter. Drink it now. We haven't got much time. We must cross soon." The wind whipped through her. Maryam's teeth were all but chattering.

Shokat took a tentative sip just as Maryam poured whiskey into Shokoufeh's mouth. In perfect unison, the girl and her horse shuddered and spit the alcohol out. Shokoufeh pounded the ground with her hooves and shook her head defiantly. Shokat shook from head to toe, the weight of the situation hitting her all at once, and sank to the ground in a puddle of tears.

"I can't do it, Mama. I can't. It's too dangerous. I don't want Shokoufeh to have to do it, either. There must be another way."

Maryam took Shokat's face in her calloused hands and looked her sharply in the eye, the way she had done with her horses thousands of times. "My dear girl, there *is* no other way. We cross here, and we cross now, or we don't cross at all. And we can't cross without that alcohol; it's too risky. If there are guns or explosions at the border, the horses, and you, my dear, need to be calm."

"But Mama, if I cross, then it's done. I've crossed over. Everything will be different. I won't see you, Ezzhat, the boys, Baba, Mamanee, or the horses ever again. That's not life," she wailed.

Maryam nodded. She had had versions of this conversation dozens of times, but she'd never expected to have it with her own daughter. Before she knew it, she was crying, too. She wrapped her arms around Shokat's small body and kissed her over and over.

When the wind stopped a few minutes later, Maryam was ready to try again with the whiskey. There was no more time to waste.

Before she could raise the pouch to the horse's lips, she heard shots and smelled gunpowder: drug lords. A moment later she heard the roar of their tanks and knew the guerrilla soldiers were close.

Maryam yanked the horses down the hill and around a ledge. There she pulled her daughter and the animals into a crevasse to wait out the gun battle. But the gunshots went on and on, stopping at dawn only because it had begun to hail. *The poppies must be really worth their weight in gold for them to be fighting in this mess.*

"We can't cross in this. We'll take the horses down the hill, wait out the storm in a cave, and try again tonight." She was trying to keep her voice calm, but Maryam knew that the longer the crossing took, the higher the chances were that someone would find them.

Tearfully, the women fled back the way they'd come and sheltered in a makeshift cave. Maryam's eyes strained against the darkness as she searched for attackers. Every crack of gunfire made Khosrow twitch, and she patted his neck absentmindedly, even as the drink kept him quiet.

Less than an hour later, three men on horseback announced their arrival, firing more familiar gunshots into the air like firecrackers. Maryam's heart leaped into her throat. Had the Soviets found them?

"We work for Mr. Sadr," one of them barked, and her heart sank. "You have something that belongs to him." It was only much later that Maryam would learn her son-in-law had been tracking her smuggles for decades, as insurance against his own misdeeds.

The men encircled the women, guns aimed at their heads. The one who had spoken jumped off his horse and approached a terribly still Shokat. The man walked slowly but deliberately. A wicked smile spread across his face.

"You understand that he will not be happy with you when I bring you home, right?" he snarled. Shokat bit her lip to stop it from trembling. "And *you*," he said, staring hard at Maryam. "You ought to be arrested for what you do." Maryam remained stone-faced, and the man went on. "You're lucky we found this girl intact. Otherwise, we were told to kill you."

Maryam narrowed her eyes. "You don't scare me."

The men burst into laughter. "You think we care what you think? You're pathetic."

"Let me shoot her!" another of the men said. He aimed his rifle at Maryam's head.

The leader shook his head. "Our orders were clear: Get the girl. Leave the mom. Kill her horse." He drew his gun, aimed at Shokoufeh. "Oh, yeah. I almost forgot about that last part." He pulled the trigger. The horse crumpled to the ground, crushing Shokat's leg. The girl howled.

"You idiot, you were supposed to pull the girl off the horse before shooting it." The first man, whom Maryam assumed was their leader, growled in frustration.

"Shut up! Just get down and help me." The shooter stalked over to a screaming Shokat and pulled her out from under Shokoufeh. "Well, she got her punishment. And now she won't be able to run away again."

Her daughter's leg was dangling, a bone jutting out from the skin. "No!" Maryam screamed. One of the men fired at her but missed, as Maryam launched herself off Khosrow and ran toward Shokat.

The ringleader grabbed her by the waist and flung her to the ground. "I wouldn't do that, khawhar," he snapped. "You're lucky we were specifically told not to kill you."

"Let. Her. Go." Maryam said between gritted teeth.

"She's coming with us. Good luck ever seeing her again."

Maryam watched the men ride away with her broken daughter. As soon as they were out of sight, she let out a bloodcurdling howl, and screamed until she collapsed on the cold, hard sand.

LOUISE, 1957

AFTER THEIR WEDDING IN VIRGINIA ON FEBRUARY 1, 1957, Narcy and Louise flew to Iran, and she knew instantly she was home. Louise fell as hard for her new country as she had for her groom.

Shiraz was heralded as the city of love, wine, and poetry. It was the birthplace and burial ground of famed poets like Hafez and Sa'adi, whose words were etched on marble gazebos in parks throughout the city. Rivers flowed to the south and mountains rose to the north, and Shiraz felt private, protected.

Narcy bought fifteen thousand hectares of land in an area just beyond the city and close to where his father had been born, called Siyakh ("thirty frosts"), which was also home to one of the oldest Persian tribes, the migratory Qasghghai. As both a wedding and a housewarming present, Narcy's cousin gave Louise a black stallion, a Turkoman-Qasghghai mix, a breed known for their alluring combination of strength and gentility, whom Louise named Kyrie Eleyson in honor of her years as a member of the Cornell choir. Narcy bought himself a bay stallion, a Qasghghai thoroughbred he named Albert.

Narcy had a degree in engineering from Yale as well as a master's from the University of Michigan and was appointed chief engineer at the Nemazee Hospital in Shiraz. The young couple had a staff house on the hospital compound but spent as much time as possible in Siyagh, where they rode their stallions alongside Qasghghai tribesmen.

Louise understood she had a lot to learn about Iran, but horses? Horses and horsemanship she knew. But riding with the Qasghghai opened her eyes to a whole new way of relating to horses. The Qasghghai rode barefoot, bareback, and hands-free through the rugged landscape. Sometimes they carried a spear, a gun, or a bow and arrow. On other occasions, they carried musical instruments like an oud, a pear-shaped stringed guitar, or a donbak, an oversize tambourine-like drum, playing as they rode.

The tribe wore rawhide leather vests, chaps, and straps around their calves, and both the men and women grew their hair long, their ponytails blowing in the wind like their horses' manes. And the *horses*. Like Kyrie Eleyson, they didn't so much gallop as dance. Rather than moving their front two feet in opposition to their hind legs and jostling their rider, their right front leg and hind leg moved in unison as the left front and hind also moved together. The horses she and the Qasghghai rode were among the oldest living breeds on earth and were often referred to as "gaited" horses.

"Our horses move like humans dance: right foot, then left foot. This is because our horses learn to walk and run like us and from us," a tribesman told Louise.

Louise hung on his every word. Since her Persian was not yet fluent enough for Louise to communicate in that way, Narcy translated the Qasghghai dialect he had picked up from his father as they spoke. "In America, the horses don't dance. They jump with their front two feet together followed by their back two feet."

"Like Arabians," the tribesman said. Narcy nodded. In the states, he had ridden quarter horses like those Louise trained, and their gait was similar to that of Arabians.

"Yes, exactly, only the American horses are not so hot-blooded," Narcy said wryly.

The tribesman laughed before clearing his throat and narrowing his eyes at Louise. "You know why that is, do you, Louise Firouz?"

Louise shook her head.

"It is said that your horses, like Arabians, learned to move from other animals. Wolves. Dogs. So, they run like animals."

Perhaps the smooth gait of the Iranian horse breeds was why their riders could float atop them hands-free, Louise thought.

Over the next few months, she mastered the art of riding bareback and hands-free while simultaneously shooting a bow and arrow. Herds of gazelle, wild sheep, jackals, foxes, and wolves roamed their lands, and while Louise was willing to hunt, she refused to use guns and spears, fearing they were too dangerous to wield and carried too much risk for the horses she mounted. She also learned to play the donbak and would join the tribe around the fire, pounding out sensual rhythms and dancing late into the night.

Just as the tribe was growing restless and preparing to move on to another region, Louise discovered she was pregnant. Roshan, curly-haired and dark-skinned, was three months old when the tribe next migrated through Siyakh. Already the infant spent her days atop a horse, swaddled to her mother's chest as Louise rode through rivers and over mountains, and already she, too, loved the fresh smell of dirt and olive trees. Soon Roshan was joined by her baby sister, Ateshe, and then, three years later, by their brother, Caren.

By the time they were a family of five, most of the Firouzes' fifteen thousand hectares had been confiscated. The US military advisers who had installed themselves in the country after the CIA-backed coup of 1953 that overthrew democratically elected prime minister Moham-mad Mossadegh and reinstalled the procapitalist Pahlavi monarchy believed the Siyakh region would make an ideal firing range. Louise's American passport—she was now a dual citizen—was no match for the shah's army.

When much of the remaining acreage became overrun with soldiers, Narcy and Louise moved their family to their southernmost ten acres and started a farm. The couple sold chickens and purchased two mares to breed their own Qasghghai horses, glad to be raising their children in an agrarian environment. But Narcy was heartbroken by the loss of his beloved valley. The nomadic tribe moved farther south, leaving the Firouz family contemplating a similar move. When he was offered a position as a building contractor in Tehran, he took it. Staying in Shiraz was too painful.

"To compensate us for the loss of Siyakh and to encourage us to continue raising horses, Narcy's father, General (Prince) Mohamad Hussein Firouz, gave him a property that had been in the family for some time," Louise wrote in her diary. "Norouzabad was one hundred and forty hectares of barren land a half hour's drive west of Tehran. There was little to recommend the situation. It was flat and drab and barely supported some scrub grass poking through the gravel and rocks."

Despite her misgivings, Louise moved the three children, four dogs, five canaries, and seven horses from their farm in Shiraz to Norouzabad, and the family dove in headfirst to make it home.

"No one had ever bothered to cultivate the land and it did not look like much," Louise wrote. "Fortunately for the success of the experiment we were too young and inexperienced to realize the amount of work and money that would have to be poured in to make the farm a success. Triumph of optimism over expedience."

One of the former owners, also a prince, had given the land its name. "Norouz," which translates to "New Day," is the name of the Persian New Year, celebrated on the vernal equinox of March 21. "Abad" in Persian means to develop—"ab" for water and "bad" for air. As Louise wrote, "taken together, the name was either a bad joke or a good omen. It was obvious that it had never been cultivated in spite of its name." But Louise and Narcy were determined, and they planted trees, thawed the soil, sifted out rocks, and made piles of manure to fertilize the ground. Slowly, they nurtured Norouzabad back to life.

Louise still missed the lush landscape of Shiraz and the tranquillity of life in the valley. Part of the majesty of the verdant Qasghghai land was that it made living harmoniously with the earth so easy. But she also came to love the Alborz Mountains outside Tehran and the way they looked in winter, blanketed in pristine white snow with their peaks kissing the crisp azure sky. While Tehran did not have all the romance of Shiraz, Louise was drawn to this city, too, which had replaced Isfahan as Iran's capital when Narcy's family, the Qajars, took power in 1789.

In 1962 Louise and Narcy purchased a small three-story town house, one that resembled the houses Louise had loved back in Georgetown in Washington, DC, and joined three million other Iranians living in Tehran. Their new house was surrounded by tall plane trees and had a fireplace in the living room and a small pool called a hozcheh in the garden. Most important, they were close to Narcy's office at the Firouz Construction Company and even closer to the Iranian Swiss school their children attended.

Though it wasn't Shiraz, Louise wrote that she still loved Tehran the way she loved Washington, DC—second to Great Falls, Virginia. "For me [Tehran] was still bearable as there were vestiges of old-world rural smells and sounds. There were horse-drawn *doroshkehs* [carriages] and donkeys carrying goods for sale piled high on their *palouns*, hawkers crying the price of potatoes and onions, mattresses to be fluffed or snow removed from roofs in winter. But there were cars and taxis and buses which made it bedlam compared to the quiet clip-clop of horse drawn carriages in Shiraz, where tribeswomen flitted quietly along the tree-lined streets offering their loomed horse blankets for sale." She focused on improving her Persian and dabbling in the Qasghghai dialect when Narcy taught her romantic phrases.

Escaping the hustle and bustle of Tehran at Norouzabad, Louise turned her attention once more to the horses. She spent more and more time working the land and training the growing herd. She built several stables, including a birthing stall for the brood mares and, with Narcy's help and construction contacts, built one of the first indoor arenas in Iran. Though she had grown up with quarter horses and warm bloods in the United States, she was a quick study of what she called "the Oriental horse." By breeding them, living with them, and learning from the Qasghghai tribesmen and -women, she developed a deep connection to their instincts and movements.

Louise's reputation as a knowledgeable and effective horse breeder and trainer spread far and wide. Several members of the American and European expat community joined Louise in running the center. They became fast friends, bonded by their love of horses. Equine enthusiasts from around the country flocked to Norouzabad to watch the tall, blonde, blue-eyed woman, "Iran's Lady of Horses," work with the majestic animals. People brought their horses to her for behavior notes, while others wanted riding lessons.

Louise and Narcy remained adamant that their children understand and appreciate agricultural life and develop their own relationships with the animals. As Louise taught and trained Roshan, Ateshe, and Caren and gave lessons to the children of other families in Tehran, she realized that while the Oriental horses—the Qasghghai and Turkoman and their cross-sections—had many wonderful traits, they weren't ideal for children. Their large size and quick feet were too much for little bodies. Sometimes Louise would help a child mount an Oriental horse only for the animal to dash right out from between their legs, the child falling to the ground in tears, though usually more startled than hurt.

"The Oriental horse is a far cry from the mixed breed Thoroughbred hunters that I had ridden in Virginia as a child," Louise wrote in her diary.

"As different as learning to drive in a Jeep and then being given a Jaguar sports car or being told you should marry a Washington, D.C. lawyer and instead attaching yourself to a Persian Prince with a passion for the great outdoors. There is a great deal to the Oriental horse and just about all of it I had to learn myself. There were no books that accurately describe the phenomenon."

Even before she realized what she was doing or where it might lead, Louise followed her instincts and immersed herself in the history and origin of the Iranian horse breeds. She interviewed historians and other breeders as well as those who were simply passionate fans, who loved the horses as she did. Louise read every book she could get her hands on and collected photographs, paintings, and even poems about the horses. No detail, no artifact, was too small for her files.

"By this time, I was beginning to discover that there was more to the Oriental horse than the Arabian," she wrote. "But the horse books at my disposal were dismally lacking in information about horses in the Middle East and, even worse, about the horses of Central Asia. I had figured out that there were Qasghghai, Basseri, and Darashuri tribal horses in Iran. There were also several types of Kurdish horses from the Iran-Iraq border as well as horses that were called Arabs but looked like the others. But I was unaware of the wealth of equine diversity that was waiting to be discovered."

The Firouz children shared their parents' love of horses but couldn't control the imposing, spirited stallions and mares their mother bred. One visitor to Norouzabad told Louise to purchase ponies, but she refused. "Ponies are for cowards. Our children will learn how to work with the majesty of a horse," Louise told Narcy when he suggested buying mules and donkeys for the farm. "Donkeys, mules, and the like are great as pack animals, but I want our children to learn horsemanship—or, in our case, horsewomanship." Louise scoured her collection of books and paintings, searching for images of horses with smaller builds. And then she remembered when Narcy had taken her to the ancient palace of Persepolis, which had been just up the road from their old home in Shiraz.

Imagined in 515 BCE by Cyrus the Great, Persepolis, or Takht-E-Jamshid, was the capital of the Achaemenid Empire when Iran was still known as Persia. Cyrus the Great was one of the first kings of the Persian Empire, and his legacy wasn't only his grand vision for Persepolis but also a stone etching that decreed the sanctity of human rights. Archaeologists and historians cited it as the first written declaration of human rights in the world, and to this day, it is the foundation of modern Iranian movements for social change. Cyrus established the site of the temple at the base of the Zagros Mountains and adjacent to the Pulvar River, flowing into the Kur River—both of which were used for trading along what would eventually become the Silk Road.

Cyrus never saw his dream for Persepolis as the greatest city in the world. A palace was erected by his successor, Darius the First, only to come up against Alexander the Great and the Greeks, who tried to destroy it in 313 BCE. Some walls and columns refused to fall to their wrath and remain standing to this day. What Louise remembered most vividly from her trip with Narcy were the horse carvings etched into the surviving stones. In fact, horses were *the* central renderings throughout the palace and the most salient motif among the remains. The animal was depicted alone, in herds, drawing carriages, and marching proudly in royal parades. Odes to the horses also predominated the poetry, paintings, and songs of Persepolis; in story after story, the power and success of the Persian Empire were laid at the feet of these revered animals.

To care for a horse is to guarantee your entry into heaven.

The first time they visited Persepolis, Narcy translated these words for his new bride, and tears filled her eyes. That was the moment Louise realized she would never want to leave Iran. This was her spirit's true home.

"Any country or culture that reveres horses in this way, that gives them their due credit in building civilizations, that is my home," she wrote to her brother David that same year.

The etchings at Persepolis depicted small horses no taller than their trainers and riders. They also appeared to keep their heads held high, even when portrayed in motion. In contrast to American horses as well as the Qasghghais and Turkomans, these horses never seemed to lower their heads. Their necks were also much wider than those of any horse she had ever seen.

When Louise asked Narcy about the horses, about their striking differences, he was, as ever, ready with an answer. "They are the ancient breeds of Persian horses. I have heard stories of them, but they went extinct long ago."

Her heart dropped, but Louise refused to believe that the breed was gone for good. She put out word, and waited. When a trader from the North arrived with stories about the small horses he and his wife rode at their farm near the Caspian Sea, Louise listened.

It was the spring of 1965 when Ali arrived in Norouzabad. He had heard about Iran's Lady of Horses and wanted to see the woman and her herd for himself.

Louise was instantly intrigued by this unexpected visitor whose eyes danced with mischief and who smiled with his whole body when he spoke of his wife and her love of horses.

All afternoon Ali watched Louise train, and when she was finally done for the day, she invited him to stay for dinner. Now was Louise's chance to ask him questions about his horses.

"They aren't as tall as Turkomans," Ali explained. "Rather they are smaller—better for someone my size, or my wife, Maryam's, size. She can jump on them from anywhere, at any speed."

"And tell me, how do they ride?" Louise asked. She was vibrating with excitement, visions of the horses at Persepolis filling her mind.

"Like riding a flying carpet," Ali told her. He stood from his place at the table, an uncomfortable position for a farmer and traveler accustomed to taking his meals from a blanket on the ground. He stretched his arms and hands out to emphasize his point, bending his knees and then straightening them, moving his arms gracefully through the air.

"And how do they hold their heads?" Louise asked, interrupting his reverie.

Ali paused to consider her question. It seemed to Louise that he had never thought about how horses hold their heads, and she wondered if his wife had. She chided herself that not everyone was as deeply horse obsessed as she.

"Well, now that you mention it, I guess they hold their heads upright," Ali said slowly. "I mean, they do bow to us when we first approach, but at the walk, trot, and gallop, they do not lower their heads."

"Yes, that's it!" Louise shouted. She jumped up and ran to get her sketches of the Persepolis horse carvings.

She thrust the notebook into Ali's hands. "They look like this, right?"

Ali furrowed his brow. He did not want to disappoint the prince's wife, but he couldn't quite make out the connection between her sketches and the horses at home.

"But Khanoum Firouz, these are from the ancient carvings of the Persian Empire, aren't they?" He shifted uncomfortably, gently passing the sketchbook back to her.

"Yes, yes, of course. But do your horses resemble these?" Louise was nearly begging.

A long silence passed between them before Ali spoke.

"Mrs. Firouz, why don't you come see for yourself? I invite you to my home. Meet my wife and our horses. You will not be disappointed."

Louise was thrilled. Years later, she wrote about this pivotal turning point in her diary, saying,

> We left Tehran early in the morning while there was still little traffic on roads that were usually a snarl of cars, trucks, horse-drawn doroshkehs and donkeys. The road to the Caspian led up the hills to the ski slopes of Ab Ali. Then it climbed steeply over the three thousand–meter pass of the shrine where the late Shah, Mohammad Reza Pahlavi, was once said to have been cured of a near-fatal fever while traveling to Tehran by horseback. We were four women travelling alone which, in those days in Iran, was unusual as it is once again in post-revolutionary days. Women are supposed to stay home, cook meals, and raise children, not stray alone conversing with strangers.

Two of Louise's friends from the riding club and fellow expats in Tehran, Penny and Jean, joined her on the trip. The fourth member of their group was Azizeh, a cousin of Narcy's who was, in Louise's words, a "brilliant woman who spoke at least seven languages and was somewhat overqualified for this trip, but she was also determined to find a pony for her nephew."

On the bumpy drive to the Caspian Sea, the four women jostled across the snowcapped peaks of Mount Damavand, Iran's highest mountain, which soars up through the Alborz range surrounding Tehran. They followed rocky gorges and admired the spring foliage that foretold the summer harvest to come. In Amol, they stopped to refuel and to sample the local varieties of goat cheese. They also met a man who described himself as a "horse dealer." When he learned the women were on a quest to find the perfect small horse, he suggested they travel the rest of the way along the "old road" and villages, where he promised there were many such specimens. Louise was dubious but up for the adventure.

"The old road was gravel and wound through rice paddies and thatched-roof hamlets," she wrote in a letter to her brothers and later in her diary.

> Geese and ducks blocked the road. Herds of horses and cows grazed the brown rice stubble in the fields, knee-deep in mud. Drainage ditches on both sides of the roads were one to two meters deep. In the slow-moving brown water, snakes writhed, and turtles moved among them undisturbed. I don't know if these snakes were poisonous. Probably some were and some weren't. What amazed me were the quantities. There seemed to be more snakes than water. The movement of the water was caused more by great swarms of snakes nudging around each other, rather than by any current.

Locals emerged from their homes to meet this curious foursome and invite them in for tea. They accepted the first several of these invitations but were disappointed when every family told them the same thing: yes, they knew the small horses they sought, but those horses were in the *next* village or the one after that one.

Finally, after many villages, the women came upon a small dirt road lined with olive trees. Louise recognized it as the road Ali had described that would lead them to his farm. She shifted into gear and swung the Jeep down the road, failing to notice that her abrupt turn had tossed Jean right out the back.

"Lou, stop!" Penny shouted. "Jean fell out!" Louise pumped the brakes and jumped out to find her friend sitting in the mud, picking earthworms out of her hair.

"This will be my stopping point today," she told Louise. "I've had enough adventure." Louise shook her head and smiled. She knew that look of resignation.

"No matter, Jean. Why not take a little walk? We'll come back for you on our way home." Jean could do what she wanted, but Louise wasn't going to let anything stand in her way today. She climbed back into the Jeep, one passenger lighter, and continued on. She could feel she was close.

As soon as they pulled up to the farmhouse, Ali and a gaggle of children rushed to greet them, and Louise knew this was the place she'd been searching for. She couldn't even see the horses yet, but the sweet scent of hay and fur filled her nostrils. She closed her eyes, relishing the moment. Her entire body was alight.

"Welcome, Louise Firouz! This is my wife, Maryam." Louise opened her eyes as Ali gestured to a slight woman with a protruding chin. From afar, Louise had assumed Maryam was one of the children. She couldn't have been more than four and a half feet tall. But coming close and meeting her gaze, she saw that the woman carried more than her years' worth of pain. Louise found herself drawn to her like a magnet. She towered over Maryam as she drew close and then enveloped her in a familiar, loving hug.

MARYAM, 1962

AFTER HER FAILED ATTEMPT TO GET SHOKAT TO SAFETY IN the autumn of 1942, Maryam stopped smuggling. The image of her daughter's bloody body filled her dreams, and she could still smell Shokoufeh's blood. When her father slaughtered her favorite horse right before her eyes, Maryam had assumed nothing in her life could be worse than that moment. But worse kept coming. After what happened with Shokat and Shokoufeh, Maryam vowed never to ride again.

Ali did everything he could to soothe her, putting aside his own pain at the fate of his firstborn, favorite child. His heart ached for Shokat, and he was guilt-ridden at having suggested such a horrible match to begin with. But he also knew that he needed to be strong for his wife and family. But Maryam remained in bed and grief-stricken for years. This time it was Maman's turn to pull her out from under the blankets and back to the living.

"Get up, daughter; your other children need you," Maman snapped. She knew the weight of the pain her daughter was battling from her own years of grief at the death of her son. Maman knew how hard it was to push past the weight of the darkness and rise. But she also knew that her daughter had given her a gift when she felt her own descent into hell. It

131

was Maryam who had helped her up, who had shone a light on the importance of moving forward. The other children and Ali worked the land while Maman cooked and barked orders, doing her best to manage the household in spite of her aging body and waning energy. She was determined now to bring her daughter back to life. "The horses need you. The farm needs you."

Two years passed without word from Shokat. Laleh, Ali's cousin, wrote occasionally to report that all was well in Mashad and that she and Shokat were both thriving, though Maryam wondered if this were true or if Laleh penned the letters under duress or pressure. Even the mention of her daughter's name would plunge Maryam back into a deep depression.

It was only when Ezzhat became a mother that a small glimmer of light broke through the darkness. Maryam was now a grandmother. As she had once hoped for her mother, the importance of the bloodline continuing and her own role in preparing a new generation began to bring her slowly back to the world.

"Get up," Maman ordered. "Be the mother your sons need you to be and your granddaughter will be proud of." In a daze, Maryam nodded. At long last, she stepped wordlessly out of bed. Once more, she immersed herself in the life of the farm. This time, she also vowed to never again leave Gonbad-i-Kavoos, her village on the Caspian Sea.

The 1950s roared into Iran, and Maryam's turmoil was soon rivaled by impending war and revolution, as the fight over oil nationalization brought the country to its knees. A new leader emerged, Mohammad Mossadegh, and he became the prime minister in 1951. Backed by the Parliament of Iran as well as a growing group of soldiers who had defected from the Royal Army, Mossadegh preached a new vision for Iran, one governed by democracy. Ali and Maryam's eldest son, Atta, was fascinated by the reforms Mossadegh preached. So entranced was he by the prodemocracy stance that he even supported Mossadegh's 1952 Land Reform Act, which required landowners to pay a 20 percent tax to fund new development and infrastructure such as public restrooms, transportation, and pest control. Not everyone in the household was so enamored, however.

"Why should we pay taxes on *our* land? This man is terrible for our country," Maman protested.

"Please, Mamanee, he wants to do good things for Iran," Atta argued. "He wants Iran to modernize, to develop."

"He wants Iran to be for Iranians," Ali added. "We don't want to go the way of Afghanistan, a graveyard of colonialism. We want Iran to rocket into the future."

"We definitely do not want to go the way of Afghanistan," Maryam said. Her thoughts drifted to the women of the caves, and she wondered how they were faring as first one country and then another invaded their home.

"Mossadegh will make Iran strong, so it can't be invaded like Afghanistan. So it will be modern," Atta insisted.

"Listen to you men. 'Modernize.' 'Rocket into the future,'" Maman scoffed. "That's not who we are. We are farmers. We live and work the land."

"But why can't we be both, Mamanee?"

"You should go join your sister in the big city then, Atta jaan, if you want modernity. I'll sit here with my horses and my crops." Maman crossed her arms and planted her feet firmly on the kitchen floor.

"Please don't think of it like that. This is good for trade. And what is good for trade is good for us," Ali said.

They were interrupted by the cries of three-year-old Mohammad. The little boy had been born just before Maryam set out on her fateful journey to Mashad to see Shokat. Upon her return, her milk had dried up completely. She looked at her son, who had been forced to grow without a mother, and felt sharp, stabbing pangs of guilt. Earlier that night, Mohammad had refused dinner, complaining of a stomachache. He didn't want to eat; he wanted to chase chickens in the courtyard, his favorite pastime. Now, he was wailing from outside.

"Come to Baba, my son. Come over here," Ali called.

"I can't!" he wailed.

Maryam rushed outside with Ali at her heels. She pulled her son up, but his little legs would not hold him, and he sank to the ground, sending a fresh wave of screams echoing across the farm. Matching looks of terror came over Maryam's and Ali's faces. Maryam pulled Mohammad's body into her arms, singing softly in his ear. Ali staggered upright and ran to the stable. Emerging astride Khosrow, he rode hard for help.

The doctor didn't make it in time. Their farm was far from town, and the polio spread quickly through Mohammad's body. He was overtaken by meningitis burning him from the inside out. Maryam was still holding him when he went cold and limp late in the night.

For two days after his death, she refused to let Mohammad go. When Maryam could fight off sleep no longer, Ali quietly slid their son's body from her arms. He buried Mohammad under the little boy's favorite olive tree.

The doctor arrived only to bring more bad news: the highly contagious disease had spread to the second-youngest member of the family. Hossein, Maryam's four-year-old son, was experiencing paralysis of his right arm. The doctor remained at the farm for weeks, working to treat the little boy while the family continued to grieve Mohammad. Maman stayed by Hossein's side from morning until night, rubbing his aching belly just as she had done for her own son, Asghar, years ago. But it was no use. Like Asghar and Mohammad, Hossein's illness was too much. He succumbed to the polio virus exactly one month after his younger brother. Mercifully, Hossein drifted away in his sleep.

In her crushing grief, Maryam went back to bed and stayed there. Maman, whose aging body had grown weak, could no longer keep up with the physical demands of the household on her own. Ali needed to keep making the trading trips that supported the family, so he left Atta in charge of the farm. With her husband's blessing, Ezzhat left her husband's home and moved back to the farm with two of her own children in tow to help run the household.

In 1953, the beloved prime minister was overthrown in a coup. Rumors of the involvement of the Americans and their intelligence arm, the CIA, spread throughout the country. But it would be years before this covert act was confirmed. Mossadegh had succeeded in nationalizing Iranian oil, setting off shock waves across the world by changing oil and gas prices and inspiring other oil-rich countries to do the same. But his efforts were not so celebrated, especially in Great Britain and the United States. The success of the coup strengthened the monarchy of Mohammad Reza Pahlavi, known as the shah, or "king." Supporters of the former prime minister—not to mention anyone suspected of supporting him—were imprisoned if they were lucky, sentenced to death if they were not. Teams of Savak, Iranian mobsters, appeared almost overnight according to the papers, turning the streets of Tehran into a bloodbath. Hundreds were killed, and divisions between shah supporters and those who believed in Mossadegh's Iran became a matter of life and death. The nation seemed to be on the brink of civil war.

Farmers and traders like Ali feared for their survival. The North was largely considered Mossadegh territory, and Ali worried that the shah would send his Savak to arrest men like him and destroy their homes and farms.

"We need to leave, start a new life in Afghanistan or Turkey," Ali told his wife late one night.

Maryam spoke only when spoken to and still would not leave her bed. She had been lying with her back to her husband but now turned to meet his anxious gaze. She sat up and took his face in her hands. "I'm never leaving this land again. I will not leave the farm. I will die here, just like my children."

"Maryam joonam, please. It's not safe here. Think of the children who remain. What of their future? We must leave."

Maryam shook her head and released Ali's face. She crawled back under the covers and pulled them up to her chin. "Ali, I can't leave here. I cannot."

He stroked his wife's dark hair. For almost as long as he had known her, she'd had the same chin-length cut. Ali loved the way it made her curls spiral in every direction like firecrackers. He thought of Shokat with her blonde curls. She wore her hair the same. Or she had. It pained him to realize he had no idea how she styled her hair now.

And then Ali had an idea. "What if we could get Shokat back here? What if she came with us?"

Maryam sat back up. Just the sound of her beloved firstborn's name sent waves of hopeful energy through her body. But then images of her daughter bruised and beaten flashed in her mind. "It will never work, Ali. She'll never get away from that man, and it's our fault."

But Ali had another idea: they would send Ezzhat with Mahmood, their third-born son, as emissaries. If they could bring Shokat home, then the whole family would move. If not, Ezzhat and Mahmood would remain in Mashad with Shokat, where they would be safe and could protect their sister while Ali formulated a new plan.

"Our country is crumbling, and the future is uncertain," Ali reasoned. "I know this is difficult, but we need to protect our family. This may be the only way."

Maryam nodded through her tears.

Ezzhat's husband, Mehdi, needed little convincing of Ali's plan. He wanted to join his wife and brother-in-law. He also hoped to resettle in the city. Mashad was brimming with possibilities for a textile merchant. Like Ali, he worried about their fate should they remain in the village.

Ali and Maryam packed Mahmood's books and the small violin one of his cousins had made for him when they learned of his love for music. They burdened him with a heavy load for a ten-year-old: succeed in what Maryam had not been able to do, save Shokat from that wretched man.

But Mr. Sadr had no intention of letting Shokat leave Mashad. When young Mahmood arrived, Shokat hardly recognized her brother. He had been just a toddler when she left the village. He had their father's eyes, and his hair matched hers in coloring. Slender, with a chin as pronounced as Maryam's, he was a shy boy. His sister embraced him and decided then and there that she would care for him and protect him fiercely. When Sadr announced that she would not be leaving Mashad, Shokat begged him to let her brother stay instead. She wanted to raise him like the child they did not have. In their ten years of marriage, they had never once been intimate. Shokat knew now it was because her husband preferred the company of men.

Miraculously, Sadr agreed to let Mahmood live with them in Mashad, but only on the condition that the boy attend a private school and excel in all subjects—a decision that forever changed the course of his life.

Ezzhat sent a telegram to her parents, informing them of the new situation and that she and Mehdi were settling permanently in Mashad. She was emphatic that all was well, that Mahmood was thriving, and that she and Shokat grew closer to God each day. They had become immersed in the mosque, volunteering much of their time in service of the Imam Reza shrine. Ali was relieved that at least two of his children were safe. He told himself that Mahmood's presence would also make things better for Shokat. But the hole in Maryam's heart only deepened. Two more of her children were now out of her sight and far away. The crippling pain kept her bedridden.

For one year, Maryam drifted in and out of consciousness. She lost count of the days, only fluttering her eyes open when one of her children came to her. But in the spring of 1954, on the anniversary of Mahmood and Ezzhat's departure for Mashad, Ali woke her.

"Your mother is sick, Maryam. You need to get out of this room right now and go to her."

Maryam, who could only half-process what her husband was saying, stood up in a trance. Still in her yellowed nightgown despite it being the middle of the day, she followed Ali to Maman's quarters. It was unclear what ailed her mother, and she refused to see any of the doctors Ali brought home. She burned with fever and could not eat, drink, or even speak. When Maryam saw how frail her warrior-like mother had become, she was filled with a self-loathing rage. She was furious with herself for being so blinded by her own grief that she had failed to notice her mother withering away, and now it was too late. Maman died the next day. A small, quiet funeral attended by the dozen remaining family members and a handful of friends was held at the burial site just under the bahar narenj tree, where the other Mahdavis had been buried some years before.

The remainder of the 1950s passed in a blur. Thankfully, Ali's fears did not come to pass, and their village remained safe in the aftermath of the 1953 coup and the bloody installment of the shah. Ali again tried to persuade Maryam to leave the farm, still uncertain of their safety under a shah who was known for his brutality, but Maryam convinced him that their family had already suffered the worst of their possible fates.

Again and again, Maryam told Ali that Iran was not Afghanistan. Iranians had the strength of generations of fighters running through their veins, she reminded him. But Ali remained uncertain, worried that the relentless invasions and unrest taking place in neighboring Afghanistan would soon be their reality, too.

"If that happens, and I believe it will not, but if war begins to ravage our lands the way it has in Afghanistan, then we will go to my friends in the caves," Maryam conceded. "We will go live and train to fight with our allies there. That will be our survival." Ali was surprised that his wife was referencing the all-female army in the caves, as she had told him that she never wanted to speak of them or the border again. Yet it seemed to Ali that the mere mention of these fighting women gave her a burst of strength. It was enough to make him agree to stay on the farm—for now.

Maryam did not return to her bed after Maman's death but threw herself back into the farm and the family's survival. She could not let another member of her clan die on her watch. Now she made sure that her boys were healthy and becoming stronger by the day. In 1958, despite having just turned forty-five, she gave birth to a baby girl, Shahla. She hoped that one day the little girl would get to meet her sisters, Shokat and Ezzhat, and her brother Mahmood. She prayed that they would all return home to the farm.

But Maryam never fully recovered her previous strength, and without Maman, the household was more difficult to manage than she wanted to admit. The farm was falling steadily into disrepair. When the coup had made trade impossible and the family was desperate for money, Ali had been forced to sell off most of the horses. Each horse that left the family brought a fresh wave of tears to the remaining family members— including and most especially his wife. The few who remained were too old to work. Maryam ached for the herd but could not make herself get back on a horse. Each time she held the reins, her entire body trembled at the memory of her daughter. But without more workers and without the assistance of the agile horses, there was no way the delicate saffron crop could thrive. The family survived on the meager bounty of their vegetable garden.

Spring brought the arrival of a new year and the Iranian holiday Nowruz. The year 1960 was here, and finally, so was some peace. Moham- mad Reza Pahlavi had grown more confident in his rule. He called off his brutal Savak police force and announced his full support for farmers and merchants throughout the country. The monarch even opened more trade routes, with subsidies and incentives for farmers to produce and sell more goods.

One afternoon just before Nowruz, Ali returned from a fruitful visit to the capital bursting with news. He found Maryam in the kitchen making yet another batch of cabbage and potato stew and presented her with a bouquet of orange blossoms.

Maryam embraced him distractedly, and Ali's heart ached, remembering the time before her sadness when her face brightened upon his return and the two would sneak away for a long embrace. He studied her heavy, grief-stricken face and hoped his words would allay her pain. "I have news, wife!"

"Tell me, Ali jaan."

"Business is picking back up, my dear. The government will pay us to hire more people. We can even get the saffron going again."

Maryam turned back to the stove, stirred the soup, and then wandered out into the courtyard to pick more herbs. Ali hurried after her, flustered.

"I know you don't believe me, or—or—you are skeptical. But it's true. We could bring our crops back to life. I know we can."

"It's not that simple," Maryam tsked.

"But we can buy back some of our horses—"

"You know I'm never going to ride again, Ali."

"Just listen. That's the other news. Please." Ali took his wife's hand. "This is the best part, azzizam. Hear me out. I met someone in Tehran, a horsewoman warrior, a Gordafarid like you, but with yellow hair."

"Okay, so you met another woman. Are you taking another wife? Is that the news?" Maryam pulled her hand from his and turned back to the herb garden.

"Maryam. She's married. To Narcy Firouz, the Qajar prince."

"Oh, so that's why you didn't—"

"My dearest wife, please, please, please. Wait. Let me explain." Ali was on his knees now, begging. Maryam stopped her gardening and arched a silvered eyebrow.

"Louise, that's her name. Louise and Narcy Firouz have opened up a riding academy in Tehran," Ali continued tentatively. "She's from America, and she studies horses. She married Narcy Firouz and moved to Iran. They started a riding academy, and they have some of the most beautiful horses I've ever seen."

"That's good for her, but what does that have to do with me?" Maryam raised her other eyebrow.

"I'm getting there. You would like her horses, but that's still not the best part." Ali stood now to face his wife. "I went to visit them, to see this riding academy everyone is talking about, and Louise told me she is looking for different horses, smaller ones, for the children she teaches. And I immediately thought of our sea horses! Small, but strong and powerful. I told her about them, and she was intrigued."

Maryam's face softened from frustration to curiosity. She nodded for Ali to continue.

"In fact, she was so intrigued that she asked if she could see them for herself. And so, she's coming! Tomorrow. She is famous, even more than her husband. Everyone talks about her skill with the horses—how she can make them dance and almost sing. I invited her to stay with us. You will love her." Ali held his breath, waiting for Maryam's response.

"We had better prepare the house, then," Maryam said flatly.

Ali exhaled. There was hope yet that this new visitor, this new year, this new decade, would bring new life to his wife.

LOUISE ARRIVED the next afternoon with little fanfare. Maryam had never seen a woman behind the wheel of a car before, but this

American drove herself. When Louise stepped out of her Jeep, Maryam was amazed to see how tall she was, taller than Ali and all his uncles. Her straw-colored hair was shorter than Maryam's, and her blue-green eyes exuded warmth.

Louise strode right up to Ali and Atta to shake hands. Maryam was shocked a woman would behave so brazenly and was even more startled when Louise pulled her into an embrace and kissed her three times on each cheek. She took Maryam's hands in hers, and Maryam felt the calluses on her palms and knew Louise could feel hers as well. This woman was a worker. They exchanged a knowing look.

Another American woman had come along, Penny. They mentioned a third friend who was wandering their village in search of an inn for the night. Penny followed Louise's lead, shaking hands with the men and embracing Maryam. She and Louise wore form-fitting trousers and knee-high boots. They looked like the magazine photographs Ezzhat had shown her of female riders competing abroad. Maryam's heart skipped a beat.

"You are welcome here, Ms. Louise. You and your friends," Ali said, breaking the easy silence.

"Khayli mamnoon," Louise responded in heavily accented Persian. Parviz and Shahla, who had rushed out to see what appeared to be a Hollywood celebrity with a fancy car, giggled at her mispronunciation.

Louise knelt to meet the children at eye level. "Salam, bacheha, man Louise hastam," she said, introducing herself. Though her Persian was clumsy, she breathed a quiet confidence. Maryam counted the creases around her eyes and mouth, drawn in by the simultaneous softness and power of this horsewoman.

Shahla squealed and covered her mouth, and Louise enveloped her in an embrace, which only further delighted the girl. She gave Atta a high-five, a gesture new to him but one he immediately adopted.

"Well, I don't know about you all, but I'm starving, and I smell a delicious stew," Louise announced in English, smiling broadly.

Ali was the only one who comfortably spoke what northerners referred to as "the language of the colonizers," which he had learned from his merchant father whose travels took him into Saudi Arabia, where English was the common tongue. He lowered his head in a half-bow and motioned their guests inside, where Maryam had set a humble table with the remnants of her wedding dishware. Penny excused herself, preferring to continue her tour of the surrounding villages after she retrieved Jean, but Louise sat right down and enjoyed every bite. When they were finished, she rose and thanked Maryam for the delicious meal. "Now, shall we ride?" she asked.

The room fell silent. All eyes were on Maryam. More than a decade had passed since she had last sat atop a horse. But Ali remained confident in his wife's deep love for the gentle, powerful creatures. All he wanted was for Maryam to return to herself, and he knew the horses were an intrinsic part of her. As soon as he had laid eyes on Louise with her horses in Tehran, he had known that if anyone could bring his wife back to life, it was this warrior woman from the West.

Maryam looked at her children's anxious faces, then at her eager, hopeful husband, and finally at Louise. She nodded.

Ali clapped his hands and sent a prayer to the sky. The children cheered and then ran out into the courtyard, arguing over who would get to saddle the horses. When Atta led Asghar and Khosrow out of the stables, Louise gasped.

"Khanoum Louise, do not worry," Ali said quickly. "They are smaller than your Arabs, but they move more quickly and smoothly."

"Worry? Ali jaan, I'm not worried. I'm enchanted. Never before have I seen such horses. Are they Turkomans?"

Maryam, who understood only that last word, thought Louise was asking for a Turkoman, and she sent Atta back to the stables to get one.

Louise stared in wonder as the boy emerged with yet another magnificent horse. This one had a longer neck, and its brown coat had an almost metallic sheen. Its face and legs were narrower, resembling the Arabians, but its back was much longer and its face narrow, almost like a giraffe.

"Here . . . Turkoman . . . Akhal-Tehke Turkoman horse . . . ," Maryam said in her broken English.

The horse's name was Saadi, and Louise wasted no time going to him, cupping his long face, and pressing her forehead to his nose, just as Maryam and Maman had always done. Next, she placed her palm to Asghar's neck and bowed. The horse drew close, resting his chin on her shoulder, and gently pulled her in as if for a hug. Maryam wiped away tears and smiled when Louise turned to her and said, "Let's ride!"

For the first time in a decade, Maryam hoisted herself onto Khosrow's back, and the stallion tossed his head in joy. Shahla had never seen her mother on a horse, and the little girl couldn't help but squeal with delight.

Louise chose Saadi, the Turkoman who was better matched for her height than the smaller horses whose strength she did not yet know. Saadi's eyes danced with a mischief she understood. "Can the chestnut one come along with us?" Louise asked, motioning to Asghar. "I want to ride him, too. I mean, if I can. If I'm not too heavy. I just want to ride them all!"

Ali turned to his wife and saw in her eyes something he hadn't seen in years: joy. "What do you think, my dearest? Do you want to take Asghar? Would you like me or one of the boys to come?"

Maryam shook her head. "This is a ladies' ride."

She whistled at Asghar and jerked her proud chin to the right in an upward motion. Asghar licked his lips and shook out his mane at her attention. Maryam sucked in her cheek to make a clicking noise and tightened the muscle of her upper thigh ever so gently. That was all Khosrow and Asghar needed. Off they went, thrilled to be reunited with their human mother. Maryam knew Louise was close behind because she could hear Saadi's clickety-clack gait, so distinct from the steady boom-click-boom of the Caspians' gallop.

She turned her face up to the sky, relishing the wind in her hair. Leaning forward onto Khosrow's neck, she dug her hands into his thick mane and closed her eyes. Maryam had tried to forget this joy, but oh, how she had missed it. The power of history coursed through her body. She could feel Gordafarid riding alongside her and feel the strength of the Persian Empire pumping in her veins, the valor of her people that had been passed down for thousands of years from horse-woman to horsewoman, from grandmother to mother to daughter. It was the strength she had lost when her eldest child, bruised and bleeding, had been carried away from her at gunpoint; it was the strength that had drained from her soul when she lost one child and then another to polio; it was the strength that died with her mother. Death and heartbreak had bested her. But now, ever so slowly, as they galloped toward the sea, Maryam felt something new—more than hope. It was the possibility of resurrection.

When at last they reached the beach, Khosrow didn't hesitate, leading her right out into the ocean until her skirt bloomed with water, and she began to laugh.

"You are amazing," Louise called from the sand, resuming her clumsy Persian. "I can't believe you ride *into* the water with them!"

"They love to swim," Maryam shouted back over the waves. It had never occurred to her *not* to ride into the water with the horses. "They love it more than you or me."

"I don't love to swim, but I do love adventure," Louise said. Maryam struggled to discern her tone through the accent.

"You will love swimming with the horses, I promise. Let Saadi come in. He will be happy, and he will make you happy too. They are, how you call it in English? 'Sea horses.'"

"Where I come from, a 'sea horse' is something else. It lives under the sea."

"A horse who lives under the sea?" Maryam furrowed her brows.

This time it was Louise's turn to laugh. "No, no. They are not horses; they are fish. Or, at least, I think they are."

"Then why call them 'horses'?"

"You know what? That's a good question!" Both women were laughing now.

"Come in, Louise Firouz! Come into the water." Maryam floated on her back as both Khosrow and Asghar swam around her. "Float with me; feel weightless." And it was true: the heavy load she had been carrying for so long already felt lighter.

Never one to shy away from something new, Louise clucked and squeezed Saadi with the full weight of her legs. But the horse wasn't accustomed to such forceful commands, and he bolted, catapulting his rider into the water. Maryam laughed and laughed, and Louise, her yellow hair plastered to her head when she broke the surface, couldn't help but laugh too. Maryam tapped the water, and Saadi bowed his head before swimming out to join them.

"Too much force, my friend, too much muscle," she said to Louise, who stared in wonder as Saadi swam toward her. "You don't need to kick them so hard or cluck so loud. Work *with* them. Match your mind with theirs."

Louise nodded. She prided herself on being a horse expert and had believed she was bringing the art of horsemanship and its tricks *to* Iran. But as Saadi circled her playfully, tossing his mane in the waves, Louise's understanding of herself and of her adopted homeland was rapidly shifting. Maryam watched her new friend drift a world away, lost in heavy thought. She knew that look.

"Tell me your story, Louise Firouz. Tell me about your world and what brought you to mine."

The American woman flipped onto her back, took a deep breath of sea air, and started from the beginning.

When Louise finished, Maryam could hardly believe it. Was this woman floating next to her real? She shook her head and swam to Khosrow, leading him ashore. Louise followed silently, all the while stealing glances at Maryam.

They were sitting on the beach, drying themselves in the baking sun, when Maryam finally asked, "So why are you *here*? In my village?"

A moment of silence passed between them.

"For them," Louise said at last, pointing to Asghar and Khosrow.

"You want to take my horses?" Maryam's eyes were wide.

Louise hastened to reassure her. "Maryam khanoum, no, no, friend. I just wanted to see them for myself. People from Tehran to Shiraz speak of you and of the horses in the North. They tell stories of smaller, stronger horses, like those carved into the stones of Persepolis. And so, when I met Ali in Tehran, well, I just had to come."

"I still don't understand," Maryam said, rising to her feet.

"Wait, my friend, wait. Let me explain." Louise stood as well but kept her voice gentle, melodic. "I have a lot of riders at my academy in Tehran. Many children. Children of prominent families—"

"I have no care for the opulence of Tehran or the prominence of Tehrani families," Maryam interjected.

"I understand. I'm just trying to explain. I try to teach children to ride, but the Arabian horses in the capital aren't appropriate for the young ones and their little bodies."

Maryam nodded; it was true. She had never understood the obsession with the hot-blooded Arabian horse, especially for children or beginners.

"And I kept hearing the most incredible rumors about another breed of horse in the Alborz Mountains and here by the Caspian Sea, about their magic. I had to see them for myself. They really do look like the horses in the carvings of Persepolis in Shiraz and in the art hanging in the galleries of Tehran. They are magical."

"These horses can*not* leave the Caspian," Maryam said firmly, her eyes dark. "They would be miserable in Tehran or Shiraz. I don't care where their pictures are. These are *Caspian* horses."

"That's what we will call them, then. Caspian horses. We will be their caretakers, under your direction, of course. I promise." Louise held out her hand.

Maryam paused. She looked at Louise and then at the horses, acutely aware of the soreness along her thighs. It was the first time she felt alive since her daughter had been taken from her. The first time she felt light enough to mount a horse. The first time she had smiled from the inside out. She did not trust strangers, especially those from abroad, and would never have invited one into her home, let alone fed them at her table, or ever let ride one of her herd. But she had recognized something in Louise. This woman may have come from far away, may have talked funny and looked different, but she was no stranger.

As she had seen Ali do hundreds of times when trading, Maryam took the woman's hand with a firm grip, binding herself, her horses, and their legacy to the tall warrior horsewoman standing beside her.

JUST AS Ali hoped, Louise's passion for the horses revitalized Maryam. She joined Louise on adventures in search of more Caspian horses. Together the four horsewomen rode the old road from Amol to Babol, winding through rice paddies and small villages dotted with thatched-roof homes. When they reached Babol, Louise purchased her first Caspian horse, a chestnut stallion named Hawk.

Ducks and geese led them on to still more villages and horses while Louise scoured her notebook in search of the most efficient way of identifying and keeping track of their burgeoning breed. The women covered the entire Mazandaran Province of Iran, rescuing one Caspian horse after another from careless and ruthless owners. That first year, they were able to identify fifty horses between them. By this time, they could tell the physical characteristics and personality traits that set the Caspian horse apart from the others. Large bulging eyes, smaller hindquarters, a slightly curved back, and wide neck. They moved their legs from their shoulders and walked, trotted, and galloped with their heads held high rather than lowering them. Louise purchased six stallions and seven mares to breed them. She had initially planned to return to Norouzabad to use these horses to train children, but her love for the North had grown so strong, she decided to abandon the suburban farm altogether and relocate her entire operation.

For his part, Narcy was relieved that Louise had found her calling in Iran, so much so that he began spending more of his time in the North as well, sneaking away from the hustle and bustle of the capital on weekends and then for months on end in the summertime. Their children loved the fresh air on the farm, adored playing with the horses from morning until night, and Louise felt the strength of the bond between the siblings growing, as hers had with her brothers when they worked the land.

As the trust deepened between the two women, Maryam shared more and more of her memories and instincts, such as the precise way she gave a horse slack by loosening her grip on the reins. She also told Louise about the all-female army battling in the caves of Afghanistan, and it seemed to the American that this Iranian horsewoman was a ceaseless fount of inspiration and knowledge. The female horse warriors fascinated her, but Maryam was evasive about the details of the army's whereabouts and their smuggling operation. Louise didn't mind. She loved the flames of strength that flickered in Maryam's eyes when she spoke of the women of the caves.

The year was 1962, and Iran was healing from civil war after the installation of the shah. For Maryam, though, the rift and distance between herself and her three children in Mashad stymied her own healing. Two decades had passed since she had last seen her firstborn child. The pain of remembering paralyzed her, but the fear that her long silence and absence might make her children forsake her forever gnawed at Maryam. She had stopped communicating with Ezzhat and Mahmood after they sent word from Mashad that they would not be returning to her and the farm. She had felt betrayed, but now she felt only longing. With Louise's encouragement, Maryam finally relented and agreed to plan a trip to Mashad. But she was afraid that Shokat's husband, Arsalan—or, worse, Shokat herself—might not permit her to enter their home.

"If she doesn't let you in, surely Ezzhat will," Louise reassured her. "It's time, my friend, you reconnect with your children."

WHEN SHOKAT opened the door and saw her mother, heavy with the grief of the last twenty years, she rushed to embrace her. Soon, Ezzhat, who had moved just down the street from her sister in Mashad, joined them. And both of Maryam's sons-in-law seemed genuinely pleased to see her. Mr. Sadr, who had once placed a bounty on Maryam's head in order to retrieve his wife, even invited her to stay in their guest room. *Perhaps time does heal all wounds*, Maryam mused. But even as she wanted to believe this, the fresh bruises on her daughter's wrists told her otherwise.

Maryam assumed Mahmood was out and would return in time for dinner, but when she realized there was no place setting for her son at the table, she testily asked where he was. Shokat and Ezzhat exchanged nervous glances.

"Your son is studying to become a doctor, Khanoum Mahdavi," Mr. Sadr told her. "He is at Tehran University. Top student in all his studies, you know."

Maryam dropped her fork. "Mahmood? A doctor? Living in Tehran?"

"Yes, Maman joon, it's true." Shokat cupped her hand around her mother's wrist. "You should be proud."

But Maryam's heart did not swell with pride. It broke—for her son. Of all her children, the one who had loved farming the most was Mahmood. How happy he had been as a child to rise at dawn and help his mother plant and prune and weed and harvest, digging his hands deep into the fresh soil. He was a true farmer. She could imagine him as nothing else.

Then again, Maryam had also believed that Shokat could never be anything but a dirt-on-her-boots horsewoman. A female warrior in the caves, even. Instead, sitting across from her was a buttoned-up woman wearing designer clothing and drinking from a crystal glass. Even Ezzhat had changed. Her sharp, wild edges were nowhere to be seen, replaced by steady softness. While her eyes still danced with mischief, she had grown into a woman who carried herself with an air of unshakable calm. Maryam couldn't stop studying her daughters' faces.

"Madar, stay here with us. Don't go back to the village," Shokat pleaded. Her cheeks had hollowed, making her look much older than she was.

"You'll stay with us. We have so much space, and your grandchildren will be thrilled," Ezzhat said.

Maryam looked to her son-in-law. Mehdi, who had grown almost as wide as he was tall once Ezzhat learned to cook, beamed at her and nodded his enthusiastic agreement. Then she turned to Mr. Sadr, in spite of herself.

"They are right, Khanoum. I suppose you ought to stay here in Mashad," Arsalan said. He held a sugar cube between his teeth and sipped hot tea after he spoke, so it was hard to discern his tone and expression. Gently and quietly, Shokat placed her hand on her husband's wrist. It was a technique she used frequently to calm him. "We would . . . we would love to have you," he concluded.

The offer was clearly a disingenuous one, but having only just reconnected with her daughters, and having discussed with Ali the strategy of enveloping Shokat to get her away from her abusive husband, Maryam didn't care. She could not bear the thought of saying good-bye again so soon.

"Then I'll stay," Maryam announced. The room, save for Mr. Sadr, erupted with excitement, and Shokat and Ezzhat found themselves bickering over who would get to host their matriarch.

"On one condition," Maryam said, raising a finger to quiet the group. "That you permit me to get my own place. You know I like my space, and I'll need to be on the outskirts of town anyway on account of the horses. But I'll dine with you all every evening, if you'll have me."

Maryam sent a telegram to Ali, inviting him to visit but asking that he and their sons continue to oversee the farm. She also asked that their youngest, Shahla, come stay with her in Mashad. Ali was happily surprised. He had often visited Shokat and Ezzhat on his trading trips to the religious capital of the country and knew how much they had missed their mother. Still, he had not imagined that Maryam would ever willingly leave the farm.

The city life never appealed to Maryam, but she knew it would take time to wedge her daughter free of the man who gripped her, and in that moment, nothing was more important than being near her girls.

LOUISE, 1984

LOUISE FELL IN LOVE NOT ONLY WITH MARYAM'S HORSES BUT also with the mountains and the sea of the Gilan, Mazandaran, and Golestan Provinces of the North. Tired of the dusty chaos of the capital, she yearned for fresh air and ached to spend her days riding, not in a ring, but through the forest and into the sea. It took three months to convince Narcy they should move, but once he agreed, Louise wasted no time creating a new life for them in the North. She had a new purpose, too: bringing the Caspian horse out of the paintings of history into the living present.

From what she could glean, these horses were stronger, smarter, and more reliable than any breed she had ever met before. After training more than five hundred horses in the United States, Louise thought she could anticipate the movements and personalities of every horse after meeting them once. But the Caspians continued to surprise—pleasantly. They rarely bucked their riders or their packs. No matter how much weight Louise piled on their backs, they continued forward, not missing a single hoofbeat, tripping, or deviating from a straight line.

Growing up in the United States, Louise had always taught new riders that the hardest thing to make an American Quarter Horse do was walk in a straight line. They always wanted to fall in to the center of an arena or pasture, favoring one shoulder or another. The main objective for the rider was to know when to anticipate the fall or deviation and correct it with leg pressure. But Caspians were different. They walked perfectly, rarely favoring one side or the other. Louise had to teach them a trick only once or walk a new road one time, and they would remember it. They were unflappable. The more she got to know them, the more Louise understood why these horses had been the perfect animals to ride into battle, to conquer empires, to deliver their riders safely.

As far as she could tell, however, they had fallen out of favor in the 1900s as locals grew taller and larger horses came into fashion. Caspians stood no more than fourteen hands from the ground. As such, riders over five foot ten would find their feet dragging on the ground. Louise had experienced this herself the first time she mounted Asghar at Maryam's house. Because of this, she worried she was too heavy for the animal. But Maryam had shown her how to fold her legs and rest them in stirrups against his sides, or how to curl her legs at the knee and lean forward so she could rest the tops of her toes on the back of his hindquarters. With the right posture, anyone of any height or weight could ride a Caspian. And sitting atop them was a dream. No more choppy gaits like American Quarter Horses. This was like riding in a rocking chair, Louise thought. It reminded her of nights curled up in her mother's lap on their favorite upholstered chair.

Everyone who met the small, mighty creatures fell in love with them. Word spread, and soon the most prominent families in Iran were asking for their own Caspians. Even Crown Prince Reza Pahlavi, son of Mohammad Reza Shah, fell hard for the animals; he particularly loved that their lineage traced back to the glory of the Persian Empire. He declared them a national treasure, founded the Royal Horse Society of Iran (RHS), and proclaimed himself the patron and protector of the Caspian horse and its history. The history of a horse that led the greatest empires of all time—Persians, Greeks, Romans, Mongols—to conquer territories and expand their reach: this horse, it seemed to the royals, was the key to geopolitics.

In 1969, the Duke of Edinburgh visited the RHS and became the second royal to fall under their spell. Prince Philip had been visiting the region on annual scouting trips where he would purchase new breeds for his wife, the queen of England, who was an avid equestrian. When he heard about the Caspian horses—word had traveled to Europe via Turkey—Iran jumped to the top of his list. He told Louise and Narcy that he simply must have Caspians of his own and tried to persuade them to export a few to England. Louise was reluctant, but Prince Philip promised not only to take excellent care of them but also to promote their story worldwide. For a devoted conservationist, the idea was tempting. It had become Louise's mission to ensure that the Caspian horse, which she and others believed was the oldest breed on the planet, did not go extinct.

Prince Philip's Caspians wouldn't be the first of the breed to reside abroad. In 1966, Louise had taken a dark-brown liver chestnut named Jehan to Virginia. The journey had been exhausting, both for Louise and for the stallion. But it had meant something to bring the Caspian to her birthplace, a piece of her heart where she had left some of her soul. Jehan would go on to father many part-Caspians, bringing the breed's legacy to the United States.

Prince Philip told Louise if she sold him the horses he wanted, he would start his own Caspian breeding program in the United Kingdom. After discussing with Narcy and exchanging telegrams with Maryam in Mashad, Louise finally agreed to his request. Between 1971 and 1976, Louise exported twenty-six Caspian horses of different bloodlines to England via a caravan that traveled through Turkey and Germany and then boarded a boat in France. With the support of the Duke of Edinburgh, these became the European Formation Herd, eventually breeding five hundred Caspians for distribution across Europe. The Europeans fell in love with them almost at first sight and took up the modern-day breeding program, as they were seen as the most reliable horses for training children. And for adventurous trail riders on the Continent, their sure-footed nature was unparalleled. The worldwide legacy of the Caspian horse was taking root.

From the United Kingdom, the horses made their way to Germany, Sweden, and then the Caribbean. Caspians were bred to Norwegian Fjord Horses, Paso Finos in the Caribbean, and, when they made their way to the United States, to American Quarter Horses.

The Iranians were not impressed with the expansion of Louise's global mission. The crown prince was particularly angry, going so far as to accuse Louise of betrayal. In 1971, he ordered the Royal Horse Society to punish her and Narcy by taking their twenty-three remaining horses. They left Louise with only her stallion and a gelding, which meant she needed to find a mare to keep her work alive. Always the picture of calm in the face of adversity, Louise became uncharacteristically distraught. It pained her to share the news with Maryam, and, as she wrote to her dear friend, "an emptiness occupies my organs."

As soon as Maryam read Louise's letter, she knew it was time to leave Mashad. The pendulum had swung again, and it was home that needed her most. Despite her daughters' protests, Maryam immediately put her house on the market. It was not an easy decision. She worried still for her daughter Shokat, who, despite a seeming détente with her husband, still shrank away from him, folding her body in two or leaving when he entered a room. Ezzhat had birthed three children, two boys and a girl. The boys' faces reminded Maryam of her father, while the girl was the spitting image of her mother. She adored being with them but was also growing homesick.

Ten years in the city had made Maryam restless. She was ready to go back to the life of soil, sand, and sea. In 1972, Maryam said good-bye to her children, saddled up her horses, and rode north.

Louise, leaving from the capital after a tense meeting with the shah, to whom she was pleading her case to have her herd returned, was also riding north. The two women arranged to meet in Kalaleh, near the border of Turkmenistan. Ali had sent word that three Caspian mares had been spotted by horse-trading merchants in Gharah Tappeh Sheikh, a village near Kalaleh. If it proved true, Louise and Maryam would be able to start a new herd with those mares and the two stallions they still had between them.

When Maryam rode into the village, Louise was out thistle hunting on the steppe plains. The toxic plant had already claimed the lives of several sheep in the village. Louise worried that her horses would be next, so she'd grabbed a pair of gloves, pulled on her boots, and started pulling the thorny weeds wherever she found them.

Maryam could've sworn she heard Louise's heartbeat before Asghar's hoofbeats thundered onto the steppes. She unfolded to stand, two bushels of freshly torn thistle in hand, and took in her magnificent friend. Just as her horse's mane had begun graying, so too did Maryam notice wisps of white curling at Louise's temples. Her previously smooth face was cracked with wrinkles from the sun.

Louise's years on horseback had worn down her back, which now curved permanently, bringing her closer in height to most Iranians. Like Maryam, Louise's hair was also thinning, though hers was less noticeable, given her blonde strands.

Maryam slid off her horse, and the two women embraced, Louise enveloping her petite friend in a full body hug. They kissed each other three times on each cheek. Maryam wiped a tear of joy as she gazed into her friend's eyes. After pleasantries, the two women got down to business.

"We need to start a studbook," Louise told Maryam, as soon as they had met up and started for the steppe plains.

Maryam had picked up a fair amount of English from Louise and Ali over the years, but "studbook" was not in her vocabulary.

"It's a record of the horses, every single one we breed," Louise explained in Persian. "Including who each horse was sired by, who the dame was, and so forth."

"But why would we need that?" Maryam asked. "I know every foal I've delivered and their parents, too."

"A studbook is crucial. It's living history, Maryam joon. It will live on long after we're gone," Louise explained.

"But it's just a book?"

"It's an ancestral tree, only for animals. Studbooks are used for rare and endangered wildlife of all kinds—tigers and elephants, for example—but horses, too. The Caspian is the most ancient breed of horse we know of. We need irrefutable records to keep track of who, when, and where we breed, making sure we can prove the bloodline."

"So, it's a record, then?" Maryam was still perplexed.

"It's history," Louise said.

"It's a business opportunity," Maryam mused. Purebred Caspians would fetch a higher price.

"It's all these things. It's how we're going to grow this herd. It's what we know, what we learn, and what we want to pass down. One day this book, not to mention the horses we breed from our studs, will be worth millions. Really, it's priceless, Maryam."

Gharah Tappeh, with its steep rock formations and mossy rolling hills, was a welcome respite when they finally reached it, and there were indeed three brood mares waiting for them. But Louise worried the mares—who were, as far as Louise could assess, older and in need of more fertile grass and less sand—might not reproduce if they moved them to Sari, near Maryam's farm, because of the arduousness of the journey. They might not even survive the trek. After much deliberation, Louise decided she would begin to breed the new herd right there in Gharah Tappeh. She hired some local villagers to build her a yurt, invited her children to join her for a year's adventure in the wild, and settled comfortably for the season. Maryam, eager to return to her farm, Ali, and the smell of dirt that filled the air as the seasons changed near the sea, left Khosrow with Louise and rode home on the gelding whom she'd named Kaveh.

Louise's new breeding efforts got off to a rocky start. No sooner had her first mare given birth than a pack of wolves attacked in the middle of the night. Louise heard them howling and rushed outside barefoot, in nothing but her nightgown, but she was too late. She arrived only in time to watch as the entire wolf pack of seven completed the attack, taking the lives of the mother mare, her baby, and the second of the three brood mares. Louise's howls rivaled the wolves as she screamed in desperation into the empty night sky. She had never felt more alone.

Left with the two stallions and only one remaining mare, Louise wrote a telegram to Maryam

DEAREST FRIEND HORRORS KEEP SETTLING ON US. SO MUCH BLOODSHED. WOLVES ATTACKED. MOTHERS AND BABY DEAD. COME SOON. NEED HELP.

Maryam immediately sent word back that she was on her way to Kalaleh. Though it had been only two weeks since her return to the farm, she agreed to return immediately, sensing the desperation in her friend's letter.

By the time Maryam reached Gharah Tappeh in Kalaleh, Louise had managed to locate another mare, and this one, small and white, looked uncannily like Shokoufeh.

Maryam's arrival further buoyed Louise's spirits. The women rode to Turkmenistan to track down three other mares they had heard about. In contrast to the Afghan border, the winding roads that led to Turkmenistan were pleasantly quiet—no soldiers, no gunshots, no people as far as the eye could see. Just endless trees shading the smooth sandstone routes around the mountains.

"If only all border crossings could be this easy," Maryam remarked.

"Absolutely. But then again, we aren't smuggling anything . . . or anyone," Louise laughed.

Maryam promised to help bring the new mares to Kalaleh before returning home to her beloved farm ahead of the fall harvest. They collected the mares and returned to Iran, praying for fertility in their new herd.

By the time the following year arrived, Louise wrote joyfully to her friend that their prayers had been answered. The white horse, whom Maryam had insisted Louise name Shokoufeh, turned out to be a wonder mare. In just two years' time, she produced not one but two sets of twin foals. Now Louise had ten new Caspians, an even better beginning for a new breed than she could have hoped. Encouraged by Prince Philip and worried about the Caspians' survival in Iran should her renewed efforts be discovered by the shah's son, Louise arranged for eight members of the new breed to be exported to the United Kingdom in 1977.

Unbeknownst to Louise, however, Reza Pahlavi, who was now King Pahlavi, had been spying on her. When his secret police told the shah about the latest export of horses to England, he flew into a rage, ordering that all of Louise's remaining Caspians be slaughtered. In the middle of the night, three of his brutes slipped silently into Gharah Tappeh, where they knew Louise was living alone, as Narcy Firouz and the children had moved to Tehran for the season. They arrived in the dead of night and found Louise asleep, surrounded by slumbering horses. They grabbed her by her graying hair and tied her hands behind her back.

"Keep your eyes open, filthy traitor," one of the men snarled.

"Ready?" another asked, his eyes glistening in the moonlight. He had taken hold of one of the twins, the smallest of the white foals.

"I'm ready," said the guard holding Louise.

"Ready," came a third voice in the dark. Louise was sure she saw the flash of a steel weapon. Suddenly, she understood her stallion had been taken hostage too.

"Eik, doh, seh." The men counted to three. Louise's heart stopped. Gunshots rang out. She started to fall, but the man guarding her yanked her back and pressed himself against her, making uncomfortable sexual gestures. Her entire body was shaking, but she could find no voice with which to scream. The gunshots went on, each followed by another corpse hitting the ground. The little white foal hadn't made a sound when he fell. But the mares and stallions screamed as their bodies crumpled in pools of their own blood.

When the deed was done, the men slipped out into the night, leaving Louise to be found by the villagers in the morning, her wrists still bound, lying in the horses' blood.

"They are dead, all of them," Louise wrote, once she was able. She hoped her friend could still read her handwriting despite the ink smears from her tears. *"I know what you would say. Don't give up, Louise. That's what I would tell you—what I have told you over the years. But revolution is brewing and things are getting worse and worse. The Shah has his men watching me day and night. And Narcy, too. I fear for our safety."* Louise wanted Maryam to smuggle her into Afghanistan, where she could build an alliance with the all-female army she had been told about over the years.

By the time Louise's heart-wrenching letter reached Maryam, it was 1978, the Iranian Revolution was in full swing, and her life was in an upheaval of its own. She wrote to Louise to share her own heartbreak—her family had been ripped apart once again. Her sons, including Mahmood, fled to the United States to escape the economic and political uncertainty brought about by the revolution, vowing never to return to their home country.

Worse still, Ali was ill. Paralyzed by a heart condition neither of them would ever fully understand, Maryam's husband now was the one who couldn't get out of bed. All she could do was watch as his immobility robbed him of his will to live. By the time the Revolutionary Guards—the army of the Islamists who had overthrown the shah and were taking over the country—were banging on doors in the northern villages, Ali had passed away peacefully in his sleep, surrounded by his wife and three of their children.

"Once again," Maryam wrote in her letter to Louise, "I have no time for grief." By 1979, the violence of the revolution was inescapable. The shah insisted he could bring Iran into the future of global markets, trade, and modernity. The Islamists accused the shah of being a puppet of the United States, of overindulging in Western culture and depravity, and of an overall sense of Westoxication. The battle between tradition and modernity was unfolding before their very eyes, and it was Iran—the land and the people—who suffered. No one knew if it was the shah's men or the revolutionaries who were burning the fields, but Louise was determined that no one would touch their farm. "Surround any intruders—any men who aren't related to you, don't trust them—and never let your guard down," was what Maryam told Louise.

But Louise and Narcy did both let their guard down. Like the wolves who had attacked the herd in the middle of the night, the Revolutionary Guards tore through their flock of sheep and burst into their home under the cover of darkness.

Louise couldn't remember if she saw them, smelled them, or heard them first. Within minutes four guards tore the couple out of bed and dragged them outside into the courtyard. As her bare feet felt the soil beneath her, Louise sent a silent prayer into the universe that someone would look after the animals, the crops, and their precious home. She inhaled the familiar scent of dirt and olive trees, wondering if she would ever return to this magical place.

"What is our charge?" Louise demanded, when the guard threw her in the back seat of their Paykan vehicle. Narcy had been taken to a separate vehicle, a Mercedes-Benz. His car departed first, peeling out of their driveway and kicking up a dust cloud in their wake.

"Your charge?" the guard snapped. He met her eyes in the rearview mirror. Louise was acutely aware she was wearing nothing but a thin, white linen nightgown. She watched as his eyes wandered to her small breasts, wishing her hands were untied so she could fold her arms over her chest.

"Yes, my charge. Why are you arresting me?" Louise returned. "And what has Narcy done?"

"We don't need to respond to you, filthy American," a second guard spat.

Louise leaned her head against the cool window. She wanted to catch one last glimpse of her farm, memorizing the peace it had brought her soul to make a life there.

"Are you taking me to Evin?" Louise asked. It was everyone's greatest fear that they would be placed inside Iran's most notorious prison. Word was that the political prisoners in Evin faced the worst kind of physical and emotional torture.

The guards smiled. Louise shuddered, and closed her eyes.

At Evin, Louise's first interrogator was a man whose round face was covered in a thick beard that seemed to grow into his collarbones. He was short and stocky, rising only to Louise's chest, and informed her that she and Narcy were both charged with espionage.

"You are most clearly an American spy," he told her matter-of-factly, "and a royalist."

Louise shook her head and crossed her arms. She knew there was no way to otherwise convince the Islamic Revolutionary Guards, an arm of the regime that had risen to power on a platform of anti-Westoxication. Her blonde hair, blue eyes, American accent, and clumsy Farsi were damning in the eyes of her captors. The revolution had unseated the shah—that much she knew and could support, for Louise had experienced the shah's brutality firsthand. She could relate to a country growing weary of royalist rule. But what had replaced him seemed to Louise far worse. An ayatollah who ordered abuse, torture, and murder, all in the name of God. A regime more focused on controlling women's bodies than solving the growing unemployment crisis.

Louise was held in solitary confinement, her only visitor the squat interrogator each morning. She paced her small cell, thinking about her husband, wondering about her children, her farm, and her dear friend Maryam. She spoke a prayer one night into the walls of her cell: *Please let Maryam continue the legacy of the Caspian. We have worked so hard to ride that horse out of the past and into Iran's future.*

Each day when her interrogator arrived, Louise told him stories about the Caspian horse. "The shah destroyed my herd. His men slit the necks of horses—God's creatures—before my very eyes," Louise told him. "I could never support a man who does not care for this wonderful country that has become my home, a monster capable of harming Iran's most precious lands and creations."

After three weeks, Louise managed to convince her captor that she was a sworn enemy of the shah. He and his men had killed her most beloved horses. An unforgivable crime, she told her interrogator. Any ruler whose cruelty extended to animals needed to be removed. She pledged her support to the regime, vowing to help ensure that Westoxication did not seep into the perfect Iranian culture. (Whatever it took to get out, she reasoned.) Whether she believed her own words, she was not certain, but she was determined to get out of prison and back to her horses as soon as possible. Fortunately, she was successful in pleading her case. They had more offensive prisoners, they told her. She simply wasn't worth their time.

Upon Louise's release, she went first to the town house they had kept in Tehran. In recent years Narcy had spent more and more time in the capital, where their children, all three of whom had married, lived. When she arrived, she saw that their belongings had been ransacked. A letter arrived three days later, informing her that their town house and farmlands in Norouzabad were also being confiscated.

Louise went to the bank where Narcy had set up an account and gotten a safety-deposit box not long after they were wed. Donning a black chador for the first time in her life, she begged the teller to give her access to the box that was in her name. It took five attempts on five separate days before she was successful. When she finally gained access, she retrieved all the jewelry she had been gifted for their wedding, along with several gold pieces Narcy had given her over the years. She sold every last one, repurchased the land in Gonbad-i-Kavoos, and returned to this home of her heart to heal and await word of her husband. Narcy remained in Evin, where he stayed for another eleven months until his body grew so frail the guards deemed him unworthy of a spot in the overcrowded prison. Narcy would recover, but was never the same. He remained weak, his spirit broken by his time in Evin, and he increasingly withdrew into himself.

The quiet life continued to elude them. As soon as the Islamist regime was firmly in place, they decided to attempt annexing Iraq. Power hungry and determined to spread their message of Islamic renewal, the regime raised armies of men and boys as young as nine years old to fight. They told them that they were fighting for the most noble cause of all—God. They sent thousands of young boys to their deaths—telling them they were martyrs and would be given the keys to heaven—to fight in a bloody war that lasted a decade.

The Iran-Iraq War infiltrated the country. Night after night, Louise, unable to sleep, paced her damaged lands as she prayed the nearby bombs would skip over her farm. She set up a tent in the middle of their land where Narcy could rest and enjoy the full fragrance of the earth. She pinned back the fabric folds during the day so he could watch her work, gaze up at the clear sky, and hopefully heal. But no sooner had they fallen into a slow rhythm than the Revolutionary Guards once again came for Louise. This time they arrived with an order not of arrest but of service. Louise was told that she needed to assist the Iranian army with breeding horses. Thousands of horses had been confiscated and deployed as a low-tech form of mine clearance, sending the animals into minefields just to watch them die.

Toward the end of the 1980s as the war wound down, Louise was drafted by the military to inspect the horses who survived the mine clearings. They wanted to know which might be Caspian or Turkoman breeding stock. Louise loathed the work, like so many other Iranians who felt tricked by the Islamist regime whose cruelty rivaled and often surpassed that of the shah, especially their treatment of women. She despised the Revolutionary Guards and the way they stood too close, breathing over her shoulder as she assessed the battered horses. They reminded her of the shah's assassins who had assaulted her and murdered her herd near Kalaleh. And they cared no more about the horses than they did the Iranian people. They only wanted Louise to help breed sturdy stock to prepare them for war once again. Whom they would invade next eluded Louise.

Desperate to see her friend and return to their quiet life in Gonbad-i-Kavoos, Louise wrote to Maryam, only to learn that she was in the United States visiting her son Mahmood. Atta, the only remaining Mahdavi child living on the farm, informed Louise that he was waiting for his mother's return from America to announce that he was moving to Mashad. Gonbad was not safe any longer, Atta told Louise.

"You should leave these lands too, move farther north, where you and my mother once started over in Kalaleh," Atta advised. Reluctantly, haunted by the memories of the disintegration of her herd, Louise said good-bye—*for now*—and moved back to the steppe plains that had once healed her and given birth to a new breed. She convinced

Narcy to join her, reasoning that the fresh country air would help calm his nerves.

Maryam returned to Iran some months later, only to learn that many of her lands had been confiscated while she was away and more than a dozen horses taken for the war effort. Heartbroken, she reluctantly agreed to move to Mashad to be closer to her children.

Before moving back to Mashad, however, she wanted to see Louise, who was now in Kalaleh. Years of tragedy had finally caught up with Maryam, and her aging body could no longer make such a trip on horseback. So, Shokat, the proud owner of a brand-new 1985 Mercedes-Benz, offered to drive instead. Mother and daughter made the familiar trek around the Caspian Sea, but this time Maryam watched the kilometers sail by through the window.

The war had been kinder to the eastern part of the North, and Louise had been able to once more reignite her breeding program. When Maryam arrived, this time *she* was the one to step glamorously out of an automobile.

Louise had already saddled up three of the horses, but Maryam declined to ride.

"I'm too old, my friend. I can't do it anymore. My hips won't allow it. But I can still enjoy them," she said, resting her head against the nose of one of the chestnut mares. "Shokat, dear, look at this one. She reminds me of the first horse I ever had, the horse you were named for."

Shokat gingerly placed her hands on either side of the mare's face, letting her fingers come to rest on those strong, round cheekbones.

"You are the daughter I have heard so much about," Louise said, and moved to embrace the younger woman.

"Khanoum Firouz, it is my honor to meet you." Shokat curtsied. "You are a legend. A Gordafarid horsewoman warrior."

Louise let out her most contagious, deep-throated laugh. "Please, dear, call me Louise. Everyone else does!"

Seeing her friend and her daughter together, and hearing Maryam's laughter after so long, Louise felt her whole body relax. "Ah, sister, I have missed you so," Maryam said.

"I have missed you, too, friend. But you look tired," Louise replied.

"I am. I'm exhausted."

Forgoing the ride, the two women sat together beside the turquoise fountain in Louise's courtyard.

"And you, too, Louise. We have both been through hell," Maryam said, with tears in her eyes.

"Let your tears fall into the fountain. That's what I always do," Louise replied, taking Maryam's hand in hers.

Maryam gazed into the clear water shimmering against the blue tiles. She told Louise of her conversation with Ali before his death, her promise that if war threatened their family, she would go to the women of the caves in Afghanistan. "Louise, we need to take horses to Afghanistan as soon as possible. Some of the Caspians and a few Turkomans."

"What? Why?"

"The women of the caves are Gordafarids like us. They need our help. They need horses. One country, then another, invades them. Men, they take *everything* from them—you understand. But the women are strong, and we can help them carry on their legacy."

"But go there now? When they are in the middle of a *drug war*? The warlords have ravaged everything."

"Exactly. Now more than ever, they need us. They need our horses. Louise, I'm not getting any younger or stronger. Your legacy is the Caspian horse. Mine is Gordafarid, helping women find their inner warrior. Without their horses, Gordafarid and the Persians would not have been so strong and would never have won all those battles. I need to know that the women I smuggled, that every dangerous trip I took to Afghanistan and Turkey, were all worth it. That the horsewomen warriors will live on."

Louise marveled that despite everything, light still danced in her friend's weary eyes. "What you are asking, Maryam, it won't be easy. It will be very, very dangerous," she said slowly, thoughtfully.

"Since when did we let that stop us?" Maryam replied, cracking a much-needed smile.

So it was that a plan was hatched. In two months' time, Louise would meet Maryam in Mashad with four horses and several vials of sperm from her strongest stallion. Maryam would go by car as far as possible until, near the border, she would switch to a horse-drawn carriage. She also planned to make a batch of home brew to calm the horses at the crossing. But as Maryam and Louise had both learned the hard way time and time again, there's what we plan for and then there's what happens.

The plan set, Maryam and Shokat said good-bye to Louise and drove to Mashad. When they arrived at Shokat's house, Maryam's children were waiting. The family feasted on lamb, chicken, and coriander stew with orange-blossom chutney. "This is perfect," Maryam told them, as she looked around the table and counted her blessings. After a leisurely meal followed by a bit of dancing beneath Shokat's pink chandeliers, she kissed her children and grandchildren goodnight and went to bed. Before the sun could rise again on the last night of spring of 1986, Maryam slipped away from this life, and the world lost another Gordafarid.

MINA, 2001

*B*OOM!

Dirt and rock exploded all around them. Mina pulled her headscarf over her mouth and nose. She looked up to see Louise putting her head down just as Khosrow II flung his head back. She heard the crack a split second before Khosrow began bucking.

Boom!

Another explosion, this one even closer.

"There is no time to wonder if your jaw is broken, Lady Louise," Mina called. Her priority now was to keep her horse calm and lead the women, as she had watched her mother do for decades. True to her promise, Mina's mother had made her the commanding general when she was no more than twenty years old. For the past twenty years Mina led the women of the caves as they fought a terrifying new enemy—the Taliban.

Mina slid off her red-haired horse, Banu, and ran to Louise, who was mounted on her favorite stallion. Mina gently pushed the horse's mane back and pulled his face close to hers, inhaling his familiar scent. Hay. Soil. Carrots. But something wasn't right; Khosrow was chewing on his bit. She peeled his lips apart. His mouth was full of dirt and rock.

Above her, Louise's hand flew to her own mouth, which Mina could see was dripping blood. The older woman moved her tongue from the inside of one cheek to the other, wincing in pain. As she tried to spit, Khosrow let out a loud whinny. Neither of them had signed up for this, Mina knew, but she was glad they were there.

Mina met Louise Firouz for the first time in 1990. She had heard stories about this mysterious horsewoman from the West when her mother's friend Maryam, the lady smuggler, would arrive for visits to the caves. In 1986, the same year as her own mother, the great general Ghashang's death at the hands of ruthless warlords, Mina received word that Maryam had died. Her daughter Ezzhat brought a letter from her mother after her death. In the note, Maryam begged Mina to work with Louise to continue building a herd of Caspian and Turkoman horses. At the end of the letter, Maryam had enclosed a postscript:

> Louise is a horsewoman warrior like you. But she will need
> guidance, protection, and, above all, patience. I do not know
> when she will arrive to you, but when she does, please watch
> over her and the horses. She is carrying the legacy of the
> Caspian forward.

The legacy of the Caspian . . . Those words echoed in Mina's soul. She loved dreaming about horsewomen warriors from the time of the Persian Empire. And when battles in her life left her depleted, she would close her eyes, imagine Gordafarid, and summon the strength of her ancestors.

Boom! Boom! Two more explosions snapped Mina out of her reverie. She stood tall and remembered the sperm bag. In one smooth motion, Mina grabbed the bag and then remounted her mare, Banu. She had a gun and two bandoliers stocked with bullets slung in an X formation across her chest. Her mother told her that she reminded her of Maryam: Fearless.

"We need to get out of here," Louise shouted in Farsi. Though different in rhythm and intonation, Farsi and Dari were closely related enough that Louise and Mina could communicate with the help of frequent hand motions and the shared language of horses. Mina could sense the urgency in Louise's voice.

Mina squinted her mischievous brown eyes and shook her turbulent curls. She was one of the few women who rode without a makeshift hair scarf of any kind. Banu reared up on her hind legs, and Mina let out a warm laugh, as if she had not a care in the world.

"Louise, if we thought like you, we wouldn't be who we are. We don't leave our lands, our *homes*. No. We make *them* leave," she said, pointing across the ridge at the men launching grenades, firing guns, and riding ever closer. "They will never take the land that is ours. Never."

"But, Mina, we're outnumbered."

"The Taliban always outnumber us. But we outsmart them."

Banu reared, and Mina roared forward. Their army of women thundered past Louise and out of the caves, trilling their tongues in battle cry. They wore bandoliers slung over traditional dress, and their heads were wrapped in checkered scarves that blew in the wind. Their scarves were not for modesty, but for keeping their hair off their faces and necks. They were for shielding their eyes and mouths from dirt.

The pink-sherbet sunrise faded into orange as dirt rained down around them. Mina had grown accustomed to a thin layer of grime coating her eyebrows and lashes from the wind, but the clumps tearing through the air from the explosions obscured her vision almost entirely. She sent a silent prayer of gratitude to her mother in heaven. She was grateful that Ghashang had trained her and the other women to fight blindfolded. Mina knew exactly what to do, and she knew she could trust her horse to lead the way while she sharpened her hearing and took shots at enemies by sound.

"Yallah yallah, let's go!" Mina shouted, cutting to the right alongside four of her soldiers. Five other women rode left. Five more rode straight, while the last five made kissing noises to halt their horses. Louise, disoriented and frightened, remained at the cave entrance halfway down the hill and watched the women surround the men.

Mina clucked her tongue, and her soldiers broke out into a high-pitched *hiiiiliii liiiiii liiiii* as they rode around the Taliban in a choreographed dance.

"Khanoumha?!" shouted one of the youngest men, who had only just registered that he and his companions were being attacked by a group of women. Mina used that brief moment of confusion to pull a knife from her boot and fling it at the man's chest. In less than a second, he was on the ground, gushing blood. His mount, the first of the enemy horses to defect, came running out of the circle toward where Louise and Khosrow II were waiting. With trembling hands, Louise coaxed the wild-eyed animal to stand next to her horse, whose calm presence worked to still the new member of the herd.

The Taliban were well armed but not well trained. None of the men looked nearly as comfortable on horseback as the women. Mina knew she, her soldiers, and her horses could outsmart them. The trick would be minimizing casualties.

Meanwhile, the Taliban couldn't control their now panicking horses, who weren't adapting well to the tight quarters. When the Arabians bucked, the men fell to the ground, and the women fired.

Rattle, snap, rat-a-tat-tat, boom!

Ghashang had prepared them well. Mina and her warrior women were relentless. They encircled the men again, firing until every last man had either fled or crumpled to the ground.

Mina let out another high-pitched trill. "Women gather around," she ordered. "Survey the damage. Take the injured women and horses up to the caves. Alert the nurses."

Mina swung Banu around with the squeeze of her right foot. The horses pounded in and out of the wreckage. Several dead horses and a half-dozen dead men. Mercifully, none of her women had died, but some were wounded. Mina fought a tear, though she wasn't sure if it was relief or the release of adrenaline pouring out of her.

THE ARMY had only just gotten back to the caves, but already Mina had moved on, asking about the studbook. "Well, is it still here? Still safe?" she asked insistently. She knew this was Louise's greatest worry: that the legacy she and Maryam had built, a book that was Louise's deepest connection to Maryam the smuggler and a book that connected Mina to her mother and her best friend, Soheila, would disappear and along with it the memories.

Louise slipped past Mina and into a secondary cavern. She found the studbook deep in the caves, just where they had hidden it. Now she held it in trembling hands. Opening it, she took care not to crack the spine of the makeshift binding Maryam had stitched nearly thirty years earlier. She smiled and turned the book so Mina could look at the hand-drawn picture of the first stallion she and Maryam had recorded in the book. Since then, the pages had filled with the hundreds of foals sired by Caspian stallions.

A drop of water fell silently to the page and onto the number seventeen, which was scrawled in Maryam's hand and indicated the seventeenth gelding sired by her stallion. Louise was so worried about the ink running that it took her a moment to realize the drop was a tear and that it was hers. The older woman hurried to dry the page. Mina curled her arm around Louise's waist and rested her head gently on the older woman's shoulder.

"This book is everything, Mina. You know that, right? This is my life's work. It's Maryam's life. It is the Caspian legacy."

Mina smiled, shaking her head in fond exasperation. "Louise, I know. My women know. It's our lives, too. Our survival depends on the horses, their magic. We trust that this book is important for them—for the horses—for their story."

Mina's mother and all the women of the caves had sacrificed everything to keep the horses safe and cared for. The herd had grown to more than fifty, mostly Caspians, but some Turkomans, Arabians, and a few mixes of the breeds. The women had increased in number as well. Maryam the smuggler brought at least three women a year, and their reputation meant that other local women facing abuse at home or who wanted to learn to run, ride, revolt, and fight found their way to the caves. The women became family, as did the equines. They fed the horses before they ate themselves, harvesting grains, vegetables, and fruits to keep the herd nourished.

"They really are magical, aren't they?"

"They're the reason we've been able to beat back the Taliban as much as we have. Our horses outmatch theirs. They keep us safe; their horses roll on them, the disgusting men."

"On TV, they're saying the Taliban may be responsible for 9/11. For the attack on my homeland. Did you know that?" Louise asked.

"I don't know what they'd be after in New York. But I know they're after our way of life here," Mina told her.

"Your way of life?"

Mina shrugged. "Women, free. On horses. Keeping each other safe; living in community. We're a threat to them. They want to control women. And of course, they also want our caves."

"Maybe you could make an alliance with the Americans. You share a common enemy."

Louise dabbed at the tear stain until it dried. When she looked up, Mina had begun pacing. She nodded, but did not make eye contact with Louise. There was a long pause, and then something clicked.

"We've actually gotten word from the Americans. They reached out to us," she whispered. "But this has to remain between us, in this cave, you understand?"

Louise nodded. "Of course, sister. But I am having a hard time understanding what I'm hearing—the Americans, in contact with you? Already?"

"Louise khanoum, I'm talking to you as a horsewoman warrior, not an American, okay?"

Mina's face was mere inches from Louise's, and she could smell the heady scent of horse and battle tangled in the woman's thick blonde mane.

Louise blinked. "Maybe I can help. Please. Let me help. Who are you working with?"

"Special forces, something called 'Green Berets,' I think," Mina said.

"The Green Berets are the best of the best of the US military," Louise replied. Part of her worried for Mina and the women. How would the United States treat them? But another part of her was relieved. She felt better knowing such strong reinforcements would be here soon.

Mina pulled out her Nokia flip phone and showed Louise the text she had received from a nearby member of her troop, who was positioned near where a group of Taliban resisters who called themselves the Northern Alliance was stationed to keep watch for the arrival of the Taliban and the Americans: "GREEN BERETS, SPECIAL FORCES COMING IN. NEED HORSES. NEED TRAINING."

"It's our time now, Ms. Louise," Mina announced. She stood up to her full height, until her head hit the jagged ceiling of the cave. She rolled her shoulders back like she had seen her mother do dozens of times when trying to find her strength.

Louise watched Mina unfold. She nodded slowly.

"The world is watching Afghanistan," Mina continued. "Now we will show the world what we are made of. And we will come together with your people—the Americans—to rid the world of the Taliban once and for all."

LOUISE, 2001

I N 1990, FOUR YEARS AFTER MARYAM DIED, LOUISE BEGAN MAK-
ing biannual trips to Afghanistan, guided by Maryam's wishes
expressed during their final reunion. It had taken her years to build up
her own herd, and Louise was insistent that she did not want to visit
Afghanistan—the caves her friend had drawn maps to for years—without
horses in hand. She had heard enough stories from Maryam that she
knew the horses were the only ones who could make the journey into
Afghanistan and that good sperm stock was also their currency. But in
1990, Louise was finally ready. Arriving atop the most beautiful Turkoman black stallion Mina had ever seen, Louise rode into their caves,
several vials of sperm and two more horses in tow. Louise then spent the
last decade helping Mina and the women breed more horses, trying to
honor Maryam's wishes.

In 1994, when Narcy Firouz drew his last breath, a grief-stricken
Louise rode into Afghanistan with a green and gold book that she called
a "studbook." Mina still did not understand its significance to the world,
but she could see that this strong woman cherished it, and so vowed to
help her keep it safe.

But now it was late fall in 2001, and these trips had become increasingly dangerous because the War on Terror had followed the 9/11 attacks

on US soil, turning Afghanistan into a battlefield. Inside Louise's woven tapestry bag was the sperm she was trying to deliver to the Afghan horse-women and their mares. After wiping the blood dripping down her jaw, Louise checked on the samples and found the sperm sloshing precariously in their thin packets. She cursed herself for not double bagging the precious liquid.

Boom! Boom! Explosions.

Khosrow II's heart was racing even faster than hers. Despite the ringing in her ears, she could hear Mina bellowing commands in Dari.

"Mina! *The sperm.*" Louise eked out a plea for her friend to retrieve the samples and take them somewhere safe.

Boom!

"Get down, Louise!" Mina shouted back. "The Taliban are relentless and will kill the horses to get to you. Watch your stallion and your back."

Khosrow II reared up on his hind legs again, and Louise threw her weight forward to level him out. Mina galloped toward them, her hips making forward circles in perfect unison with Banu. Even in the midst of the firefight, Louise marveled at their natural horsewomanship.

"Wait, I'm sorry, Mina. Did you say *Taliban?*" Louise demanded.

Like countless others around the world, terror had gripped Louise when she saw the Twin Towers fall on television just a few weeks earlier. But until this moment, she hadn't connected the turbaned men on the BBC with those who had been threatening the women in the caves for decades. She had seen the large groups of armed men in the hills of Afghanistan but hadn't realized that they were a threat not just to her Afghan sisters and the horses, but to the world.

"Take this—you're going to need it." Mina threw Louise her large rifle, and miraculously, Louise caught it, her wrist buckling with the weight.

Boom! Rat-a-tat, boom!

The men were even closer now, and Louise saw that there were about forty of them. They were after the caves, which offered seclusion and space and from which you could see anyone coming, with hours' warning. Taking the caves would strand the women and would give the Taliban an ideal stronghold in the North to train their army to fight off the Americans and turn new recruits.

The men, their white dish dasha robes blowing behind them, pounded across the hard earth on half-starved Arabian horses, and Louise and Khosrow II picked up their pace, doing their best to keep up with Mina. The Taliban were gaining, but Mina remained unfazed, gripping Banu's mane with one hand and firing into the scrum with the other.

Terrified of getting shot, Louise leaned forward, pressing her body against Khosrow II. The horse, without breaking his stride, lowered his head and neck to further protect her. Mina dropped back, but Louise kept going. Only when the familiar scent of the caves—rosewater mixed with homemade citronella—enveloped her did Louise sit up. She was safe, for the moment. But for the rest of her life, the smell of citronella candles would send her reeling back to this harrowing ride.

Mina, the warrior women, and the horses bounded forward fearlessly into battle. Louise watched, slack-jawed, as they fired shots across the cliffs, bullets reverberating off the sandstone.

"Khanoumha?!" shouted one of the youngest men, who had only just registered that he and his companions were being attacked by a group of women. Mina used that brief moment of confusion to pull a knife from her boot and fling it at the man's chest. In less than a second, he was on the ground, gushing blood. His mount, the first of the enemy horses to defect, came running out of the circle and up the hill toward where Louise and Khosrow II were waiting near the caves. With trembling hands, Louise coaxed the wild-eyed animal to stand next to her horse, whose calm presence worked to still the new member of the herd.

The Taliban were well armed but not well trained. None of the men looked nearly as comfortable on horseback as the women. Louise would never forget the first time she saw Mina ride her stallion Saman. His legs seemed to move as an extension of hers. All she had to do was glance in a direction, and Saman understood where she wanted to go. She never needed to grip his reins or mane. Her hands were free.

Louise had always thought she was an accomplished equestrian, but the women of the caves taught her a whole new style of riding—breakneck speeds and bareback, no less. She learned to knit her abdominal muscles in concert with her pelvis and that the slightest tightening of one buttock was all the information a horse needed to move. If you had to kick, beat, or whip, you were doing it wrong. Louise came to see that it was this nuanced knowledge, this reverence for the relationship between horse and rider, that gave the women such grace and fortitude in battle. They trusted their horses, and their horses trusted their riders. Mina didn't even have to think about riding; it was more natural to her than walking, which meant she could devote her energy to fighting.

Meanwhile, the Taliban couldn't control their now panicking horses, who weren't adapting well to the tight quarters and uneven terrain. When the Arabians lost their footing or bucked, the men fell to the ground, and the women fired.

Rattle, snap, rat-a-tat-tat, boom!

The smell of the men's blood filled the air, but all Louise cared about was that none of the horses were hurt. Some of the women began to corral the animals who had lost their riders, shepherding them up the hill. Louise dismounted and lightly slapped the rump of the Arabian who had sidled up to her and sent him to follow.

Louise was standing beside Khosrow II when his delayed fight-or-flight instincts finally kicked in, and he went careening back inside to the safety of the caves. Louise let him go. She was too busy staring at the lone man left below in the firefight, with a grenade in his hand. If ignited, all of them would die. Now her own instincts kicked in. As if in a trance, she held Mina's rifle up to her face. Resting the butt at her shoulder, she lined the gun up with her cheek as she had seen Mina do a dozen times.

Her left hand helped her take aim, while she used her right index finger to pull the trigger.

The rusted bullet sliced the air. It missed the man's heart but hit him in the shoulder and knocked him to the ground.

Louise had never shot a man before, but she had fired a gun. When she was a little girl, her uncle had wanted to make a hunter out of her. But the first time she shot a deer, she had cried for hours and refused to go again.

Louise's index finger pulsed where she had pulled the trigger. Was she feeling the departed heartbeat of the man? Was his soul haunting her? As her emotions swirled, she heard the ululations of her Afghan sisters keeping time with the horses' hoofbeats, and she realized that her bullet had almost certainly saved lives. That was enough. It had to be.

As the remaining man and horses retreated the way they'd come, Louise lowered her weapon. She caught Mina's eye, and her friend nodded proudly. The battle was over—they had won. For now.

"Ladies, gather 'round," Mina called. "Survey the damage. Grab the enemy horses and nurse them and our women back to health. This should hold the Taliban until the Americans arrive."

Louise's worlds were colliding. Americans. *Here*. In the caves, on horseback. She couldn't explain the tingling sensation she felt in her spine but knew that whatever history was about to unfold, she—and, more important, the Caspian horses—would need to be a part of it.

HAVING SURVIVED the battle with the Taliban and delivered the sperm for the mares, Louise was more than ready to go home to Iran. She and Khosrow II were all packed and about to depart when Soheila, one of Mina's deputies, and the first woman that Maryam had ever smuggled, came racing out. The woman was panting by the time she reached them.

"Louise . . . khawhar . . . Mina says not to . . . not to . . . take the studbook back to Iran."

"Slow down, azzizam. Catch your breath," Louise said, her voice reassuring and calm.

"I'm so sorry, sister, sorry to come running like this. It's just the . . . the . . . studbook . . ." Soheila's voice trailed off.

"Dear kawhar, don't ever apologize for caring about the studbook."

Louise always wore her woven tapestry messenger bag slung across her body, the strap tight against her chest. It was where she carried her most precious belongings—photographs of her children and Narcy, her passport and identifying documents, emergency medication for her and the horses. She'd emptied it of the precious sperm vials, but now it held something just as valuable, if not more so—the studbook. She let Soheila lead her back toward Mina's compound, and as they walked arm in arm, she took comfort in the weight of the book and its spine pressing into the side of her body.

"Thank goodness Soheila caught you before you left," Mina called out. Louise nodded and jostled her hip and arm to swing her bag to her belly. Mina slid the book out and caressed its cover.

"You really think it will be safer here?" Louise asked, her brow furrowing.

"Not only that. I think your stallions and mares will be safer here, too," Mina replied. Already deep in discussion, neither woman noticed as Soheila slipped out of the cave, returning to her post guarding the horses.

"But the Taliban? The impending invasion?" Louise pressed.

"Invasion means US troops. These Green Berets will be here any day. And when they see what our horses can do, they will be invested in keeping them safe. That's more than we can say for the people in power in Iran."

A long silence fell between them. Louise sat. She stood. She paced. She sat again. At last, she spoke.

"Okay, fine. The studbook stays. But bury it, Mina. Bury it well. There can't be *any* risk of it being found. The Americans, the Taliban, the more they all realize what the Caspians are capable of, what they can do for their armies, what they're *worth*, the more everyone is going to want this book. We cannot lose it."

Louise knew that like Maryam, who had been skeptical about the need for a studbook, Mina still did not understand fully. In time she would learn that in the West, horses were a business, their prices tethered to their bloodlines, whose histories were held in books like the one Louise was so desperate to protect, despite her hatred of the horse-trading business.

"It will be buried. It will be safe. You have my word, Louise Firouz."

Though she remained uncertain, Louise stood to go, leaving the studbook in Mina's arms.

"What about your herd? And you?" Mina asked.

Louise shook her head. "Iran is my home. The Caspian Sea is Khosrow's home, the herd's home. We won't abandon it. Just protect the book, Mina. Protect it at all costs."

STEVEN, 2001

T HEY ARRIVED IN THE DEAD OF NIGHT, HOPING THE DARKNESS would protect them. But the roaring whir of the Boeing CH-47 Chinook propellers was rapidly blowing the cover of the Green Berets' Operational Detachment Alpha (ODA) 595 group.

Steven squinted. He could just barely make out the waves of mountains, their soaring peaks rolling into one another along the horizon. With a lurch, he bent his head and vomited the meal he'd eaten back at the US military base in Uzbekistan. *Hypoxia*, he thought grimly. A sandstorm had forced their pilot to fly at a higher altitude than advisable, and the oxygen masks were all broken. Half of the twelve men onboard had fainted. The other half, like Steven, remained alert only to be sick.

The chopper descended, and Steven donned his goggles, praying the night-vision mode would work—it had failed in Kuwait, or was it Somalia? On this mission they had a new captain, Mark Nutsch. He'd led their training through the rivers and forests of Kentucky, and he was clearly talented at bringing out the best in his men, but he'd never served in combat. He'd had a staff position, a highly coveted desk job, and it was only when the Twin Towers fell that Nutsch realized combat, and Afghanistan specifically, was his destiny.

On the morning of September 11, Steven had been at home. The television had been on in the background as he applied a Band-Aid to his daughter's skinned knee. Not until he finished did he look up and spot the first images of the smoking towers. Five weeks later, on October 17, 2001, Steven and his squad were landing in enemy territory, uncertain who and what awaited them.

Nutsch told them that the only way to emerge successfully from a fight like this was to have a reason worth fighting for. He'd held a piece of rubble from the World Trade Center—no one knew where he'd gotten it. That was his reason. Steven clutched his pocket watch, inherited from his father and grandfather before him; his reason was a family legacy of fighting to protect the freedom he was raised to believe in. He tapped two fingers from his head to his chest and to each shoulder, making the sign of the cross, and then kissed the pocket watch. He spit out more bile and shook his head, his knee bouncing, adrenaline coursing through his veins.

Nutsch may have been new to combat, but none of the members of ODA 595 had ever done anything like what they were about to do. They were going into Afghanistan to partner with General Dostum, a warlord of the Northern Alliance, whose only allegiance to them was their mutual hatred of the Taliban. The Northern Alliance was a rival group to the Taliban, who wanted to control Afghanistan so they could control the opium trade. They were rumored to be only slightly less brutal, but certainly more malleable to American cooperation than the Taliban. But if this general felt like it, if he changed his mind for any reason or no reason at all, Dostum could just as easily kill each and every one of them. Their nearest base was nine hours away. There had been no test flight, no in-depth mapping of the terrain. There hadn't been time. *They* were the test flight. And the twelve elite soldiers were about to put the strength of their alliance with an unlikely bedfellow to a very real test. They saw no other choice. The Taliban had to be challenged. The pain of 9/11 needed to be avenged.

Nutsch shouted for the men to rally. The choppers wouldn't be landing, and this was not the agreed-upon deposit spot, either. But that was life as a Green Beret, the elite of the elite in the Army. They were the squadrons sent into enemy territory before the strategists and risk mitigators had a chance to fully map the terrain and challenges. They were the guinea pigs. Steven checked his weapons one last time, knees nearly buckling under the weight of his gear. He made one more sign of the cross, then jumped.

One by one his teammates hit the sand beside him, some more gracefully than others. No sooner had the chopper pulled away than the all-too-familiar sound of gunfire echoed off the mountains. The men dropped to their bellies and maneuvered for cover.

Steven's nine-year-old daughter had once asked what gunshots sounded like, and he had told her that the first time he heard gunfire in an open range, he'd looked up, half expecting to see fireworks shooting across the sky. "The rat-a-tat-tat doesn't sound anything like distinct bullets or a drumbeat; it's more like a hum. Or the soundtrack of a Tupac album."

Bullets exploded into the darkness like fireflies, and though the squadron didn't know if they were friendlies or bogies, the men were already cocking their weapons.

"*Stop!*" an American voice rang out in English. "Hold. Your. Fire."

"Is that our escort?" Steven asked his captain in an undertone.

Nutsch had said a CIA operative would meet them and take them to a safe house to await the arrival of General Dostum and his warlords. What no one had mentioned was that this operative had a squadron of his own—former Northern Alliance men, who were now firing gunshots into the sky as some sort of signal. It was unclear to Steven if this was a part of the coordinated effort against the Taliban. He often lamented being in the dark when it came to the bigger picture of how intelligence and military operations worked—or didn't—together.

The Green Berets lowered their weapons. Nutsch scrambled to his feet, but Steven remained on the ground a beat longer. The sand here smelled surprisingly like the trails of his favorite hikes back home in New Mexico, but this dirt was heavier, grittier, already making its way into his pores and settling on his scalp. In the days and weeks ahead, it would turn his black, wavy hair nearly blond. And he'd discover, too, that no amount of soap or scrubbing could ever entirely remove the grit of Afghanistan from his skin.

"Captain Nutsch?" the operative called out. The men now lined up on the uneven terrain, jamming their boots into the soil to stop themselves from slipping. The Green Berets stood facing the CIA operative and his men. Steven could see the man's breath. It was only October, and the temperatures were already near freezing.

One of the men began speaking to Steven in Dari. His brown skin, inherited from his Latina mother, had long helped him assimilate in the Middle East. But there were times like now when he wasn't sure he wanted to blend in. He shook his head at the militiaman.

"They dropped you in a bad spot. We need to get out of here—fast," the operative told them. He yelled in Dari, and his men began hustling toward the horizon. Nutsch motioned for the squadron to follow.

Seven hours later, at daybreak, they reached the crumbling compound. Inside were basic furniture and some supplies sent over from Uzbekistan, but the real gift of the safe house was its geographic location. They were on a landing midway up a mountain range. This was the closest they would come to a plateau. Surrounded on three sides with elevation and a clear line of sight on the fourth, its advantages were obvious.

Their long trek to safety had made many things clear to Steven. He had read about how the various Afghan armies used the topography of the country as both weapon and shield, but landing here and being in the middle of it was a completely different beast. The terrain was vastly different from the rolling sand dunes of Kuwait and the sweeping tundra of Somalia. The ground was rockier, more rugged and uneven, and he struggled to find a rhythm of steady movement the way he had on the sand dunes and in the marshes. This soil dipped unexpectedly, and all the men were decidedly off their footing. The mountains forced them up and down elevated treks, and it seemed like they were almost always out of breath.

But about those mountains: nothing Steven read, no photo he saw, had prepared him for the sight. If the elevation didn't take his breath away, their beauty certainly did.

Not long after they arrived, the operative and his squad bid farewell. Seven of his men, however, would stay behind as guards for the Alpha team.

"I thought he was going to be with us the whole time," Steven said. His captain shook his head, tense.

"Good luck, boys! Try not to get killed," the operative called over his shoulder as his group began their steep descent. Steven and his men watched wide-eyed as they half-slipped, half-walked down the badlands of the mountains. It was no surprise that vegetation could not grow out there, but Steven couldn't help wishing for at least a few bushes to break his inevitable fall when losing his footing.

The one exposed side of the compound provided quick escape and gave them a lookout point to spot incoming danger. Steven told Nutsch that he'd take the first shift on guard. He dug a small hole for his pack and rested against it as he got into position, grateful for all the sandcastles his daughters asked him to build on their beach trips in San Diego where they went for vacations to visit family.

Rock and gravel dug into his back, and he closed his eyes, wishing he was still in San Diego with his family. But the thought of his daughter and his wife snapped him back to attention. After all, it was their freedom and lives he was trying to protect. He was convinced that if he and his team failed here, there would be more attacks like 9/11 across the United States and around the world.

Below and partway down the mountain, the operative's trucks had just reached a flattened bit of terrain when a high-pitched sound began reverberating off the cliffsides and mountain walls. Loud and forceful, it rang like a battle cry in Steven's ears. Nutsch and the other members of ODA 595 came running, but the seven Afghan men that the operative had left behind were unfazed.

"What the hell is that?" one of Steven's teammates asked. The trilling died down, replaced by something like thunder. Something like hooves.

Slack-jawed, Steven peered through his binoculars at a group of women pounding across the sand on horseback. Their black hair and colorful scarves blew in the wind and matched the manes and fabric coverings of their horses. These riders were *nothing* like the cowboys Steven had seen on the rodeo circuit in the American Southwest. No, these women, who rode bareback and hands-free, were practically floating atop their mounts, and some of them held guns, while others had their bows and arrows drawn. A decade later, Steven would sit with his daughters watching as Daenerys Targaryen led a group of horse warriors on the television show *Game of Thrones* and remember the surreal scene from his own life.

The horsewomen split into two groups, each encircling one of the operative's trucks. The rest of the riders, led by a woman with multiple guns slung across her chest, galloped toward the operative himself and the few of his men who were on foot. The women remained on their horses, riding in circles around the men and belting out a high-pitched trill. The operative and his squadron weren't going anywhere unless these women wanted them to, that much was clear.

Hi-li-lilililili! Hi-lilili!

Steven's tongue sat heavy at the back of his throat. *How did they even make that sound?* It was the truest battle cry he'd ever heard.

"Are those . . . women?" one of Steven's teammates asked, interrupting his reverie.

Nutsch told them that he had heard rumors of women living in the caves who were freedom fighters.

Steven sighed. Never in his wildest imagination could he have pictured this when he considered women in Afghanistan.

The men were transfixed. Steven watched as one of the women—their leader, he suspected—dismounted and spoke to the driver of one of the trucks. Unwittingly, Steven had taken several steps forward, as if he could step right over and join the women below. Now one of his friends pulled him back before he walked right off the edge of the jutting cliff.

"God, look how they ride," someone said. "Wild. Bareback. Hands on their weapons."

"The horses look like extensions of their bodies," Steven mused. It was almost as if the horses' legs were the women's legs, almost as if they were a pack of exquisite mythic centaurs. Steven shook his head, preventing his thoughts from drifting too far into the realm of folklore.

"Those don't even look like regular horses," one of the men said. They were smaller, with shorter legs and longer necks. "Are they mules? A cross between a pony and a horse?"

"I wonder who their daddy is?" another soldier quipped.

"The horses or the women?" yet another chimed in. The Berets erupted in a fit of laughter until one look from Nutsch silenced them.

"Now they're coming toward us!"

The women had broken their circles and were riding in a V formation. Black, white, brown, tan, and red horses swirled against the backdrop of the hills, and the hoofbeats grew louder in the Berets' ears.

Nutsch ordered the men to stand guard.

"Cap, we aren't really going to shoot at a bunch of girls, are we?"

He repeated his order to stand guard, and the men followed.

Thirty horsewomen were riding effortlessly up the hillside that had nearly bested the men. They didn't slip or trip as Steven himself had.

Nutsch instructed them to hold their fire as the women encircled them. The women slapped their hands against their thighs. Up close, Steven could see that the horses did have reins after all; they were made of fabric, and some were coiled with coins and small jewel-like rocks, which clinked in tune with the pounding hoofbeats. It was one of the most spectacular symphonies Steven had ever heard. He found himself nodding along, struggling to resist their siren song.

After a beat, Captain Nutsch lowered his weapon, and his men followed suit. Steven had assumed that Afghan women were ghostlike figures swathed head to toe in dark fabric, their heads low, curling in on themselves in fear. In fact, if he was being honest, one of the reasons he'd believed he was here was to save these women. "No one should have to live like they do," he had told his daughter when she asked why he had to leave just weeks before her tenth birthday. He wanted to fight for a world where every girl could go to school and no woman would have to walk the streets in a haunting veil, terrified of the fate that might befall her every time she left the house—or when she returned home.

But here before him now were women defying every one of those stereotypes. Warriors, fearless and powerful. Steven was transfixed.

Their commander nodded and introduced himself, turning with the women as they rode around the men, their weapons pointed to the sky.

A slender, slightly older woman broke through the circle on a black horse. She held up a hand for the women to stop. They came to an instant halt and stared at the Berets, unblinking. Steven felt deeply out of place.

"I know who you are," said the woman on the black horse, whose name he later learned was Mina. Mina spoke in heavily accented but grammatically flawless English. "Welcome to the North. And good luck." Steven would later learn that other American commanding generals had been communicating with this woman when they were seeking support for the mission. They thought these warriors were breeders of military horses. No one had thought that these women were an army themselves.

The woman looked each of them in the eye and then made a turning motion with her hand. She thrust her hips forward and galloped off to join the other women gathered in a *V* formation. The horsewomen who still surrounded them went back to moving in a tight circle, this time picking up their pace. They made three more circles around the men—as if they were sizing them up, assessing whether they were friend or foe—then broke into a line to join the *V.* Altogether now, the women galloped up the nearly vertical face of the nearest mountain. Steven had been certain the only way to enter or exit their safe spot was from the one exposed side where he stood guard, but he knew now he was wrong. The women, their torsos practically horizontal with the earth, had already reached the mountain peak. Steven watched as they disappeared over the other side and were gone.

STEVEN WAS still thinking about the women the next day—the whole squadron was—when another group of horses was spotted making its way up to their compound. This time the riders were male.

It turned out to be General Dostum and his men; Nutsch commanded his men to stand down. Everyone knew Abdul Rashid Dostum was a ruthless killer poised to fight outsiders. But they had also been told that the one group of people Dostum hated even more than foreigners was the Taliban. They were determined to take control of the opium trade that the Taliban had cut off—the main source of economic prosperity and power in a war-ravaged land.

"My enemy's enemy is my friend?" Steven had asked during the briefing, and the tent had erupted in nervous laughter. They were being asked to put their lives and the fate of their country in the hands of an unpredictable warlord who might or might not kill them or trade them as hostages. Following those orders was part of the job.

Which one is Dostum? Steven wondered, as the riders closed in and the sound of hoofbeats filled the air for the second day in a row. As he listened, though, he realized these horses sounded different. Uneven. Their beats were all off. Unlike the women, Dostum and his troops were not riding in sync, and many of the men were having difficulty maintaining control of their animals. They rode horses of all different shapes and sizes, but every one of them struggled with the terrain. Several of the horses even slipped on the final ascent. Had Steven not just seen the harmony of the horsewomen less than twenty-four hours earlier, he wouldn't have noticed anything amiss. But he had, and now it was impossible not to cringe watching these men bounce and sway, aggressively whipping their horses' backsides (to little avail). And they rode in no type of formation Steven had ever seen, but haphazard and wayward.

As the group pulled their horses to an awkward halt, one man dismounted.

"General Dostum?" one of the men asked.

The man nodded, and the two leaders shook hands. There was an audible exhale from both groups; even the horses seemed relieved as they licked their lips and relaxed their ears while some of the tension dissipated. Nutsch towered over the trim man whose body wore its age with a curled spine and neck. He put his arm around Dostum's shoulders and ushered him into the safe house for tea. Two of Steven's teammates joined them, while Dostum motioned for four of his own men to follow as well.

When they reemerged almost an hour later, Dostum addressed his men in rapid Dari. Not for the first or last time, Steven cursed himself for studying Arabic instead of a Persian dialect. Only one of the Berets spoke any Dari, and he had completed only the first level of language training.

Nutsch called his men to gather. Steven would have preferred to keep a close eye on Dostum and his men but did as he was told.

As they shuffled toward their leader, Nutsch announced that Dostum would be taking them into Taliban territory.

The squadron erupted in adrenaline-fueled cheers and fist pumps, but Nutsch raised his hand to quiet them.

"But only half of us," he continued. The men's excitement snapped to agitation, and their sudden distress was palatable.

"You're going to split us up?" Steven asked.

"Have to," Nutsch said, a hint of discomfort in his tone. "Now," their captain went on, his voice loud and confident again, "which one of you yahoos can ride a horse?"

Silence.

"I went on a trail ride on vacation once," one of the men finally volunteered.

"I rode horses at my uncle's ranch a few times," another said.

"Okay, great. You two will be coming with me," Nutsch said. Steven thought again of the women riders.

"I'll ride," he heard himself say, before he could change his mind. Inspired, two of Steven's friends also stepped forward, if somewhat more dubiously. Nutsch nodded and led the men to Dostum, who was placing makeshift blanket saddles across the backs of half-starved horses.

Steven approached a brownish red horse who was nodding the way the women's horses had. It almost seemed as if the horse was bowing, the lids of its bulging eyes half lowered.

"How come your horse is looking at you like that, *man?*" one of his friends asked, smirking.

"That horse is female," Dostum corrected.

"Hah! You gonna ride a *girl* horse, man!"

"All of you will be riding females," Dostum said curtly, in heavily accented English. He shook his head as he turned and mounted his own mare.

Nutsch climbed atop a black horse, patted the mare's neck, and sat up straight, ready to ride. His horse shook out her mane with pride, like she knew she'd gotten the leader. Nutsch looked at his men and signaled for them to move out.

Steven slid his M4A1 block gun to his back and walked to the side of his horse, trying to decide how to mount up.

"Come on, men, use the stirrups," Nutsch prodded. "Put your left foot in the left stirrup and then stand up into it and sit *down*."

All those long years of impossible training the Green Berets had endured: running, jumping, climbing, swimming. Always faster, higher, harder. But never riding. No one had ever suggested they might need to depend on an animal as an ally. Men—and apparently women—had fought on horseback for centuries, but Steven's superiors had assumed that was all behind them. The horse standing before Steven now begged to differ.

"What's her name?" he asked of no one in particular.

"The fuck you care what her name is? Just get on the damn thing," one of his friends quipped.

"You get up on your own damn horse," Steven snapped back. "I want to know my horse's name."

"It's Jane, okay? Now hurry up! All of you! We're embarrassing ourselves," one of the men yelled.

"I know your name isn't Jane," Steven whispered in the mare's twitching ear. "I'll figure out what it really is."

He grabbed his left ankle and guided it into the stirrup. Then he placed his hands on the makeshift blanket saddle, prayed it would hold, and hoisted himself to stand. The weight of his vest and weapons was too great, and he fell forward in a belly flop onto the horse's neck.

"Face on the ground, ass in the air!" one of his friends laughed, quoting a popular rap song.

"If it's so easy, you do it, man," Steven replied through gritted teeth. He pushed himself off the horse's neck and swung his leg over to straddle her back. Upright at last, he let out a triumphant exhale.

"Congratulations. You got on the horse. Now you gotta ride it," laughed one of his friends.

Steven felt the fear in the pit of his stomach expand as one, then another, of his fellow Green Berets fell to the ground while trying to mount.

When, finally, they were all on their horses, more or less, they jostled up and down and tried to move in a straight line, praying they wouldn't fall. Steven kept picturing the women who had floated as one with their animals. Up ahead, Dostum and his men didn't so much ride as jerk and career their way down the same hill the women had ridden so effortlessly. *Where had those horsewomen come from, and where had they gone?* he wondered. *If I am going to ride into battle against the Taliban, it's the women I want by my side, not these men.*

After four hours, Steven's entire body throbbed with an exhausted, drained pain, the kind new cadets experience in the first weeks of training. But they were only ambling through the Afghan countryside. He couldn't believe how challenging it was just to stay on the horse. Over and over, he saw the women riders in his mind and tried to make sense of how they did it. He wished he had taken a photo or video of them. *How could they possibly have ridden these powerful creatures without a death grip, let alone hands-free?*

A loud *bang* interrupted his reverie, and a gush of sand burst high into the sky like a geyser, followed closely by another burst. Then another, and another. The sky filled with the haze of sand falling like dirty snow. They had ridden right into a minefield. Steven prayed that he, and, more important, the horse on whom his survival depended, would not be injured. During the journey, he had learned from one of Dostum's men that his mare's name was Atash, or "fire." Steven was glad he knew her name and took comfort in its fierceness.

"Welcome to hell," Dostum shouted over the rhythmic explosions.

"I can't see *anything*," Steven yelled into the dust. He cradled his head in his hand, curling into himself, and Atash, sensitive and attuned, mimicked her rider, bowing her own head down.

Steven's ears were ringing, but he thought he heard Nutsch shouting. He sat up straight and tried to steer Atash toward the sound of his captain's voice.

Suddenly, a firm hand grasped his shoulder. "Get down!" Nutsch yelled in his ear, shoving Steven's head into Atash's neck. "Gunmen coming." Steven was struggling to make out his commander's words. "We gotta move, but just keep your head down and hold on tight. The horses know what to do."

Steven heard gunfire in the distance. "Taliban!" someone shouted. And then came the roar of tanks rolling in, rockets being fired into the sky, what sounded like a thousand men stampeding. They were outmanned and outgunned. *How was that possible?*

They had come to fight the Taliban, but now that the Taliban had found them—and brought the big guns, literally—they were forced to turn and flee the way they had come. Dostum led them back up the jagged peaks, through the same harrowing twists and turns they'd just survived. They rode up and up along the cliff edge, and more than once, Steven nearly fell to his death when his horse lost her footing, teetering on the edge of a jagged mountainside.

Finally, after hours, they stopped. Nutsch, Dostum, and the Afghan men dismounted with ease. Atash halted and knelt but still Steven struggled to get down. His muscles had turned to jelly.

"Grab yourself some mane," someone called back sarcastically.

PARDIS MAHDAVI

Steven held tight to Atash's thick black hair and slowly slid off her back. But the ground did not feel solid; his world was spinning, his adrenaline crashing. Steven looked to the sky. The bright sharpness of the stars steadied him. He was still gripping Atash's mane, and he leaned into her, grateful for the horse's support. He knew they'd have to try the crossing again tomorrow.

Dostum woke them at dawn, shouting, "Time to kill some Taliban!"

Even before he opened his eyes or moved a single muscle, Steven felt pain from his head to his toes. He could not begin to fathom how he was going to climb back on the horse and stay there, upright, for hours, let alone fight and kill while he was up there. But he knew he would find a way. He had no choice.

They chose a different path this time, following Dostum along a narrow ridge through a series of smokestack-shaped rock formations. Steven marveled at the way Atash and the other horses expertly navigated the twists and turns, taking each without hesitation or fear.

After three hours, Dostum came to a halt. "Welcome to the Valley of Hell," he told them.

It took Steven several sharp pulls of the reins to get Atash to stop. When the mare finally did, she did so so abruptly that Steven fell forward onto her neck. Nutsch glared at him.

"Don't do that to me again," he whispered into Atash's ear. "If you want to make a fool of me, fine. Just do it when no one is looking."

They were at the top of a mountain. Down below in the valley were hundreds or maybe even thousands of Taliban soldiers.

The valley below them was the Taliban supply route, Nutsch explained. And Dostum's plan was for the Americans to blow it up to cut off their legs.

"It's where they bring their weapons in and store them," one of the men said. "We destroy that, we wipe them out."

"Sure, we're only outnumbered a hundred to one," Steven mumbled under his breath.

Dostum looked through binoculars at the scene below and listened to someone on his walkie-talkie. "Americans! We ride now!" he shouted.

In a flash, Atash was off and running, herd-bound, as Steven would later learn it was called. Sometimes the horses would go without any prompting; they just wanted to run and be with their group. Not unlike soldiers in an army. And like soldiers, horses were at their most vulnerable when separated from the pack.

As they galloped downhill, Steven knew he would have to shift the reins to his left hand so he could draw his weapon with his right. Clinging to the horse with his thighs, and heart pounding, he thought yet again of the women floating atop their horses, both hands free. Atash, as if reading his mind, lowered her head to make it easier for him to steer one-handed. He took advantage of the momentary give in the reins, transferred them to his left hand, and drew his gun. And he was just in time.

The Taliban spotted them. *Boom. Rat-a-tat-tat. Boom.* By the time Steven took aim, the Taliban were shooting off their rockets. Back-to-back explosions filled the sky, enveloping them in thick clouds of black smoke. Steven was grateful for his goggles. *Where were the Taliban getting these weapons? And from whom? Why hadn't he or his teammates been told they were so well armed?*

The thick smell of blood and dirt filled his nostrils. Memories of Operation Desert Storm came rushing back, and Steven shook his head, trying to clear his thoughts. He needed to focus.

"The rocket loader, men!" Nutsch yelled. "We need to take it out!"

Steven tried to make out his enemies through the heavy black smoke, but all he could see were Dostum's men and their horses falling, one after the other. The man who had told him Atash's name fell to the ground and was crushed by the weight of his own horse, both covered in blood.

Steven watched the horses fall, but the sound of their magnificent bodies hitting the earth was lost to the ceaseless rockets.

"Cover me!" Nutsch shouted, and the sound of his captain's voice shook Steven out of his death trance. Nutsch and his black mare were riding straight into the lion's den, and Steven knew he had to follow.

The rocket loader that Nutsch was targeting was a behemoth. The only other time Steven had seen one this big had been in Iraq. *Were the Taliban's networks larger than they thought? Were the same people who supported Saddam Hussein now sending weapons to Afghanistan?* Steven didn't have time to dwell on these unsettling thoughts, not while he was staring down an apparatus that could fire a dozen rockets simultaneously and be reloaded in under two minutes.

Atash buckled to the ground, but Steven didn't fall. His body remained sutured to hers. *But had she been shot? Had he?* In the adrenaline of battle, you never knew if you were really wounded until hours later.

"Please, Atash, please get up," he begged, desperate. He wouldn't stand a chance of survival on foot. It was only in this moment that Steven grasped the true power of the horses. The reason horses created empires. How very dependent man was on this animal. He needed Atash now more than he had ever needed anyone else before.

"Come on, earn your name. You are *fire*. Get up and get us through this," Steven roared. *No, this could not be his end.* He tugged gently on her reins and squeezed her ribs with the full force of his legs. He had to cover his captain.

Whether it was his squeeze or the emotion in his voice or something else entirely, Atash shook out her dirt-caked mane and stood. She wasn't giving up, and neither was he. Steven took aim and began to shoot as he rode, taking fire and ducking and weaving with renewed confidence. His captain and his teammates were back in his line of sight, and they were taking aim at the rocket loader.

Nutsch pulled a grenade from his vest pocket. He told his men to ride away as hard and as fast as possible once the explosive hit the ground.

Steven pulled the reins to turn Atash's neck, and she obeyed. He felt the heat of the fire behind them and knew the grenade had exploded, but he didn't look back, keeping his eyes trained on the steep cliffside ahead.

They'd been successful in destroying the rocket loader and the large weapons stash, but the Taliban had numbers. Their gunmen weren't going to stop. Steven heard the sound of more tanks rumbling in the distance.

Two steps forward, one step back.

"We got their stash but pissed them off!" one of his teammates confirmed.

"They're gaining on us, and with tanks, too," another called.

Nutsch rode up, and Steven was relieved to see him.

"Dostum says we'll be safe at the jagged part of the mountain. Their tanks can't reach there," Nutsch told them.

And that's when Steven heard a sound he'd heard before, one that halted Atash and the other horses in their tracks.

"Hi-li-li-li-li-li-li!"

Steven couldn't help but smile as he watched the horsewomen descend on the Taliban. But then Atash and the other horses began to run, galloping up the cliffside to safety, and the women disappeared into the smog of battle.

MINA, 2004

"WE'RE BLEEDING, MINA. WE'RE AT THE EDGE," SOHEILA said.

For three years they had been fighting, and they were losing. The summer of 2004 had arrived fast and hot, and Mina felt the heat of oppression in her body, mind, and heart. She looked at Soheila, still unused to the girl's scars. The accident had happened the year before, in battle—a land mine in the Tangi Pass. Her horse hadn't made it, and Soheila had barely survived.

The Americans had come and gone and come again. In 2001 they had helped defeat the Taliban in the North, but like a bad insect infestation, the Taliban were constantly coming back stronger and in larger numbers. Mina still wasn't sure the Taliban were responsible for 9/11, but she was grateful for the Americans' help beating back the enemy she and her comrades had been fighting for decades.

The Northern Alliance had referred to the first Green Berets, the ones who arrived in October 2001, as the "Alpha group." Their arrival had been celebrated throughout the North. Eager to see the Americans up close, Mina and thirty of her riders had ridden right into their makeshift camp the day they arrived, but the women had been shocked to discover only a dozen soldiers. *Where were the rest?* And then they had learned that it was General Dostum who was going to take them into battle on horseback.

"Untrained men on untrained horses," Mina described them to her army family. Several of her women burst out laughing. "Pssst," she hushed them. "It may be funny to you, but these men are our only hope for bigger weapons and American support fighting our enemies."

Mina and her lieutenants knew the American soldiers needed backup, but to the women's great surprise, the foreign group succeeded in destroying a significant portion of the Taliban's most deadly weapons in their very first confrontation. By the time Mina and her group reached them on the battlefield, the Americans had already taken out the rocket loader and were headed back up the hills to safety. Dozens of Dostum's men were killed in that battle, while all of the Americans on the mission survived. But it was the women of the caves who finished the job and defeated the Taliban that day. While the Americans had ridden home, it was Mina and her army that rode into the Taliban base camp in the middle of the night and stole their horses and weapons to weaken them.

Celebrations had erupted throughout the North. *The Taliban had been defeated!*

Or so everyone thought.

The Americans returned to their country as heroes, Mina supposed. No doubt they were heralded at home just as Dostum and the Northern Alliance were in Afghanistan. The women were seldom seen, let alone celebrated. Not that they minded—for the most part, anyway. They lived in the caves for a reason.

The feeling of victory was short-lived. Two weeks later, the Taliban were back, relocked and reloaded. They pulverized their way through the North, taking out entire villages and warlord armies in a nationwide bloodbath. Afghanistan became a graveyard yet again.

The United States sent more troops, and this time they brought the world's attention with them. Air supplies of food and water and basic medical equipment were dropped daily. Some boxes were more valuable than others. Estée Lauder teamed up with the first lady of the United States to send kits of makeup and lotion. Mina and her commanders had laughed and laughed the first time they saw those boxes. The women of the caves laughed not because it was funny but because what they really felt was too dark to entertain.

Still, there was no denying that the weapons and tactical support the Americans brought were useful to Mina and the women. The soldiers led air strikes and had a seemingly endless arsenal of helicopters and rockets. They also had tanks. But their tanks, much like those that al-Qaeda had sent to the Taliban, were no match for the rugged Afghan terrain. For that, you needed well-trained and sturdy Caspian horses, ridden by well-trained and sturdy riders.

The bloody battles stacked up and dragged on, and soon there was more blighted land in the North than not, which made travel increasingly difficult. But the horses adapted, learning the new divots and rockier roads scarring their homeland. The women trusted their horses without question. Mina's stallion, Khosrow II, whom Louise had left behind when she left the studbook, could even sniff out land mines. On at least a dozen occasions he had refused to cross a valley that Mina would later learn was riddled with them. And then there was the one time that fearless, determined Soheila had ridden ahead and she—and her horse—had paid dearly for it.

By 2004, the war had taken more than a dozen of Mina's women and twenty of their horses. Supplies were low, and while several groups of American troops remained in Afghanistan, the world had grown weary of the war. Shipments of food, blankets, and weapons dwindled. The winter of 2004 proved especially brutal—hundreds of people lost their lives to cold and famine. Mina lost two dozen horses to starvation alone. At least the carcasses provided food and sustenance.

"We're bleeding women, food, supplies, horses," Soheila said, a conversation she'd struck up with Mina before. Since her accident, her voice had developed a hateful edge. Mina understood, but she also knew this bitterness clouded Soheila's judgment and might eventually get her—or someone else—killed.

"Do you think I don't know that?" she spat back.

Mina marveled at how war had changed her friend so much. She was far from the first woman in their ranks to experience trauma, and she certainly wouldn't be the last, either. Soheila, Mina's best friend, had taught her that women must embody a toughness beyond men's comprehension. Like Mina's own mother, Soheila had been beaten and raped repeatedly by her husband. In Soheila's case, it had driven her to flee Iran and find a transformational purpose for her wounds, reshaping herself into a warrior and one of the most formidable forces on the battlefield that Mina would ever witness.

"The problem with hate is that it seeps into your heart, making you hate yourself. You need to remember to separate it from your organs," Soheila had told Mina many years ago. "Let it live under your skin and fuel your strength, but never let it consume you." Looking at Soheila, Mina wondered what had happened to the girl who spoke those words.

"General, I mean no disrespect," her friend said, seeing Mina's face darken. "I am just worried. We've nearly depleted our supplies. The women are tired and the horses even more so."

"We need more horses," Mina agreed. She rubbed her scarred, calloused hands. In 2002, a bullet had grazed her fourth and fifth fingers during a particularly harrowing battle. She'd since developed a tic of opening and closing her hand, stretching the skin over her knuckles, until a satisfying sting rippled across her old wound. The familiar pain comforted her.

A silence passed between the two women, the same question—and answer—coalescing in their minds. *Who could help them get more horses?*

"Louise?" Soheila said aloud. The general nodded.

"Things aren't exactly easy in Iran, either, though," Mina said, sighing. "But Louise might be our only hope. We need more sperm and a few brood mares. Khosrow has run dry, and our mares are in no shape to carry foals."

"We need to breed what Caspians we have left with the Arabians and Turkomans we've amassed from the Taliban. We need a sturdier herd," Soheila reflected.

"Send word to Louise. Immediately," Mina instructed.

BY THE time the women's message reached Louise, summer was fading, and a mercifully cooler breeze was rustling the trees on her farm. Louise had returned to Gonbad-i-Kavoos at last, abandoning her breeding operations in Kalaleh in favor of the farming life. She had rebuilt the herd enough for now, she wrote to Mina. Twelve horses would do, and she longed to plant crops again and work the earth. It had been a bountiful year. The spring rains had brought a lush crop, turning the land a shimmering shade of velvet green that had shone against the blue sky all summer.

Louise wasn't the only one enjoying the fruits of the rain that year. The horses grazed greedily, and the herd grew steadily, she reported. Several of the mares had birthed twins, and a horse Louise had been certain was infertile had given birth to a perfect chocolate-brown colt. Even the stallions were more virile.

The memory of riding into Afghanistan and witnessing the terrors of the Taliban firsthand was still raw, and this year more than most,

Louise was grateful for the beauty and reassurance of new life. She'd also received an unexpected visit from an old acquaintance, she noted, an Englishman and diplomat who had once helped her pass horses to His Royal Highness Prince Philip. Stranger still, accompanying him was a young Iranian American who reminded Louise of her long-deceased friend and partner, Maryam.

2004

I FIRST MET LOUISE FIROUZ IN THE DWINDLING DAYS OF THE summer of 2004. I was dating an English diplomat named Josh, who was working at the British embassy in Iran. He and I had little in common, save for a love of horses and a keen interest in Iran's underground scene.

I had spent the last four years researching the country's sexual revolution, following young Tehranis into darkened, emboldened corners, but it was the weekends I spent riding horses with another group of young women that solidified my love for my homeland. A mutual friend from London introduced us, and Josh wasted no time whisking me off on heady, whirlwind trips to Europe and Africa. Dating him was exciting. There were countless late-night parties. Long, invigorating days at his summer home in Kordan, where we rode horses for as long and as far as we wanted. But by late summer, his orientalism had grown tiresome. He looked at me with centuries of colonial fetishism in his eyes. The way he spoke about Iranian women could be charming, but it also made me uneasy, steeped as I was in the literature and ideas of my renowned university professor Edward Said.

I had begun to question our relationship when Josh's life and mine were threatened. The presidential election was in full swing, and hard-line fanatics were pushing an aggressive anti-Westoxication campaign. One Saturday morning, after a long night of drinking at the British compound in Tehran, Josh and I were heading out of the city for our usual weekend ride in Kordan when bullets started pinging off the doors of his Range Rover. The pulsing, rapid-fire *rat-a-tat-tat* reverberated in my skull, and I slunk down in the back seat, covering my face. Josh's driver, Amir, floored the engine, and the car fishtailed as we peeled away and sped down a quiet side street.

"It's not safe for you in Tehran, sir. Or in Kordan. We need to get farther away," Amir said, glancing back at us in the rearview minor.

"Let's go to Louise's, by the Caspian Sea. I'll call and tell her we're coming," Josh replied. He pulled out his secure cell phone.

"Who's Louise?" I asked, a hint of jealousy lacing my question.

"You don't know Louise?" Amir asked. He lowered his Ray-Bans, a gift from Josh, and winked one of his hazel eyes. "I thought everyone knew 'Iran's Lady of Horses,' even if she is an Amricayi."

"Louise Firouz is an American equestrian who married an Iranian Qajar prince," Josh said flatly. He took my hand in his and kissed my wrist. "Sweetheart, she's like seventy years old."

"She lives in Gonbad-i-Kavoos. Isn't that where you said your father was from?" Amir asked. I nodded, but I was distracted, deeply rattled, my heart still pounding. We'd just been *shot at*. Josh and Amir might have been used to it, or at least unsurprised, but I didn't live in their world—nor did I want to. Certainly not like this.

Which side was I on? Which side should I be on? These were fleeting thoughts. I knew I wasn't going to figure out the answer sitting in the back of that car holding hands with Josh. Instead, I focused on the fact that I was about to see my family's village again. In the summer of 2002, my father, Mahmood, had agreed at last to return to Iran and to visit his childhood home. But when we finally reached it, he refused to stay even a single night. He said the smell of the sea, the salty sweetness of the olives, and the sight of the farm where he was born were too much for his heart to bear. We'd spent an hour looking around and then gone straight back to Tehran.

Pulling up to Louise's farm, I rolled down the window to inhale the familiar scent of horses and dirt. Six of the most beautiful horses I had ever seen were moving around the pasture, running and tossing their manes, stopping only to munch on lush green grass.

"Befarmayin doostan," Louise called out, welcoming us brightly from atop a white horse. She whispered something in the mare's ear, and we watched as the beautiful creature bowed to us, bending her front legs so that her rider could slide elegantly to the ground. When Louise dismounted, I realized how tall she was. Despite her curved spine, I could tell she was nearly six feet tall and towered over me, her short blonde hair flopping into her gleaming blue eyes.

Louise's horse reminded me of the one my riding instructor, Mastaneh, rode—small and stocky, with a large head. In contrast to Arabians and Turkomans who bow their heads when trotting or galloping, Louise's and Mastaneh's horses kept their heads high while carrying their riders. I locked eyes with the white mare and curtsied the way I had seen Mastaneh and the other women in Kordan do.

Louise was watching me closely and nodded in approval. "Have you ever seen a Caspian before?"

"Once, in Kordan. My friend rides a sorrel horse just like yours—only hers has a red mane and tail like fire."

"I bet Khosrow's the daddy of that one," she replied, taking my hand in hers.

"Who?" I murmured, but she just smiled. My interest was piqued. How could she be so sure of a horse's origin from one throwaway description?

We left Josh and Amir behind and went directly to her stables, home to twenty more of the most gorgeous horses I had ever laid eyes on. They were different shapes and sizes and colors, and it would have been impossible to name the most majestic one. Each was perfect. Something was pulling me toward the horses, but I couldn't put my finger on what. I watched as Louise waded into their midst, whispered in their ears, and fawned over them.

Louise invited us to stay the weekend, and I couldn't say yes fast enough. When I climbed atop a Caspian, a buckskin gelding named Tondar—meaning "thunder"—I shivered, despite the late-summer heat. As we rode off the farm and onto the trail, I felt a clapping in my heart, a cheering pitter-patter as real and strong as my pulse.

While the Turkomans that Josh introduced me to had pried open my love for horses, the Caspians leaped in and nestled deep in rooms of my heart I hadn't known existed. Every night when I fell asleep, they whispered the long history of my people to my dreams. I remembered stories my paternal grandmother had told me about horsewomen warriors in Iran and the carved wooden horse she'd given me long ago when I was only five years old.

On what was supposed to be our last night with Louise, I took her suggestion to sleep outside in the turquoise-tiled courtyard. Josh was nonplussed, but I was beyond caring by then. As I stretched out on the bed of blankets and saddle pads Louise had made up for me, one of her horses tried to lie down right beside me. I laughed so hard I woke my hostess.

"You live in heaven," I told Louise, when she came out to investigate and decided to join me, laying out a bed for herself next to mine.

"You know the Persian proverb 'The wind of heaven is that which blows between a horse's ears'? I guess that's me," Louise said, curling her lips into the half smile I'd come to recognize as her signature expression.

"You know Persian better than most people," I observed. "Horses, too."

"I don't know, I think horses are pretty good at Persian," she joked.

We talked until the sun rose: about passion, dreams, Iran, horses, our families. When my new friend looked at me, she did so with deep curiosity, studying my face for clues to a puzzle I did not yet know. It would take me more than a decade to realize that all that long night, Louise had been putting together the pieces herself. She figured out then that I was the granddaughter of her dear friend Maryam—the legacy of the Caspian horses living within me. At what moment it all clicked into place and why she chose not to tell me, I don't know. What I do know is that she took a keen interest in me, inviting me to stay on longer and learn everything I could about the horses.

In the morning, when Josh announced it was time to return to Tehran, I told him I would not be joining him. Louise explained to my soon-to-be-ex-boyfriend that several of her ranch hands had left for Europe and that she could really use my help. Josh reluctantly agreed, and Louise and I high-fived as soon as his Range Rover was out of sight.

I spent the next week learning the intricate details of what Louise called "horsewomanship," and what in other parts of the world is referred to as "natural horsemanship." The principles were similar to those I had heard from the women in Kordan. Live and ride *with* the horses; be in unison with the horses rather than trying to control them; learn the language and cues so you don't hurt the horses or yourself; be in harmony. The true art of horseback riding was to understand the self, not to dominate the horse. That had to remain the core.

That was just to start. There was more, so much more. Big, lofty ideas and values as well as small, nuanced practices and subtle shifts in carriage, posture, and placement. All of it intricately bound, each necessary what and its why paving the way for the next.

Louise showed me how to place my index and ring fingers between a horse's ears to get him to lower his head and open his mouth for the bit and reins. She was quick, too, to notice my growing bond with Baran—the chestnut gelding who had tried to climb into bed with me that night in the courtyard.

"Baran. His name means 'rain' in English," she said. I arched my eyebrow. *Had she forgotten Persian was my first language?*

"That wasn't meant as an insult. What I was trying to say is that Baran is a rainmaker, which is also how I think of you, Pardis. Powerful energy follows you both. You're well matched."

Louise was insistent I learn to ride Baran bareback. But when I stepped up onto a rock to more easily reach the horse's back, she shook her head.

"Bow to him. Place one foot behind the other and lower your knee. Then he'll bow low enough for you to easily climb on. This will help you on the trail, even more so if you're in a tough spot or being chased, and there's no time to find a rock. Get ready to get strong, kid."

When I sat atop Baran, I felt his body suture with mine, and all I wanted was to squeeze my legs and go galloping into the wind, catching the sea breeze in my hair.

But Louise read my mind. "No, you're not ready for that yet."

She handed me the woven red and white reins. I started to choke up on them, curling my fingers tightly around the yarn. Louise stopped me again.

"Let go," she commanded. "In more ways than one."

I stared back at her, confused.

She laughed, head flung back. "Okay, we'll get there. For now, loosen that death grip you've got on the reins. How would you feel if someone was pulling on your face like that?"

"Not great, I guess."

"You're darn right, not great. Horses don't respond to pressure; they respond to the *absence* of pressure. You won't condition them by yanking on them, squeezing them, or trying to pull them in. That desensitizes them. And confuses the shit out of 'em. So, stop it."

I uncurled my fingers slowly, then dropped the reins altogether.

"No, no, no, I didn't say drop them." Louise curtsied to Khosrow II, and he lowered so she could mount him. She held the very end of the reins loosely between the thumb and middle finger of her right hand and made a kissing sound until she and Khosrow II were fully facing Baran and me.

"Okay, watch me, kid." She was still holding the end of the reins in her right hand. With her other hand, she pulled slightly to the left while leaning her body to the right. Khosrow bent his head all the way around her leg and kissed her left knee. Louise repeated the same motion on the other side, this time holding the reins with her left middle finger and thumb and gently pulling with her right hand, leaning her body left. Khosrow kissed her right knee.

Now it was my turn. Baran didn't budge.

Louise laughed and shook her head. "You need to give him slack with the right when you're pulling with the left. You still have that death grip. You gotta loosen up."

After about a dozen more tries, I finally got the steering. Then came "changing gears," which I needed to do without using my legs. By shifting my body weight, clenching my buttocks, and leaning my head more forward or backward, I could get Baran to speed up or slow down. The movements were mystifyingly slight, but eventually they became second nature, which was the point. I learned that by shifting my weight in these subtle ways and relaxing my waist and stomach, I could also guide my hips in a swiveling motion. Louise was right. It was all about letting go and becoming *one* with the horse.

On our seventh day together, the four of us rode out to the Caspian Sea. I could feel Baran's excitement growing the closer we got to the beach. Khosrow II galloped right into the ocean, and Baran didn't hesitate to follow. I was stunned. I'd had no idea horses could swim or that they might want to.

Louise and I joined them, floating on our backs in the calm water. When a wave came, she took my hand, and I remembered our first day only moments after we'd met, when she had taken my hand in hers and led me to the stables. *Had that really been only a week ago?*

Back on shore, we built a fire, and I told Louise about my research on Iran's sexual revolution, a new type of global justice feminism on the rise. We talked about orgies and sex work and about clandestine feminist gatherings, like the underground dance classes I'd attended. Louise listened with an intensity I wasn't accustomed to, and it took us a while to notice that the temperature was dropping, the sun setting. We rode home, tired and hungry, but buoyed by the sea, the horses, and each other.

Our exuberance was short-lived. A cryptic, ominous voice mail awaited Louise on her half-broken answering machine at the farm. A group of women in northern Afghanistan needed help. They were called the "women of the caves," Louise explained, and they were part of an all-female army that had been fighting the Taliban for decades. Now the War on Terror had brought an ever-increasing level of threat and violence to their caves and way of life.

Louise excused herself and spent the next few hours in her room, where I heard her making several phone calls. She reemerged for dinner, but her brow remained deeply furrowed. Several times she opened her mouth to speak, only to close it again without uttering a word. The lightness of our day by the sea felt a million miles away. An endless war and a whole region in turmoil. Not to mention Iran on the precipice of civil war, fanatics practically assured to win the upcoming presidential election.

As Louise told me about the women of the caves in Afghanistan, I hung on her every word. Late into the night, Louise paced the courtyard. "The women are depleted in every way. They need weapons, which I certainly don't have. And more horses. More sperm."

"We can get them those," I blurted. Now that I knew about these mysterious and fierce female warriors, I had an impulse to go to them, to help ease their unimaginable suffering in any way I could. There was much I didn't yet understand, but one thing was clear—these were modern-day Gordafarids, and I yearned to meet them.

"The borders between Iran and Afghanistan, and Iran and Turkey, have tightened. I imagine you're aware?" Louise asked, her eyes narrowing.

"Of course. I lived through 9/11. I was in New York."

"And I was in Afghanistan," she replied, putting me in my place. "This war, it's not over, not by a long shot." Louise's deep voice ricocheted off the ceramic tiles of the courtyard.

"I know. Like the war on drugs, the war on trafficking. America's wars never end."

"Endless wars. Exactly right."

"Lou, the women need our help. We can bring them mares and sperm. We can ride Baran and Khosrow."

"Ride into Afghanistan *now*? That's a suicide mission."

The unflappable, indestructible Louise I had spent the last week with was rattled. She continued pacing, and for the first time, I noticed a limp in her left leg. Maybe she wasn't up for such a trip. It was true that she had mentioned her body ached after long rides, but I hadn't given it much credence. She'd always seemed so energetic and sharp. But could she really make the harrowing border crossing? She was well past seventy, after all. And what about me? I had youth on my side, but I'd barely learned to ride outside of an arena. Riding into the sea was one thing, riding into a war zone, something else entirely.

"It's not that simple, kid. We'd have to drive several horses in and across the border at once. You're not that good, and I'm not that healthy."

She had read my mind. But I wasn't ready to give up.

"So we get some more people together. We can all ride and drive the horses in. Safety in numbers."

"That would take time, planning," Louise said, but she had stopped pacing, and I sensed a shift. She was considering it. "Time isn't something Mina and the women have much of. Soon the winter will come, and the border crossing will be all but impossible. We would need to find the right riders to go with us, and quickly. And they must be women."

"I wouldn't dream of asking Josh, if that's what you're worried about."

Louise shook her head. "It's just got to be the *right* team. There's no margin for error. This will be one of the hardest things any of us has ever done. And most of the best female riders I know aren't exactly spring chickens."

"What about the women I ride with in Kordan?"

The horsewomen I had been training with were some of the fiercest, strongest, and most capable I had ever met. And I knew from Mastaneh, my teacher, that they were also training in combat skills, in case civil war did break out. They were, as they liked to remind me, children of the Iranian Revolution raised against the backdrop of the decade-long war between Iran and Iraq. Fighting was in their blood.

"You know, that's not such a bad idea, kid." I thought I could detect a faint trace of hope in Louise's voice. "But I still need to organize the sperm, pick the mares. Do some thinking." With that, Louise ended our discussion. In the morning, she sent me back to Tehran and told me to wait there for further instructions.

I broke up with Josh and tried to focus on my research. Instead, I found myself digging into the history of horsewomanship in Iran and Afghanistan by spending days in the library, reading every book I could get my hands on at Tehran University. I was thankful that my day job as an anthropologist allowed me the freedom to pick up and follow any string I needed to. And at that point I needed to follow the horses.

Four long weeks later, just days after mourning the third anniversary of 9/11, Louise finally called. I'd been avoiding the horse ranch in Kordan, worried about a run-in with Josh, but Louise told me it was time to go back.

I had missed the horses, the wind in my hair, and the sight of the lush green hills. And I was excited to reunite with Mastaneh and all of the women I had so loved riding with on my weekend escapes from the city.

"Well, well, well, look what the horse dragged in!" Mastaneh called out when I pulled up in the tiny lime-green Peugeot I had borrowed from a friend. I ran to her, tripping over hay barrels and uneven gravel. We held each other in a long embrace.

"I thought you had forgotten us," Mastaneh said, not entirely joking.

"Josh and I broke up. It got complicated."

She cocked her head and bit her lower lip, studying me. "I always thought the worst thing about you was that you were with *him*. A khareji. A foreigner and a colonizer."

I laughed with relief. My body was buzzing with the excitement of seeing Mastaneh again, of inhaling the familiar scent of jasmine and farm, and of being back among horses. I kicked myself for letting incon-sequential fears about an ex keep me away. I wanted to make up for lost time and suddenly couldn't wait to wrap my legs around one of the horses and ride up into the mountains. I was so eager and distracted, I almost forgot the real reason for my visit.

Mastaneh and I sat down under an olive tree, and I told her the story of my time with Louise. At first, she couldn't believe it. She had heard stories about the legendary Louise Firouz and had a million questions about what she was really like. I told her about riding into the sea and how the horses were like members of Louise's family. Mastaneh relished every detail, until I got to the part about the women of the caves, and she fell silent, looking out at the farm and the horses, everywhere but back at me.

One of my favorite horses at Kordan, Sia, so named for the blackness of his mane, fur, and tail, had fallen asleep beside me. So had several of the other horses who had made their way to us and laid down under the olive tree. I stroked Sia's head, entangling my fingers in his mane, and waited for Mastaneh to speak.

"Tell me about the studbook," she said at last. "Where is it?"

"The studbook?"

"Yes. It's legendary, Pardis. The studbook is the only way to trace the lineage of all the best horses in Iran, maybe even the world."

Louise had mentioned a studbook at some point, but I hadn't realized its significance. There had just been so much to take in and absorb in such a short amount of time.

"Did Louise show it to you? I heard once that the horsewomen war-riors, the same ones you're talking about, had it. You know Louise's health isn't good? I've heard that, too."

"That's why she needs us," I said.

"I get that the women need us to bring them horses and sperm, but what about what they might be able to give us?"

According to Mastaneh, there was speculation in the Iranian horse community about two things: first, that the studbook was somewhere in Afghanistan, and, second, that Louise was unwell and therefore the future of the Caspian horse was uncertain. Without Louise holding together warring factions claiming ownership of the breed, Mastaneh and others worried that Caspians would be bred to other horses rather than continue the lineage.

"Pardis, I know you spent a special week with her, but you've only just met her. You have no way to judge whether she's declined or not. Everyone talks about it. She's not well. I used to watch her ride when I was younger, when she would show in Tehran. No one could ride like her. But the last time, when she came to a horse show in Shiraz, I could tell just from how she sat on the horse that something was wrong. And . . . well . . . she dropped out of the competition."

I didn't want to hear any more, but maybe I could use this to convince Mastaneh to help the women of the caves and Louise.

"Okay, you're right. If Louise couldn't complete a ride in a competition, then there's no way she'd survive that hellish border crossing. And we both know *I* can't do it alone."

Mastaneh was standing now, her black hair falling into her brown eyes, fastening a saddle onto Banafsheh, whose fur, as her name suggested, shaded from gray to purple in the sunlight. As she snapped the saddle cinch into place, I thought I saw the urgency of the moment click in her mind.

"*We* need to go, Masti."

"What do you mean, *we*? It's a suicide mission."

"You, me, and whoever else can come. We need to help the women. And we can earn our stripes to help protect the studbook."

Mastaneh kicked at the ground with her spur-fastened boot, and I knew better than to interrupt her thoughts. Moments later, she pulled her phone out and began texting furiously. And then it rang. It was Rhana, the best rider—and sharpshooter—in Kordan.

By the time the sun had splintered into twilight, we had a plan. We would trailer the horses close to the border and then ride from there. For Mastaneh and Rhana, the studbook was a big draw. I wish I had thought to ask Louise where it was when she mentioned it to me. *Was it in Afghanistan? If so, would she even want us to bring it back to Gonbad?* I tried calling her half a dozen times from Kordan that afternoon, but she never answered. *Where was she? Had her failing health landed her in a hospital?* She had told me about going to see a doctor in London for some kind of treatment the day she called me in Tehran to send me to Kordan. But I didn't know when she was going or what the treatment might be. I was nervous to ride into a potential gun battle without her.

"That is precisely why we have to go *without* her," Mastaneh had said. "We can't let Louise, the keeper of the studbook and the lineage of the horses, die in a gun battle. We'll just need to get our team together so we are a big-enough group to keep eyes out for each other."

Rhana had been easier to convince than Mastaneh. She already knew about the women of the caves and had heard that their commander, Mina, was the best sharpshooter in the world. She was dying to meet her.

I suggested we try to contact Mina to let her know we were coming, but Rhana explained, as Louise had tried a few weeks earlier, that for safety reasons, Mina had stopped carrying a cell phone. Occasional radio contact was still possible but only from within Afghanistan. Our options were either to ride into the country and find her or to ride in and try to make radio contact then.

At Mastaneh's suggestion, I returned to Louise's ranch in Gonbad-i-Kavoos to retrieve the vials of sperm and the two brood mares she had selected for the journey in the hopes that I could convince Louise to remain in Iran while we completed the mission. I hoped that Louise herself would greet me, but when I arrived, I was told she had left for Europe just two days earlier. I sent a silent prayer to the universe that she would make it to London and be restored to her full health. The world needed Louise Firouz. I needed her.

In the end, four of us—myself, Mastaneh, Rhana, and Rhana's younger sister—made the journey. We took six horses, one for each of us plus the two brood mares Louise had chosen. And of course, we were also carefully guarding seven meticulously wrapped vials of sperm. It was five hundred miles from Kordan to the outskirts of Mashad, where we parked the trailers. The last hundred miles of the journey were on horseback.

As we rode closer to the border, I felt the chill of the high desert snake through me and shuddered to think of crossing in winter. My whole body was tense, my legs squeezing Sia's withers. Sia was part-Turkoman and part-Caspian. The Turkoman in him gave him elongated legs and a thin neck, but his Caspian ancestry ensured that the ride would always be a smooth one, regardless of the terrain. Attuned to my cues, he galloped toward the border. The other five horses, herd-bound after a year of being turned out together in Kordan's pastures, rushed to follow.

I needed to relax. My buttocks had become a rock, the worst thing for a rider, according to Louise. I took a deep breath and sent a desperate plea from my brain down to my glutes. *Please, please, relax.* I told myself that the border was calmer now. That three years had passed since the Twin Towers had fallen. *But how would we find the right path? How would we avoid border skirmishes?* My legs tightened again, and Sia tensed in response, quickening his pace once more.

This time Rhana and her Akhal-Tehke horse, Javid, were ready for us, and they smoothly rode ahead of Sia to calm him. Rhana had a deep appreciation for Caspians, but because of her height and muscular weight, she favored the Turkoman horses who stood at fifteen or sixteen hands from the ground. Javid, a dark-brown gelding with a black mane, was the tallest of our horses by far, and he, like his rider, exuded strength and confidence. Sia halted instantly.

"You must stay calm at this crossing, Pardis. You must," Rhana reminded me. She and Javid were riding close enough now that she could grip my wrist, if necessary.

"I'm worried," I confessed.

"Trust the horses," Mastaneh said. "Sia and Banafsheh know the way. And Javid is fierce. Trust them like they trust us." Sia bobbed his head as if nodding in agreement and encouragement.

Rhana suggested Mastaneh take the lead with Banafsheh. Sia and I were to follow, then Rhana's sister Azar and her Turkoman mare Laleh, with Rhana bringing up the rear on Javid. Rhana and Mastaneh were armed, but Azar and I were not. Rhana said that with guns up front and in the back, we would be safe. I tried to summon all the courage I could muster.

With the subtlest click of her tongue and squeeze of only her right thigh, Mastaneh sent Banafsheh forward. We were off, galloping toward the border at full speed. I braced myself for explosions, eruptions of earth, and a ringing in my ears. But they didn't come. The landscape, however, was just as Louise had said, and my heart dropped, remembering the rising smokestacks of mountain rock, the steep hills, and the deep valleys she described. Waiting ahead were tight turns and jutting rocks. But I knew we couldn't dare slow down, no matter how treacherous the terrain became.

Mastaneh kept Banafsheh at a full gallop, and the rest of us followed. I knew Louise would be disappointed in my inability to let go, but I couldn't help gripping Sia with every muscle in my body, praying I wouldn't fall to my death off one of these cliffs. After what felt like days but was only a few hours, the horses came to an instinctive halt. I sat up straight and pushed away the hair that had blown into my face.

The caves.

I could almost see Louise ducking to avoid hitting her head at the opening and could practically feel the vibrations of the earth from the countless explosions of the last three years. I let myself imagine the look on Louise's face when I told her that we made it in.

Rhana instructed us to dismount and told Mastaneh to have her gun at the ready. But even before our boots hit the ground, a voice roared out of the caves.

"Who dares come here?"

I was mid-dismount and couldn't figure out if I should climb back on Sia to ready myself for an escape or step to the ground. Instead, I chose to lay awkwardly on my stomach across Sia's withers, my legs dangling in the air.

"Get down!" Rhana whispered through gritted teeth. "You're embarrassing us."

Not as much as I'm embarrassing myself, I thought. I jackknifed my body with the help of my hands and dismounted in time to see a band of women striding toward us. Barefoot, with leather straps lining their calves, hair blowing behind them, they marched in a *V* formation, guns drawn. A tall, muscular woman led the way, ammunition across her chest.

"We're friends of Louise Firouz!" Rhana called out. She had tucked her gun away as soon as she caught sight of the women and raised her hands in surrender. "I'm Rhana. You must be Mina? I think Louise radioed to you about us coming?"

The tall woman at the front used her right hand to slice the air, motioning to her crew to stand down. Mina was roughly my height but took up so much more space than I ever would. She had long, cascading waves of black hair and calf muscles that burst through the leather straps on her legs. Her black eyes blazed with fire and fury.

"Yes. She told me you are horsewoman warriors," Mina replied, coming to stand mere inches from Rhana's face. The rest of us lowered our hands and watched them.

"An aspiring warrior, my friend," Rhana corrected. The two women studied each other. The air was thick, until finally, Mina pulled Rhana into an embrace, and every one of us exhaled.

They invited us inside the caves. I straggled, following slightly behind the group, trying to hide how sore my inexperienced thighs were. My stomach was still tight with anxiety. *Were these women really welcoming us? How long would it take this group of strong, fearless women to realize that I was barely a horsewoman, let alone a horsewoman warrior?*

The cave was nothing like I had imagined. Instead of a sandy floor, there were overlapping carpets. The jagged walls I had pictured Louise leaning against were padded with woven pillows that had tiny mirrors sewn into them. Candles and lanterns illuminated piles of artillery. The cave was not dark and quiet but bright, pulsating with energy. Women moved through various openings, carrying food, hay, weapons.

Mina led us through a series of caverns into a large space open to the sky. I squinted to avoid the suddenly penetrating sunlight and had to rub my eyes to make sure that what I was seeing—more than two dozen horses of all shapes, colors, and sizes—was real.

"We keep the horses secluded here to protect them. They are our most valuable asset, and our family," Mina told us. I wanted to run to them to figure out how many were Caspians, but Rhana put a hand on my shoulder and held me back. I turned to catch her eye, and she shook her head.

You must build trust with the humans and with the horses before you approach, I could hear Louise saying, her spirit with us every step of this journey but even more so now that we had found Mina and the women. I closed my eyes to send her a thought across the hills, hoping she would know where we were and how much we missed her.

Mina graciously invited us to stay for dinner. She asked Rhana to bring our horses out back to the pasture so that they could also refuel. Their supplies were low, they told us, but large buckets of water and discarded food scraps awaited the eager horses.

After a humble dinner of boiled rice and yogurt made from the cows they kept onsite, Mina invited us to lie back against the tattered pillows and instructed one of the women to bring tea as well as a hookah so we could have a smoke. Once the puffing began, Mina got down to business.

"So, ladies, why are you here? I know you didn't risk your lives crossing just to deliver some vials of sperm and a few horses. Or even for my lamb stew that people speak about across borders."

"The border crossing wasn't as bad this time," Rhana blurted out. Mastaneh shot her a death stare.

"This time?" Mina arched a perfectly plucked black eyebrow. "So, you've done this before? I didn't give you enough credit then."

Rhana's younger sister Azar, who'd been stuck in a terror-stricken, awe-inspired silence, now let out a nervous laugh. "It wasn't exactly easy, though," she said.

"Borders are never easy. Especially ours." Mina exhaled one perfect O-shaped ring of smoke after another. "But I repeat my question, what are you doing here?"

The four of us looked at one another uncertainly.

"We wanted to help Louise," Mastaneh said.

Mina arched her tattooed eyebrows and pursed her lips. "Do you take me for a fool?"

My stomach tightened, and Azar's face went white. Rhana took a deep breath, rolled her shoulders back, and cleared her throat.

"We're here . . . we're here to get the . . . ," Rhana fumbled. I wasn't used to seeing her flustered. She chewed the inside of her cheek, drawing in her lips and accentuating her jawline.

"For Louise. For the horses. For the history and the legacy," Mastaneh relented. Her voice quivered, but her eyes held Mina's. I braced myself for the blast. All during our journey I hadn't allowed myself to imagine Mina's reaction to our mission. *Would she be grateful for our help or distrustful of it?* I had pushed the thought from my mind, reasoning that it made no difference because we might not even make it across the border or ever be able to find this powerful woman and her command. But we did and we had.

On the power of Louise's name alone, we had been granted not only admission into the caves and the hospitality of a shared meal but enough of Mina's trust to sit with her, weapon-free. She had invited us to stay the night, which we desperately wanted to do. *But would she now kick us out? Would we have to make the treacherous journey back to Iran at once? And were we even right to think that our presence here was helpful?* The questions stabbed at me, and I had to sit on my hands to stop them from visibly shaking.

"And the studbook," Rhana said at last.

A pregnant pause hung in the air. Mina inhaled several more drags on the water pipe. Rhana tentatively reached for the hookah, but Mina pulled it out of her reach.

"The studbook, huh?" Mina looked each of us in the eye. Then she fixed her gaze on Rhana.

"I noticed *you* didn't ride in on a Caspian. The other two horses, I recognize. Sia and, what was the mare's name?" Mina didn't blink as she spoke, refusing to break eye contact with Rhana.

"That's Banafsheh," Azar squeaked out from the corner, where she was attempting to melt into a pillow. The other women who had been scurrying about the cave had now left, presumably to finish their evening chores.

"Right, Banafsheh, purple for the color of her fur. She's a real beauty. But you," Mina pressed her index and middle finger into Rhana's chest, "you rode in here on an Akhal-Tehke."

Rhana nodded. She held Mina's gaze. I wanted to intervene, to explain why Rhana favored the Turkoman horses. But I heard Louise's voice in my head, telling me to keep my mouth shut.

"Pretty impressive that you navigated the twists and turns of the terrain on one of those guys," Mina said. Rhana let out an audible exhale. "I understand why you aren't riding a Caspian. You're too tall, too big, too much—"

"I wouldn't say—," Rhana attempted to interject, scrambling to her feet.

Mina held up her other hand and shook her head. "It was just an observation," she said, standing and tilting her face to meet the taller woman's gaze. Rhana looked down, her hands balled into fists.

"The studbook is precious. We know that," Rhana said through gritted teeth. Her nostrils flared the same way our horses did when they were angry.

Mina took Rhana's hand gently and guided her back down to the pillows. "Relax," she said. She placed the pipe in Rhana's hands and changed the hot coal at the top of the hookah. It was only then that I realized I had raised myself up on my knees and that Mastaneh was in a runner's lunge. Now we slowly, tentatively, slunk back to the cushions.

"I don't have it." Mina exhaled a long stream of apple tobacco smoke into Rhana's face.

"What do you mean, you don't have it? We were told it lives here," Mastaneh said incredulously.

"I mean, it's not here. I don't have it."

"Well, where is it?" I wanted to wade into the conversation gently, but instead belly-flopped in, full of accusatory tone.

Mina raised her black eyebrows and then pushed herself up from the cushions to stand over us. Rhana began to stand again too, but one of Mina's women appeared from a neighboring room and pushed her back. Mina opened her mouth to speak but changed her mind. She shrugged her shoulders, turned on her heels, and walked out of the cave and into the night sky. A few other women trickled in as we stared after her in disbelief.

"It's not like she's hiding it. Calm down, American girl," one of Mina's guards, a woman named Afri, said.

"I'm not American, I'm—"

"We can all hear it in your accent," Rhana snapped. She took a deep inhale on the pipe and blew smoke out her nose.

"Don't worry, friend," Mastaneh interjected. "We're legit. Pardis is a protégée of Louise's. And she spends most of her time in Iran now. So, we forgive her the Americanness."

"I don't have a problem with Americans. Other than the ones who just wanted our horses, not our strategies," Afri said, and told us the story of the American special forces that had been deployed to her region to fight the Taliban.

"Imagine: They show up, and it's their first time fighting these bastards. Meanwhile, we've been fighting them for *decades*. My mother, my mother's mother, my mother's mother's mother. We know the Taliban. But did the Americans want to hear from us? No. They wanted our horses, and then they wanted to find *men* in the area who would help them fight. The blasted Northern Alliance."

I thought about all the news coverage that had followed the events of 9/11. Men in turbans wielding large weapons; American troops dropping into Afghanistan. Women in blue veils facing brutality from all sides. None of those thousands of stories ever mentioned an all-female army that had been fighting the War on Terror before it even had a name. Nor was there ever anything about Mina's success in beating back one of America's most elusive enemies.

"I don't have a problem with this American. Yet." Afri gestured toward me. "I don't want her making any uninformed accusations."

"I didn't mean to accuse," I replied clumsily.

"Fine. And I should tell you, I have great respect for many of the Americans who did come to fight alongside us. It's just that the Americans have been . . . uneven. As for the studbook, I'm sorry, ladies; it's really not here."

Mastaneh buried her face in her hands. I fought back tears. Rhana exhaled several smoke O's and then cleared her throat.

"When was the last time you saw it?" she asked flatly.

"I haven't. But rumor has it that it was moved back here when we returned for the winter of 2002. Then there was a three-day battle. Some Americans came and fought with us." Afri directed this last sentence at me. I nodded obediently, apologetically. "After the battle, apparently, it was gone. Like a cloud of smoke into the air." Afri made swirling motions with her hand and blew smoke up toward the ceiling.

"We heard that Louise left it here with your general, with Mina?" Rhana offered.

"I remember hearing Louise and Mina speak of it before the Twin Towers fell and the Americans arrived—maybe a year before, in 2000. Louise told Mina to bury it. But when we returned from battle, right before the first Nowruz after the Americans came in 2002, I heard it was gone."

Rhana drew a sharp breath, and Mastaneh's eyes widened.

A contradicting mixture of emptiness and hope gripped us. *Had we failed Louise?* We would have to return to Iran empty-handed, without the studbook. The lineage of the horses would be lost, their stories dead, their bloodlines questioned. *How would we break the news to her? Or did she know that the studbook was missing? Had Louise retrieved it herself? Why would Mina be cagey about the studbook and its whereabouts?*

A loud *boom* interrupted our uneasy silence. It sounded as if the sky were being ripped apart. The cave shook violently, and several pieces of dirt crumbled down from the jagged, waxlike ceiling.

"Get down!" someone called out. The explosions continued.

"Taliban?" Azar cried.

"Could be Taliban, could be Northern Alliance, could be Americans," Afri said, her tone casual.

I wondered briefly where Mina was and if she was safe, but then there was no time to think anymore. I was paralyzed by the pounding of my own heartbeat. Afri grabbed me and dragged me down a small opening at the back of the cave. Mastaneh followed. Rhana carried her terror-stricken sister. The cave was shaking so much that I kept falling. Afri pulled me up a half-dozen times or more before she ordered us all to drop to our stomachs and crawl. I winced as my knees dragged along the floor of the caves where the carpet ended. We wound our way down two more tunnels before reaching an opening, which spit us out into a lantern-lit cave deep in the recesses of the earth. Several other women were already in the room. Two were pregnant. Three had young children.

"Stay here," Afri ordered, before disappearing back the way we came.

After a few hours, I fell into a fitful sleep, cold and shivering. When I awoke, Afri was calling my name. It was time to go, she announced. They had formed a plan to help us ride out of harm's way.

"This could be a long one," Afri said, as we crawled back through the endless twisting bowels of the cave. *The battle or the tunnel?* I wondered.

We had succeeded in our primary mission. The vials of sperm were delivered safely, as were the two brood mares. We would be returning without the studbook but in one piece, which seemed like a victory in and of itself. Assuming we managed to ride past what sounded like a fierce gun battle above.

Black smoke filled the sky and our lungs when we finally stepped out of the caves. Our horses were waiting. Sia reared and neighed at the scent of us.

"Three women will accompany you," Afri said. "You'll ride up the face of that mountain there." She pointed to the steepest sloping peak in the distance. "It will be a longer, more difficult ride. But it's the only way to get you out of here safely."

Waves of fear kept crashing over me, but knowing I would be back on a horse calmed me enough to focus.

Rhana nodded obediently, mounting quickly. Both rider and animal appeared unfazed by the pulsing gunshots in the distance. She jerked her head and the horse shifted to indicate her place at the lead, and we took a collective deep breath, mustering all our courage.

"Don't look back," Rhana said, as she rode forward. "Ever."

2008

THE NEVER-ENDING WAR ON TERROR CLAIMED MORE LIVES and spread more sorrow. The grief knew no borders, consuming countries and hearts. By 2008, grief was the only language I spoke. I had been arrested, accused of espionage, held for thirty-three days by the morality police, and then kicked out of my ancestral homeland for writing a book about sexual politics in modern Iran. I was in a failing marriage. And I had all but stopped riding horses, unable to re-create the flying feeling I had felt atop Caspian and Turkoman horses in Iran.

Don't look back . . . ever. Rhana's words echoed in my ears as I tried to press forward with my life, the pain of exile threatening to be my undoing.

We had done as Rhana said back in 2004; we didn't look back when we left the caves. We had followed three women whose names we never learned on an eight-hour ride up the mountains and swimming through the Harirud River. We didn't stop throughout the entire ride, not even for food. The ride to Afghanistan had been filled with nervous laughter and conversation. The ride home was in contemplative silence. I processed the events I had just witnessed, trying to understand the lives of the women I met, their horses, and the challenges they faced daily, from warlords to weather. As my horse moved beneath me, I closed my eyes and imagined Gordafarid, riding into the past and bringing her spirit forward to give all of us strength. We rode hard for the border, determined to reach Iran before nightfall. Mina's women bid us farewell at the border. We were far from our previous crossing, but at least we were back in Iran. We made camp near the river that night and then rode for three more days to reach the trailer and begin our drive back to Kordan.

Our arrival home was met with a flurry of calls from worried friends and family. Word was spreading that the Taliban had reorganized under one of their founders, Mullah Omar,[1] and that their violence had increased exponentially. We were lucky to have escaped, we were told. The last four days had been nothing but nonstop war.

Rhana sent word to Mina through a group of Iranian men riding out to sell grenades to various fighting factions in Afghanistan, but never heard back. She asked around about Afri and the women of the caves, but no one had any news. None of us wanted to articulate the unthinkable. We could only pray that the women and their horses remained safe.

I returned to my familial home in Tehran, where I tried—and failed—to call Louise. Each day I rose in the morning and called every number I could find to reach Louise so I could recount what had happened. Every day I was met with busy signals or dial tones. I knew that I had to return to the United States soon to continue my studies, but I hoped to see Louise one last time before leaving.

While violence in the North of Afghanistan was increasing, America's presence was waning. Thousands of lives were being lost year after year, and President George W. Bush was the subject of mounting criticism. Worse still, he had instructed the American military to spread their presence to Iraq and throughout the Middle East. Democrats pointed out that none of the members of al-Qaeda who had carried out the 9/11 attacks were Afghan. The whereabouts of the identified leader of al-Qaeda, Osama bin Laden, a Saudi, were still unclear, but bin Laden's ties to Islamic extremist groups had been revealed, and now Saudi Arabia was a target. The Bush administration, carrying long-standing grudges against unfinished business in Iraq, also used the 9/11 attacks as a reason to invade Iraq on a manhunt for Saddam Hussein. Bush made his case to the United Nations General Assembly in 2002, and the invasion in Iraq began in 2003. The entire Middle East was in turmoil.

Even Iran became a target when, in 2002, President Bush referred to what he called an "Axis of Evil" composed of Iran, Iraq, and North Korea during his State of the Union address. Many Iranians blamed this speech for the emboldening of the Islamic hard-liners in the lead-up to the election of the brutal Mahmoud Ahmadinejad in 2004. America's targeting of Iran—even if only in rhetoric—added fuel to the burning flames of those running on a campaign to fight the "Great Satan America." Moderates like Mohammad Khatami, they reasoned, gave too much to the West and threatened Iran's very existence. Internal unrest was ignited as hard-liners, moderates, and reformists battled for the soul of the country. Young people, whose social movements I had been following in my research, were dismayed that their cause, their sexual revolution, which they believed had the power to overthrow the regime, was now going to fall, another casualty.

"We're in a bad situation," Rhana had said back in 2004, when we gathered for our weekly ride a month after returning from Afghanistan. "Not as bad as Mina and her crew, but bad. Iran has unrest from all sides, and we might be on the brink of civil war."

We continued to worry about Mina and the women. With American troops scattered throughout the country, not to mention the region and even into the Philippines, we knew the women's supplies must be dwindling, as were their previous advantages over the Taliban. During the first year after 9/11, the special forces had worked successfully with the Northern Alliance to beat back the Taliban by destabilizing them and cutting off their supplies of weapons. But the American invasion of Iraq had awakened a sleeping dragon among Islamic extremist groups, who were now banding together to defeat a common enemy.

"We don't even know if Mina is still alive," Mastaneh said. She was only saying what all of us were thinking, but still, a bone-chilling shiver wound its way down my spine.

"Or the horses," I said.

An uneasy silence settled among us. Mercifully, the sound of my cell phone blaring an Iranian pop song broke the tension. Mastaneh and Rhana laughed nervously as I answered.

"Heard you did it, kid. Nice work." Louise's soul-nourishing voice filled my ear, and my entire body relaxed for the first time in weeks.

"Louise! Where have you been? What's happening?"

"Slow down, kid. I don't have all the answers. Why don't we start with you telling me what happened when you rode into the caves."

I told her everything, with Mastaneh and Rhana jumping in to fill in details. Louise stopped us when Rhana mentioned the studbook.

"It's safe; no need to worry about that," she said. "I don't want to talk about it."

She was being evasive, but I'd come to realize she got that way whenever the studbook was mentioned. I would learn later that Louise frequently moved the book around without telling anyone when, where, or how. But at that moment, I was just so happy to hear her voice, I let it pass.

"Lou, have you heard from Mina?" I asked, chewing my lower lip.

The silence was so long, I wondered if we had been disconnected.

"I don't know how to tell you this, kid," Louise said at last. Mastaneh and Rhana crowded around my small Nokia. The speaker was turned all the way up, but Louise's voice had dropped to a whisper we strained to hear.

"Don't say it," Rhana interjected, twisting her hands.

"You need to hear it," Louise said, clearing her throat. "Mina is dead."

My phone slipped from my trembling fingers and hit the ground. Tears flowed down my cheeks. Rhana sat in stunned silence. It was Mastaneh who picked up my cell and asked, "And the others? The horses?"

"Not sure. Just received word from a contact in the American military that it was a long battle you all escaped and that there were many casualties on all sides."

"So, it *was* the Taliban we were fleeing," I said, stunned. It didn't elude any of us that had we been captured, we would have immediately been put to death.

"Taliban, Northern Alliance, Americans—everybody is shooting guns out there," Louise replied. I could tell she was trying to reassure me, but I could hear the grief in her voice, and I didn't feel any better.

Another long pause. I hung my head. Rhana paced, snapping olive branches underfoot.

"Kid, I'm not doing so great myself. I gotta go," Louise said, her voice still faint. I had detected the tremble and the grief, but it hadn't occurred to me to ask about her own health, shocked as I was by the events of the past few weeks.

"Wait, Lou, what's wron—," but my question was cut off by the silence at the dead end of the line.

LOUISE STRUGGLED with her health for the next two years, and our calls became fewer and further between. Worse still, a terrible car accident in Croatia prevented me from returning to Iran the following summer of 2005. I was on my way to watch the Iranian soccer team play in the World Cup in Germany. My spine split in half in the town of Split. I lay in bed in an abandoned Hapsburg palace turned hospital outside of

Dubrovnik with a fractured spine, cursing my luck and wondering if I would ever ride again. As they encased me from head to waist in a Frida Kahlo–like torso brace, I realized that my spine would likely never be the same again.

By the time I was healthy enough to make a journey to Iran, it was 2007. The shifting sands of the regime caused me to lose my footing on what would be my final trip to my native homeland. I arrived in Tehran only to meet members of the morality police, who held me in detention as soon as the plane landed. They released me the following morning. The detention should have been a warning, but I didn't heed it.

Instead, I dove back into my research on Iran's sexual revolution with voracity. My friends partied with a hungry anger that was contagious. Some nights people raved as they raged about their worlds ending. Other afternoons feminists lamented the tragic state of affairs of a regime that was shattering their souls. I was so wrapped up in the movement, I kept ignoring the siren call of the Caspian—the horses and the sea. Finally, one evening after a particularly harrowing escape from a party raided by the morality police, I decided I needed to travel north, to get away from Tehran. I called Louise the following morning and made plans to visit her after my lecture at Tehran University the following day.

I didn't know it then, but that was the last time I would ever hear Louise Firouz's silky, deep voice. My trip and my entire life were put on hold when I was arrested thirteen minutes into my lecture at Tehran University. Charged with the crimes of espionage and trying to foment a "velvet revolution" due to my research on sexual politics, I was held under house arrest for thirty-three days. At the end of this harrowing time, I was put on a plane, stripped of my Iranian citizenship, and told never to return. When I landed in the United States, filled to the brim with trauma, I decided to lock Iran away forever. I compiled all of my notes, clippings, photographs, and journals—including the horse-embossed leather one Louise had given me through Mastaneh—and threw them into a large banker's box.

The weight of the box was too much for my healing spine to manage, so I called on my parents and brother Paymohn, who, like me, was living at our family home in San Diego for the summer, to assist me.

"I want to burn everything in here," I announced quietly. "Never look back." My parents and Paymohn exchanged glances. My brother shook his head.

"How about we just lock it away in storage?" my mother offered. "You never have to see it again, but I just can't let you destroy memories of my homeland."

Of course, my mother, who carried a small bag of dirt from Iran in her wallet everywhere she went, would never understand. I kicked the box over and over until the tops of my feet went numb.

I shoved Iran in a box the way that leaders lock history away from their people. I wanted to erase everything about my homeland, to be numb to the memories.

I threw myself into policy work around the War on Terror and its hyperfeminine antidote, the war on trafficking. After Barack Obama was elected president in 2008, I was invited to move to Washington, DC, to advise on strategy for the Middle East. My work on Iran's sexual revolution as well as my research on human trafficking helped policymakers get a more complete picture of the disconnects between governments and the lived experiences of people on the ground in the region. The War on Terror continued, filling the newly erected detention center at Guantánamo with hundreds of prisoners from Afghanistan, Iraq, and Saudi Arabia. So little did the United States understand its enemy, there were reports that the wardens didn't even know that the prisoners didn't share a mother tongue.

On the eve of my move to Washington, just months after I had been arrested and kicked out of Iran, a slim envelope marked "airmail" arrived from Iran. Inside was a newspaper clipping from the *New York Times* obituary pages, its light weight betraying the heavy news it carried.

"Louise Firouz, Horse Breeder, Dies at 74" was the headline. I blinked back the tears and forced myself to keep reading.

"Louise Firouz, an American-born horse breeder who while roaming a mountain range in Iran in 1965 discovered a pony-sized Caspian horse, long thought to be extinct, died on May 25th. Caspian horses were found to be a precursor to modern racehorses." The opening paragraph of the obituary was largely correct, but the black-and-white ink of the paper felt so sterile. Louise had lived the most colorful life of anyone I had ever met. How could her experiences be captured in these few hundred words?

I read and reread the article, trying to make sense of it. I opened my laptop to see if it was true, scanning other news sites, including the Caspian Horse Society pages as well as newspapers in Iran. All of them confirmed the tragic truth. Louise had indeed died of liver failure, according to her brother, David. Not wanting to leave her beloved horses alone in northern Iran, she had stayed on the farm, refusing to return to the United States for more testing and examination.

"In her 70s, living in Northern Iran, Mrs. Firouz continued to ride," the *New York Times* article continued. "Some years ago, she was mounted on a tall Turkoman horse when it tripped on a mountain trail, dislocating her shoulder. 'People said she should stop riding,' Mr. David Laylin, Mrs. Firouz's brother, recalled. 'She said, "I beg your pardon. The horse fell. I didn't."'" I smiled through the tears. That sounded exactly like the Louise I knew.

But had my dear friend really left this world—and ten months ago? How had I not known? I'd been so steeped in policy and trying to make sense of the crumbling region where my ancestral homeland was under threat, I hadn't been checking in on my friends. I'd even stopped riding, the trauma of our escape from Afghanistan ever present. My heart couldn't bear to ride without my Iranian companions. I didn't want to ride alone.

And I couldn't bear to face a call with Louise where I would have to admit that I'd stopped riding, my heart sinking as I heard her weakening voice.

But I wasn't ready to carry the weight of this grief. I tucked the clipping away in the heavy wooden nightstand my grandmother had given me and shut the drawer, closing my mind and heart off from the graveyard of grief. I was surrounded by pain. I had to shut Louise, the horses, and Iran away before they tore me apart from the inside.

2017

IRAN STAYED LOCKED AWAY FOR YEARS. ON THE TENTH ANNI-versary of my arrest and expulsion from my native homeland, I smelled the orange blossoms in the air during an unusually cool California summer. The year 2017 had been a difficult one. A new American president announced his arrival with a hunger to eliminate difference. He swore to rid the United States of all threats—and threat number one happened to be my people.

My then seven-year-old daughter came home from school on the eve of his election in tears. When I asked her what had happened, she gasped, in a mixture of grief and panic.

"This . . . this . . . this boy at school. He said to me, 'When Trump is president, he'll send you all back where you belong,'" Tara choked out. She wiped her eyes vigorously with her purple sleeve. "But, Mama, where are we supposed to go? Where would he send us?" Her question hung in the air. A few weeks later, the new president's pick for secretary of state, John Bolton, announced that he wanted to wipe Iran off the map.

Somehow, Trump and Bolton's desire to erase Iran actually erased my resistance to Iran. For the first time in a decade, I felt a deep love for a homeland I had lost. I wanted Iran back. It was the only way to survive the fascism we were now living under in the United States. And the irony of the similarities between Trump and the hard-liners who kicked me out of Iran didn't elude me.

It was time to dive back in and sort through the memories. This meant unearthing boxes I had locked away in a storage unit for years. It also meant unearthing trauma I had repressed for over a decade.

For more than ten years, I had not been able to speak—let alone write about—my arrest in Iran, being kicked out of my native country. Body trembling, I approached the cardboard cubes, box cutter in hand. I couldn't face my diaries from the early years; they were too optimistic. The latter years: too traumatic. But 2004 stood out as one of the good years. That was the year I fell deeply in love with horses and rediscovered Iran on horseback. I opened the "2004" box and fished out a leather-bound brown notebook that had a picture of a horse emblazoned on it. I smiled as I recalled a name: Louise.

As if saying her name out loud conjured her spirit, a piece of paper fell out of the front insert of the notebook—one I had never seen before. I unfolded the nearly see-through square parchment and squinted at the childlike printed handwriting. Louise had never been good at school and swore she missed the two weeks when they taught cursive because the weather was too good not to be out riding. It read:

Dear Pardis,

Treasure this journal as you treasure the Caspian horse. Remember, the story of these horses is your story. It is your legacy. You have to take this story forward. Tell the world of how the women riding these horses changed and will continue to change history. And look at your history.

Love, Louise

Like the turquoise fountain at the center of Louise's home, tears poured out of me and made the ink on the page run. I quickly wiped the paper with the top of my sweatpants and started blowing on it to dry. I folded the paper back up and placed it inside the journal Louise had given me all those years ago. I closed my eyes and called up the memory of Louise, the smell of horses, lush green grass spilling into flooded rice paddies, the taste of seawater as we rode close to the Caspian, and my favorite memory of all, riding into the Caspian Sea on the back of Baran.

Seeing this letter for the first time, I was overwhelmed. I thought about her words: *"The Caspian horse is your legacy."* What did she mean? I dove into one of my familiar black Moleskine notebooks filled with meticulous daily field notes. I set the horse-emblazoned leather book to the side and went swimming into the memories of my time in the North of Iran with Louise. My joy leaped off the page as I thumbed through my notes. I laughed and cried at the scenes I had described in such painstaking detail. I could feel the horses between my legs. I sensed, too, Louise's hand on my shoulder as she instructed me to arch my body sideways as we swam with the horses—preventing our bodies from becoming entangled and ensuring I didn't end up with a hoofprint in my abdomen. I laughed when I came to a passage about the first time I fell from Baran. Louise and I had been out riding toward the sea, and somehow Baran and I had galloped in front of Louise and Ostad—her new favorite stallion, who would later become a favorite of Her Royal Highness Princess Anne. Louise called out a correction to my posture. But instead of keeping my eyes forward while listening and adjusting my body, I turned my entire torso around to look at her. My horse was still galloping at a fast clip.

"Face forward! Look out, kid!" Louise commanded.

I turned my body and eyes just in time to see the olive tree before one of its lower-hanging branches made contact with my forehead and knocked me to the ground. Louise rode up, shaking her head and tsking.

"Serves you right, kid. Now, go get back on."

Baran had stopped and was taking advantage of a moment's rest to graze on the lush grass growing out of the side of an irrigation canal nearby. He was swishing his long black tail to swat away flies. He raised his large head and looked at me with his bulging brown eyes as if to scorn me for not paying closer attention.

"You're right, of course," I said to him. The minute I was mounted, Louise and I both burst out in laughter.

On the last page of the last of the 2004 notebooks was a key: *Louise said to talk to my aunties about the horses. Note to self, ask them on next trip to Mashad*. But I had never done that. And a decade and a half had passed.

My aunties, both in their nineties now, were still living in Mashad. Both were growing increasingly frail each time I spoke with them on our weekly calls. They had been diagnosed with various cancers. I grabbed a handful of notebooks and the horse-emblazoned leather diary and ran out of my parents' storage unit. I burst through the front door of my La Jolla home in search of my father.

"I need to speak with the amehs, Baba," I announced. I needed to talk to his elder sisters immediately. He pulled out his phone, but I put my hand on his.

"Baba, this is gonna require Facetime. Please, it's important."

My father nodded slowly. I felt like a samovar about to boil over. While my father called his eldest brother, Atta, who had the best Wi-Fi connection and could help get the older aunties on Facetime, I texted my cousin Nilou, begging for her help. Between texts, phone calls, and intercontinental arrangements, my cousin and uncle finally connected us so I could look my amehs in the eyes.

"Ameh joons, this might seem like a strange question, and I can't believe I've never asked before." I didn't know how to broach the subject.

Rather, I had just been letting my excitement guide the way. I took a deep breath. "Ameh joons, do you, I mean, did you know a woman by the name of Louise Firouz?"

Their faces broke into the widest smiles I had ever seen. Between their missing teeth and the laugh lines that spilled into wrinkles punctuated by dimples, I could see their souls filling with the same wonder I felt each time I thought of Louise.

"The Amricayi with the horses! Of course, we remember Louise!" they said. My auntie Ezzhat slowly disappeared down a hallway, promising to return with photographs from fifty years earlier.

My other auntie's face beamed at the first mention of Louise's name. But now, worry furrowed her brow and her chin trembled.

"Ameh Shokat, are you okay?" I ventured. I saw my aunt look past my shoulder to see if my father was still there. Sensing an unfamiliar discomfort with her brother, I turned and asked my father to leave. Shokat let out a long exhale.

"It is a story. A long, long story, my dear girl," she finally said.

"I want to hear it, auntie."

"You won't believe it."

"Try me. Please," I begged. I scrambled around to find the horse-emblazoned leather diary and held it up to the screen. "Please, auntie. I knew her too. Rode with her. She gave me this."

Electricity pulsed through my veins. The tears came as quickly as sweat poured from my pores. My heart pounded into my throat. The pieces were all coming into focus now. Louise. The Caspian horses. My grandmother. The legacy.

My aunt Shokat was still crying when Ezzhat came limping back in with a tattered photo album that she set down on the dining room table where she and her sister had been having a midnight snack of bread and cheese before I so rudely interrupted them.

"Shokat joon, come now, it has been years," Ezzhat whispered. She stroked her sister's shaking shoulders and pulled her tiny frame into an embrace. I had never wanted to crawl through a screen so desperately. I wanted to hold them both in my arms.

"Pardis jaan, you have opened a Pandora's box, and I'm glad," Ezzhat said.

"Those horses saved us from death," Shokat sobbed. Ezzhat kissed her sister's forehead. My second cousin Amira, Ezzhat's granddaughter, hurried into the frame.

"What's going on?" Amira asked.

"Pardis wants to hear the horse stories . . ."

"Ohhhhh . . . the drunk horses, right?" Amira smiled.

"The drunk horses?"

"But it can't be today. It is a long story. An important one. But not today. Your aunt isn't ready," Ezzhat said. I nodded and sent my love as best as I could through a two-dimensional screen. I had never felt the pain of exile so acutely as in that moment.

I hung up the phone, overflowing with emotions. How had my story unknowingly intertwined with theirs? How had no one told me in the twenty years I had been riding horses that it was in my blood? I had met Louise Firouz through happenstance. It was sheer luck that I was dating a British diplomat when he was attacked and decided to drive north to my father's village. I had been to Gonbad a half-dozen times, but would never have met Louise, never have sat on a Caspian horse, if not for him. And then I spent months with a woman who had spent years with my grandmother and aunts. And no one had put it together except for Louise? Or had they genuinely not known? And why didn't Louise tell me the moment she figured it out? Excitement and sadness stabbed at my insides. I would never be able to ask Louise. Would never know how much she knew, when she put the pieces together, and why she never told me herself. But, surely, my family would have at least some of the answers.

Over the next several months, my aunts told me stories that made my head spin. It turned out that my paternal aunts and my grandmother Maryam were avid horsewomen. Against the better judgment of everyone in their village, they were some of the earliest female riders. The deep relationship they created with the horses made them outcasts in the community.

And as if that weren't enough, not only did my grandmother and aunts ride horses, but they also smuggled goods and later women in need of help across the borders of Iran, Turkmenistan, and Afghanistan on horseback. To keep the horses calm while crossing the borders, Ezzhat explained, my grandmother would give them some homemade aragh-saggi, or "dog vodka," the liquor having earned its name for the terrible taste it left in one's mouth. Thus, the tale of the drunk horses. I could almost taste the whiskey swirling through my mouth. I was overwhelmed by the intergenerational strength coursing through my veins.

I thought it was only the revolutionary young Tehranis who home-brewed and drank dog vodka. Even the name of the bitter drink conjured up memories not of horses or the North, but of the parties I had attended when descending into the world of Iran's sexual revolution. I thought about my friend Raya, who would take a shot of aragh-saggi before going to a rave or underground political gathering. I remembered the first time I tasted it when we were doing our makeup to prepare for a megaparty with a DJ.

Dog vodka was a different world than the villages of the North, the horses, the sea, my aunties. Or was it?

"There was Iran and there was Persia," Louise had told me once. "Must look for the bridges between."

Iran was the glamour and glitz of Tehran, Shiraz, and Esfahan. From the moment Louise arrived in Iran in the late 1950s, she was struck by the high fashion and opulence of the cities. Parties overflowing with champagne. Women dressed in the latest Paris haute couture. This was her Iran. But when Louise left Iran in search of horses, the landscape quickly changed from high rises to the high peaks of the Alborz Mountains, and overflowing rice paddies replaced champagne parties. As she drove north toward the Caspian Sea, she watched as women squatted in the open sewers, washing clothing or hawking their goods, while men led pack animals towering with merchandise or their belongings.

This was Persia. Roads that ended in orchards. Mountains rising and rivers tumbling in white and blue. All shades of green contouring farming fields and jagged peaks. And village women who swathed themselves in dark sheaths of fabric from head to toe in Gilan Province or those who layered their bodies with colorful fabrics and prints with accompanying headdresses that jangled as they walked. Iran was politics; Persia was poetry.

And then the revolution came. The Islamists in power eschewed the glitz and the glamour, accusing Iran of Westoxication. Iran—where the seats of power were, in the capital, in Shiraz, and in the city of Esfahan— had to return to Persia. The new regime needed to claim a narrative of the history of Persia steeped only in their interpretation of religion. Not surprisingly, Iranians across the country did not agree. This imagined past did not comport with their understanding of Iranianness or Persianness. The Islamists pushed back, clamping down harder and harder on their people. They wanted to own the past, present, and future. The new generation, born during and after the revolution, could not stand for this. And the dissent started in the cities.

If Iran was the heart, Persia was the soul, and I was caught in between.

I met the horsewomen in Kordan who took me into their worlds. They rode through ruins while talking about revolution. They lived a deep connection with animals, the land, the seasons, and the earth. They were also committed to feminism, to change, to justice, and to each other. The horses they mounted each day were a living testament to the greatness of the Persian Empire, the resilience of our heritage, and the desire to constantly move forward. The horses and their riders galloped between Persia and Iran, bringing past into present, dreaming of a fused future.

Unbeknownst to me, a war was brewing quietly for the soul of Persia. The Caspian horse, the key to empire, was becoming a battleground for owning history.

2018

I HAD TO UNDERSTAND WHAT HAD HAPPENED TO LOUISE, WHERE the story of the Caspian had started, and what twists and turns the journey had taken. And most important, where were the Caspian and Turkoman horses my grandmother and then Louise had been caring for all this time?

Fortunately, Louise had been working on a memoir. Unfortunately, she hadn't been able to publish it due to run-ins with the Iranian authorities. But her desire to write her story meant that she had kept detailed diaries and sent many letters, including the note she left me in the journal she had given to me. After her death, her remaining papers had been distributed among friends and colleagues in the United Kingdom. Between the Royal Caspian Society, the International Caspian Horse Society, and the International Museum of the Horse, I was able to start piecing together her story.

I kicked myself for not asking her more questions when we were together. I had never thought to ask how she fell in love with and bred Caspian horses. Had never wondered what she must have gone through to become a breeder of the world's most ancient horses. I hadn't even understood how special these fascinating horses really were. I knew even less about the history of the Caspian horse than I did about my own family history. The sexual revolution had sucked me in, and I saw my time with Louise as something separate from Iran altogether. But reading Louise's diary, hearing her raspy voice in my head, now brought a concert of chaos inside me.

There was Iran and there was Persia. And the Caspian is the love affair that holds their marriage together, Louise wrote.

I could almost feel the fibers of a rope forming, bringing together inside me the woven threads of empire, equine, and the quest for revolution. Maybe Persia and Iran were not disconnected, but rather a bridge that had been broken. And maybe the women in my family were a part of that bridge.

I needed more answers. I went back to my field notes from 2004 again, and I scoured Louise's papers—the ones I could find through her friends and our mutual contacts. I continued to grill my aunts, too, even though I knew our conversations wore them out. The search went on for years, and none of it was enough. I needed to talk to more people who had known Louise well.

Brenda Dalton and Liz Webster were two of Louise's closest friends in the United Kingdom. Brenda had gotten some of Louise's story published four years after her death, in a book titled *Riding to Revolution*. Liz had bred Caspian horses in the United Kingdom. She was also the secretary of the International Caspian Horse Society and had self-published a book about the history of the Caspians and her time with Louise. Together, Brenda and Liz had started an online version of the studbook in 2011 to ensure its life span globally. While the original had to be protected to root out controversy over equine bloodlines, Liz told me, creating an online version would allow Caspian breeders to continue updating the living history.

Poring over Louise's notes in her diary as well as the papers she left behind with Liz at the Royal Caspian Society, I learned that Louise's life had many twists and turns. Her story was that of the Caspian horses, but it was also the story of riding through revolution. She fought political pressure and social expectations and helped reshape a thousand-year-old history of empire. Not only did she face resistance from the Iranian authorities during and after the revolution, but she was also up against competitive European and American horse breeders who tangled like snakes in the open sewers of Iranian villages.

Louise had known the Caspian horse was an endangered breed. Ensuring their survival meant sharing the Caspians with the world—in body and story. Her first step had been to send Jehan, one of the stallions she found on a trip visiting my grandmother, to Texas. Jehan traveled across Europe and on to Virginia, Louise's home state, and then eventually to a breeder in Texas, who bred him with a variety of horses with strong genetics. A new US bloodline was born.

His Royal Highness Prince Philip had also fallen in love with the Caspian horses during his trip to Louise's Norouzabad home before the Iranian Revolution. To honor his adulation, Louise had sent a number of stallions and brood mares to the United Kingdom. When the horses reached England, Prince Philip's daughter, Her Royal Highness Princess Anne, an Olympic equestrian, became as smitten as her father. A Caspian breeding program was born at the royal stables. The UK program was so successful that Louise arranged for a number of Kurdish Iranian grooms to travel to England to help care for the growing herd. To this day, the royals in the United Kingdom maintain a small herd of Caspian horses, tended by Iranian grooms. Many members of the royal family have learned to ride on Caspians. Started by Prince Philip but carried on by his daughter, breeding and conservation efforts for the Caspian horse to be bred out of extinction formed that were supported by the royal family. This was when the Caspian Horse Society was born, and Brenda Dalton took the helm with Liz and others at her side.

In Iran, the shah, and the rest of the royal families—the ruling Pahlavis and the line of Qajar royalty—had long been enamored with the story of the Caspian and were avid supporters of Louise's work. With the help of equine geneticists and archaeologists, Louise had proven that the Caspian was the descendant of the horses depicted in the carvings on palaces like Persepolis. In other words, they were the world's oldest living domesticated horse breed. These equines were the success of the Persian Empire. And as a national treasure and marker of great history, they had to be protected.

Louise had every reason to fear for her horses' safety and did all she could to ensure the international horse community was invested in the future of the Caspian. In addition to the United Kingdom and the United States, she sent breeding mares and sperm from her stallions to friends in Bermuda, New Zealand, Germany, Hungary, and Turkey. Her attempt to bring semen to Afghanistan on that last ride may have been thwarted, but she and my grandmother had been passing horses to Mina and her predecessors for decades. Throughout the Iran-Iraq War, Louise identified one horse carcass after another but took consolation in knowing the Caspian and Turkoman horses were being bred around the world. The Caspian would not go extinct on her watch.

What she did not anticipate, however, was the infighting among the international horse community that ensued after she died. From London to Auckland, no one could get enough of this mysterious little horse who, when bred to local horses, produced fiercely strong bloodlines. Cross a Caspian with a Tennessee Walker, and you get a horse with more dexterity and a stockier build. Breed a Caspian to an Irish Cobb, and you get a more refined bone structure. Mix a Caspian stallion with an Arabian mare, and you get a calmer, more reliable horse, who will bring home trophies and fat victory checks. The success of the Caspian horse had been a reassurance to Louise and a triumph on the global stage. But the fighting that followed threatened to undo decades of care and effort.

Louise herself had been a bridge. With her calm demeanor and drive to do right by the horses, she had directed Brenda, Liz, and others to stay the course. They continued their work abroad and in Iran, slowly building and rebuilding herds as quickly as they could.

Louise even managed to bring the Iranians back into the fold. She insisted on creating a Caspian Horse Society chapter in Iran and was adamant that all competitions and assessment of the Caspian had to be done in tandem with the Iranians. By the early 2000s, even the Islamist authorities had come around; Louise's never-ending well of patience and charm combined with the prominence the Caspian was gaining globally piqued their interest. The Ministry of Agriculture reached out to her, as did the Ministry of Culture. By the time I met Louise in 2004, she was working with Iranian officials to elevate and secure the status of the Caspian. The government agreed to start a national breeding program—which continues to this day—and invited Louise to join, but she'd had enough of authorities and chose instead to remain secluded in the hills of northern Iran. So long as the Caspians weren't in danger, Louise had no use for Tehran's political scene. Instead, she gave much of her attention to organizing international Caspian and Turkoman riding tours to show Westerners a more authentic version of Iran: Persia.

She and her husband, Narcy Firouz, had been a bridge not only between Iran and Persia, pulling the history and strength of the Persian Empire into present-day Iran through these horses, but also between East and West, securing a future for a storied history. When Louise died in 2008, the Caspian world mourned. From the jagged mountains of Afghanistan to the tumbling rivers of Wyoming, horse breeders who knew the story of Louise Firouz grieved the loss of the American woman who, with the help of my grandmother, rediscovered and reestablished the world's most ancient breed of horses. The mourning also brought a silencing of the discord, if only temporarily.

It was as though the drive to keep writing the story of the Caspian died with Louise. For the next several years, Caspian breeders mainly kept to themselves. Without Louise's infectious enthusiasm, the conference and event circuit quietly fizzled out. This had the domino effect of impacting demand for the horses worldwide. The global market for buying and selling the rare breed declined, plunging the price and the breeding efforts. By 2015, the Caspian that had been bred off the endangered breed list was once again in danger.

Perhaps it was this renewed threat that spurred the international horse community to act. Or maybe it was that seven years had passed since Louise's death, and there was a feeling that a new chapter could finally begin. Whatever the case, as 2015 drew to a close and a new year beckoned, the silence around the Caspian was broken by new conflicts.

The veracity of the digital studbook that Brenda and Liz had published online was questioned. The women were accused of falsifying records, since they refused to say where the original was. As Mina and Afri had told me all those years earlier in the caves, perhaps the studbook was truly lost forever. Perhaps Louise had hidden it too well.

2019

My QUEST TO UNDERSTAND THE INTERTWINING HISTORIES of my grandmother and Louise occupied me day and night. What *had* happened to that original herd? The one Louise, and my grandmother Maryam before her, cared for and bred in northern Iran?

My aunts told me Louise distributed the herd of one hundred Caspian horses to women across the region. One group went to Turkey to help female Kurdish equestrian javelin throwers train in combat and the ancient Ottoman sport of cirit. These women defied patriarchal authoritarianism to train, and they did so on the lighter, stronger Caspian horses. When their village was attacked by ISIS in 2019, they used their cirit and combat skills to defeat the all-male army. In 2021, I visited their village in Turkey and met a group of young women who were indeed riding Caspian and Turkoman horses that had been passed down to them. Every one of them knew the story of Louise Firouz, too. Their mothers and grandmothers had made sure of that.

The women I met had begun to gain national attention, not for their success fighting terrorists, but for their ability to compete against men in cirit. The all-female team was being heralded for their javelin accuracy and their bravery in taking life-threatening blows that most men didn't have the stomach for.

"Our grandmothers gave us brave blood and fighting skills," Banu, the lead javelin player, told me. Banu and her teammates were all Yoruk, members of an ethnic subgroup of Oghuz descent, nomadic mountain dwellers in the Anatolian region. They took me to meet the elder Yoruks, including a woman named Annahita, who showed me photographs of herself fighting men as a sharpshooter on horseback.

"The Caspian horses." Annahita smiled, and her crackling voice dropped several octaves. "They are the perfect horses for us because of their size. I mean, look at me." Annahita was no more than four feet tall. When she smiled, her leathery skin burst into laugh lines, and her mouth revealed five remaining teeth. "Our size meant people constantly under-estimated us," she said, referring to both women and horses. "We used that to our advantage."

My aunts also told me that some members of the herd were sent to Afghanistan to help women train in the art of bozkashi, or "goat grab-bing." The sport, dating back centuries, is played when riders catch or grab a goat carcass and attempt to put it into a goal. Like cirit, bozkashi is traditionally a male sport played on horseback. And like their coun-terparts in Turkey, the Afghan women who inherited Caspians used the horses to train in both sport and combat. In 2021, when Afghanistan's future was once again at stake, these women defeated members of the Taliban to take back their village.

During that Taliban takeover, a group of women escaped Afghanistan by running bravely through battlefields and smuggling themselves across borders to reach safety. Seventy of these young women came to Arizona State University to finish their studies, and two of them became my stu-dents. I met with them at the hotel in Phoenix where they were living and told them about my love of Caspian horses. Their grief-stricken faces lit up.

"You ride? You know Caspians?" Samira gasped. A shy young woman who was studying economics, Samira's round face and thick, straight hair reminded me of old Persian paintings featuring scenes from the *Shahnameh*, the *Book of Kings*. In an uncanny coincidence, Samira was from the same village in northern Afghanistan where Mina and her army had trained for years.

"Those little horses kept my entire village safe," she said. "Men and yes, women, use them for everything from trading to spying to fighting."

Zahra, Samira's roommate, was from Mazar-i-Sharif and had heard tales of the horses. She was as excited as I to hear Samira corroborate the legend. "I always heard about the horse soldiers but never knew it was true," she marveled.

"Most people think they were all men," Samira said, casting her emerald-green eyes down. "But they weren't. It was the women who were badasses."

"Of course it was the women," Zahra said. She stroked Samira's back and leaned her forehead on her friend's shoulder. "Look at all of us." She gestured to the dozen other Afghan women in the hotel lobby. A group of twenty-five Afghan refugees had joined Arizona State to finish their studies when the universities closed to women earlier that year. "It's the women who carry strength"—her voice dropped to a whisper—"more than the men. Always."

But what continued to plague me was the mystery of the studbook.

Puzzled, I finally called Liz Webster in England, one of Louise's oldest friends and the secretary of the US branch of the International Caspian Horse Society. I asked if she would help me sort through all the stories I'd been told but couldn't make sense of. I would be in London for work the following week, and Liz agreed to travel from her home in Somerset to meet me in Chelsea.

We sat outside at a café near the Chelsea football stadium. Liz's blue eyes and white-blonde hair reminded me of Louise. But it was the calming demeanor and good-natured humor she shared with our mutual friend that made my heart ache. I wished Louise was with us.

We ordered wine, and Liz shared her own stories to help fill in the gaps in my research.

"Liz, I'm sorry to have to ask you this," I said at last, stiffening and suddenly nervous. By now, I knew that even uttering the word "studbook" could send people spiraling in about a million different highly charged directions. I had never wanted to ask Liz or Brenda because I didn't want them to get the impression that I was only after the studbook like so many greedy Americans. But I hoped by this point I had earned their trust. I took a deep breath and voiced the question I had been longing to ask for more than a year. "Do you know where *the original* is?"

"What, the studbook?" she asked. "Why, it's right here in England. Just up at Brenda's place in Bury, at the farm."

The piercing sound of glass shattering on the patio turned all eyes on us. It took a moment for me to realize that I had been the one to drop my drink. I froze as waiters scurried about picking up the pieces around us.

Liz remained unperturbed, slathering a slice of bread with cheese before continuing. "Well, yes, of course Brenda and I have it. Louise gave it to us during the Iran-Iraq War for safekeeping. I can show it to you if you like."

My eyes widened, and my heart was pounding. *Had I truly found the studbook at last? Had it been sitting in Manchester all this time? How had no one I interviewed known it was there? And why had Liz taken so long to tell me?*

"My dear, I had to be sure you weren't one of the crazy ones," Liz said, reading my mind. "I couldn't just tell you where the studbook was until I was sure you weren't going to come and steal it. I can't tell you how many people want to own it. I suppose because it's such a romantic story, the story of the Caspian. Everyone wants to own that romantic history."

"So, you and Brenda own it?"

"No, my dear. We take *care* of it. That's why we put it online, so it can live on. And when we can ensure it will be safe in Iran, we will return it to its rightful—well, original—home.

"There are claims it's fake because there are errors. A horse is listed as a Blue Rhone when it should be Speckled Gray. One is listed as a Sorrel, but it should be Chestnut. Some of the measurements are wrong, and on and on. Okay, yes, two old women make mistakes based on the information we're given or based on hard-to-read handwriting. But that doesn't mean we're frauds."

Liz made a fair point, but I could also understand people's skepticism. Before I could ask her to, she was dialing Brenda's phone number.

"Brenda, dear, I'm with Pardis, Louise's friend. I just learned that she is Maryam's granddaughter."

My heart was in my throat. These women had known my grandmother, too? Everything was slowly, very slowly, coming into focus. Liz put the phone on speaker.

"Pardis, dear, is that true? Are you really the descendant of Maryam, the great warrior woman?" I heard the familiar crackle of Brenda's voice.

"How did you know my grandmother?" I whispered. My voice was trembling with excitement.

"Louise talked often about Maryam. She was a big part of the story of the Caspian horse. We never met her, but we knew all about her," Liz said. The puzzle pieces were falling into place for her more quickly than for me.

I sat silently, taking it all in.

"So, you really are a Gordafarid?" Brenda said.

"Brenda," Liz interjected, "it's time to pull out the studbook."

THE STUDBOOK'S green and gold cover shimmered in Brenda Dalton's trembling hands as she held it up to the camera. I leaned in close to my computer until my nose was almost touching the screen. We had arranged this Zoom date because Brenda was too frail for visitors, but she and Liz understood how much I wanted to see the book.

"Could you . . . could you open it for me?" I asked, my voice quivering.

"Of course, dearie. But I'll warn you, Louise's penmanship isn't the greatest," Brenda said, smiling.

"Because she was more interested in chasing horses than in school, right?" I said, returning the smile. Louise had told me this herself, and later Brenda would recount Louise's words in her memoir.

Brenda opened the book, taking great care not to crack the spine. Each delicate parchment page seemed to sing with history, even on Zoom.

"Oh, look, it's Shahrya," she said, pointing to a line of Louise's slanted handwriting.

SHAHRYA: MARE. SIRED BY OSTAD. SPECKLED GRAY

"Sounds like a real beauty."

"She was," Brenda replied. "At least Her Royal Highness Princess Anne thought so. Shahrya became her horse."

I asked Brenda to flip to the front of the book, or, rather, the back, as Iranians open books from left to right so they can write from right to left. There, we scrutinized the Persian writing that definitely did not belong to Louise.

"Someone else must have written this part," Brenda said.

"I think it was my grandmother Maryam."

Seeing the studbook, the very pages my grandmother had written so long ago, flung me back in time. Suddenly, I was crying, tears running down my cheeks and onto my keyboard. I would never understand the true significance of these incredible horses, let alone my family's story, my story, unless I went all the way back to the beginning. I hadn't gone far enough. Not yet.

I returned to the notes from Louise and her team of archaeologists and historians, tracing the identities and lineages of the horses. In her own research, Louise learned that the ancient Greeks had been impressed with Persian horses—Caspians, she realized—and had praised them for their unusual size and speed. Writing in the sixth century BCE, Timotheus of Gaza described two different horse breeds he observed in the region that today is known as Kermanshah in northern and western Iran. Timotheus wrote that "the horses of the Medes are of moderate size with small ears and heads unlike those of a horse: they are courageous but tire easily in the heat through difficulty in breathing. The Nisaean horses are remarkable for their great size and feet that shake the earth."

Most of the breeds in the Middle East are descendants of those two ancient types. The Oriental horse, as it was termed until the nineteenth century, is now called the Plateau Persian in Iran. The modern Caspian is the descent of the Nisaean of the Achaemenians, a stocky horse with strong bones and a short neck and back. In her diary, Louise wrote about this lineage:

By now I had been in Iran for ten years and, spurred on by my fascination with the archaic forms of horses I saw around me, had read many of the books on Persia's history that were in Shahzadeh [her sister-in-law] and Narcy's libraries. Shahzadeh and Safiyeh Khanum [Louise's mother-in-law] were also ardent collectors of ancient artefacts dug up by amateur archaeologists, better known as grave robbers. Legitimate archaeologists were regular guests at dinner and tales were told of strange finds and lost civilizations. My fascination with bones was dismissed although I gradually found myself consulted on Lorestan horse bits and the identity of animals in carvings and seals.

Through her in-laws, Louise had met well-known archaeologists from Harvard, the University of Pennsylvania, and Oxford. David Stronach and Carl Lamberg-Karlovsky were two archaeologists whom Louise followed on digs in Azerbaijan, Kurdistan, and Iran. It was their work that led her to begin piecing together that the history of the Caspian horse was tied not only to the history of the Persian Empire but to that of the Greeks and Ottomans as well. This was the horse who had ridden through it all. Revolution. War. Conquest.

In going back through Louise's notes and her leather-bound journal, the one emblazed with a horse, I realized she'd told me exactly where and how to start; I just hadn't been ready to listen. "To understand the Caspian horse, you have to start at the beginning," Louise had written in her letter to me. I was trying now to do just that. But was I missing something still?

2022

IN JANUARY 2022, I RECEIVED AN INVITATION FROM ONE OF THE Yoruk women I had met in Turkey the previous year. Banu wrote about a ride that she and five others would soon be embarking on that would take them to the northeasternmost part of Turkey and up the jagged peak of Mount Ararat. Did I want to join them? she asked.

Did I ever. In fact, I couldn't think of a better way to heed Louise's words than to ride with a group of fierce horsewomen to the final resting place of Noah's Ark and the possible cradle of civilization. I booked my passage to Dogubeyazid the next morning.

To get there, I would first have to travel through Van, which proved to be an adventure in and of itself. The town, named for the largest lake in Turkey, sits at the water's edge, surrounded by mountains. A Turkish friend of mine who was interested in visiting Mount Ararat joined me in Van. When our driver picked us up from the airport, he insisted on taking us straight to Lake Van, despite a cruel wind and a temperature below freezing. The lake is the pride and joy of the locals, he told us. Apparently, we couldn't pass through town without paying homage.

The loud, pulsing beat of a familiar Persian pop song greeted us as we stepped out of the car. Docked in the water was a boat with two blasting speakers and a group of men and women dancing onboard, gyrating their hips through layers of wool coats, hats, and scarves. Drawn to the music, the people, and the idea of twirling my way across the largest lake in Turkey, I couldn't help but sway my hips as I headed for the dock. I wanted to know who these people were and if they might let me join them. The driver and my friend followed along.

It was a tour group of Iranian vacationers, who had come to Van to celebrate Nowruz, the Persian New Year and my favorite holiday. I love that the holiday is an announcement of a "new day," which is the literal translation of "Nowruz." It's a new season and a new year full of new chances.

"Nowruz mobarak!" the Iranians called to one another, and I allowed myself to be enveloped in the moment. Everyone assumed I was part of the tour group, and I made no effort to correct them—I was too busy savoring this unexpected opportunity to celebrate Nowruz with fellow Iranians; it had been so long.

The boat floated across the lake and then deposited us back at our starting point. I bid my fellow countrymen good-bye, and my friend and I continued on our way north from Lake Van to Dogubeyazid. As we drove through the mountains, all my adrenaline from the fresh air and dancing on the boat evaporated, and I remembered how jetlagged I was. Soon, I was fast asleep. I woke as we slowed to a stop and rubbed my eyes. The craterlike top of Mount Ararat burst through the cloud cover and filled my window. *Was I still dreaming?* The mountain's crown kissed the sky against a bursting sun. We had arrived.

At our hotel, I recognized the perplexed glances of the men who filled the lobby. It was the same look I'd gotten on the flight to Van. On the plane, I was a woman traveling alone among a sea of men. Fortunately, upon arrival, my Turkish friend helped translate our presence, and together we made our way to a bar with live music. We pushed past throngs of men to find two tables in the back filled with women—we'd never met any of these women before. We were strangers who happened to be in the same place at the same time, but it didn't matter—they stood to embrace us like old friends. We were women out and about in a male-dominated town. That was enough. Before I knew it, we were sharing glasses of whiskey and vodka that smelled like what I imagine my grandmother's home brew might have.

"So, what are you doing here?" a woman named Mona asked me through half-drunken, lowered lids. Her blue eyes reminded me of Lake Van.

"I'm visiting," I yelled over the music. Mona slid close.

"Yes, visiting from the States, I think?" she said, speaking carefully into my ear and then pulling back to look me in the eye. She tossed her hair behind her bare shoulders, and I caught a scent of something like peaches and jasmine. I nodded slowly, not wanting to break eye contact.

"I came to find the horses," I told her.

"The horses?" Mona arched a perfectly groomed eyebrow. Her blue eyes began to shimmer in the pulsing bar light.

"They're my legacy," I ventured. I had to remind myself to breathe.

Mona chewed on her lower lip and leaned back, taking me in. It was her turn to nod slowly.

"Then you must ride into the past. That's where you'll find answers." She lit a cigarette and pressed it to my lips, our intimacy solidified both by everything (two vocal women in a land inhospitable to our kind) and by nothing (two strangers in a bar).

It was good advice. It also wasn't the first time I'd heard it. Exactly sixteen years ago, when I'd asked Louise what she was doing in my father's hometown, she'd said the same thing.

"I RODE into the past. Rode into Persia. And settled here," Louise told me. It was 2006, the day before Nowruz, and I had left my work in Tehran for a short trip to visit Louise. She and I decided to celebrate the holiday with a two-day ride in the moss-covered steppe plains that frame the Caspian Sea. We rode through small villages where horse-drawn carriages still outnumbered cars, and I smiled at the children splashing in the creeks and open sewers—or juubs—that wound their way along the roadside. Olive trees provided shade on the village paths and gave way to open rice paddies where women worked with babies tied to their backs.

"When you ride through rice paddies or rows of corn and see them," Louise said, pointing to the women in the field, "the temptation is to think, 'Thank goodness we don't have to work like that anymore.'"

I turned my head to face her, but Mumtaz, the mare I was riding and struggling to get along with, tossed her head and shoulders and catapulted me forward. Louise's white stallion, Hafez, was an alpha male who was never bashful about his size or stature, and now he watched Mumtaz and me, unfazed, content to go right on swishing his silver tail back and forth, quietly swatting away flies. I squeezed Mumtaz gently and dug my fists into her mane to get her to settle. We rode back to Louise, who continued talking as if nothing had happened.

"That's the kind of thing my mom would always say when we moved from Virginia to New Hampshire. She'd say, 'Thank goodness we are in the modern world now.'" Louise rode Hafez in circles around me as she spoke, but Mumtaz paid her no mind, rooting her hoofs deeper into the earth, unwilling to budge.

"When I first got to Iran, I was torn between Iran and Persia. Iran was the shimmering dinner parties, Persia the roadside villages."

"I came expecting to fall in love with Iran," I agreed. "And I did. But then I started falling for Persia."

"Exactly, kid." Louise winked at me. She gave Mumtaz a slap on her hind legs, and now we were both off and running, splashing through the rice paddies at a heart-accelerating speed.

"Modernity is a tempting and fickle bitch," Louise called over her shoulder. I squeezed Mumtaz with all the strength I could muster from my thighs to my heels, desperate to catch up to Louise and hang on to her every word.

"You came for the techno parties of Tehran, did you not?" she asked rhetorically. "I can see how those are seductive. But there are things that the glitz and glamour of progress lose. Or forget."

"Like what?" I asked.

She pulled Hafez to a halt, and Mumtaz stopped instinctively. Louise shifted her weight and placed a long leg up on the saddle so she could turn and face me. She held up her left hand and began counting with her thumb.

"First, connection with the earth. Look, it's Nowruz, and the earth is changing, stopping, healing. But in the quest for modernity, we miss these delicate moments." She lifted her index finger. "Second, the will to survive. You see these glass snakes, the legless lizards crawling over one another to get to the water in the rice fields? They are like the women who crouch by the roadside selling fruits. They have a strength that no one at any of your techno parties does, a resilience and hunger for life." She unfurled her middle finger. "And third, third is that sense of peace and community. That being in the flow of the universe. With the seasons. With others whose feet sink into the ground."

"So, we should pull these threads through, then? Pull the past into the present?" I asked tentatively.

"Iran is the heart, but Persia is the soul. You need both. You must find the connective tissue."

In the smoky bar sitting next to Mona, I was celebrating two Nowruz holidays, the present one and that fateful one sixteen years earlier. Stepping back into Persia through the stories of the Caspian horse was my best chance of understanding my past and my best hope for my future.

Sitting in that bar with its view of Mount Ararat, I realized that the war inside me was so much bigger than just me—it's the same war that has always raged through time: battles between the old and the new stoked by the flames of thwarted passion. Clashes that bifurcated the past and the present instead of the strength of one providing the foundation for the other so that an even stronger future might take hold. This was what the mighty Caspian has been trying to show us with its forged path full of twists and turns, which have nonetheless never stopped pulling the power and might of empires into tomorrow.

Iran owed its Persian soul to the Caspian horse.

The Caspian reflects Persia—a place where women warriors best domineering men, where those with reverence for the earth and each of its seasons win the day.

When the world stands divided, pushing and pulling between progress and stasis, the Caspian reminds us that there is always connective tissue that links the past to the future and can help us heal in the present.

DEEP IN whiskey-soaked dreams, my alarm blared in my ear. I hit snooze and tried to pull myself awake and into the present. The hypnotic energy of the bar from the night before and the spark of connection with Mona had devolved into a dry mouth and piercing headache. But whether I felt like it or not, the horses were calling. It was time to ride.

Our group shivered in the early-morning cold despite our coats and our fur-lined hats and how close we clung to the horses, who were draped in thick felt. Mount Ararat rose stark and white against the crisp azure sky, and we could hear jackals crying in the distance. Riding a tall and slender black stallion named Kaveh, Banu had tied the traditional floral Yoruk scarves to almost every part of her body, and the colorful fabric billowed in the wind as Kaveh pounded up the jagged mountainside. Banu was a bright rainbow beacon, and I was happy to be following her again.

My horse, Javan, was a younger, feistier version of Louise's stallions, and he was ready to take off the moment I swung my body atop his. Our rearing energies would have been a recipe for a potentially disastrous fall, but the snow slowed us both down. The fearsome weather was good for something after all. My body was so cold I couldn't get any of my muscles to grip or kick with my usual force. The wind whipped at my cheeks and turned them red. My eyes, still sore from the smoke in the bar, watered, and the moisture froze my eyelashes. Hours passed, and I lost feeling in my hands. I dug them into Javan's fur, and he careened faster toward the peak. And then, finally, we slowed, and Banu called out *"iiiiiisst"* to signal a collective halt.

We were at the top of a cliff, inches from the deep. Banu slid off Kaveh and tied his reins to a rock. I worried swinging my leg to dismount would send Javan over the literal edge, but I had no choice. Thankfully, he was as concerned about the cliff's edge as I was and stood motionless as I slid down his back.

Banu called me over. She pointed to an enormous formation that appeared to be growing out of the mountainside but looked as if it might also be partially man-made. It was an oval-like mound, easily the size of two football fields if not more.

"That's Durupinar, our site," Banu explained. "It's 164 meters and made of limonite. Legend tells us that what we are looking at is the final resting place of Noah's Ark."

Maybe it really was only lore, and it was just a coincidence that this rocklike structure had the same dimensions as the ark and was located where stories told us its final resting place was. But even from this distance, it was impossible not to feel the magic of the spot, the horses utterly still, all of us holding our breath.

From Durupinar, Iran was just five miles to the south; Armenia, thirty miles to the north; while we technically stood on Turkish ground. So many empires had come through this spot—building, destroying, and rebuilding as they went. Maybe this wasn't the cradle of civilization, but there was no denying it was the cradle of empires.

Meanwhile, Afghanistan, a thousand miles to the east, had become the graveyard of empires. On my way here, I'd had a connecting flight at John F. Kennedy Airport in New York City, and as I had wound my way through the hallways and terminals, I had seen dozens of Afghan refugees with identification cards dangling from their necks. There were men, women, and children, and they carried only small handbags and matching plastic "UNHCR" bags. One small group sat on the floor huddled over a stack of papers. I knew Dari, and overheard bits of their conversation. The airlines appeared to have gotten their names wrong, and now they did not know which family was supposed to transit to which US city.

I sat down with them to see how I might be able to help and expected to see pangs of grief and fear on their faces but instead saw hope. Their eyes betrayed fatigue, but their resolve and resilience shone brighter.

"The Taliban are the latest to threaten us and our people, but we Afghans have survived much worse," one woman said to me, her sleeping son cradled in her arms.

"Iranians, too," I replied. She held my gaze, and we understood each other.

"The crash of conflict doesn't always destroy," she went on, gathering her things and standing, ready now to find her flight to Detroit. "Sometimes it brings strength."

I nodded, feeling the pulse of intergenerational strength I had inherited from my grandmother Maryam and the long line of women who had come before either of us. It coursed through my veins, and I knew a similar unstoppable force coursed through this Afghan woman, too. For so much of my life, I had been preoccupied with the intergenerational trauma I'd inherited from parents who escaped revolution. But reconnecting with this wave of power, which had seen every kind of trauma and refused to be kept down, quickened my pulse and gave me new life.

Something in the woman's face reminded me of the pictures I had seen of Mina, the commander of the all-female Afghan army. The Afghans were gathering in groups now to disperse to their respective gates, and I thought about the wave of refugees who had arrived in 2001. No doubt they too had walked these same halls, while back home Mina and her women prepared their horses to serve with the American special forces in the early days of the War on Terror. And now here we were, all these years later, and Afghans were still being displaced, leaving their homes behind.

In 2021, on the twentieth anniversary of 9/11, we saw a Taliban resurgence after two decades of American military operations. The US withdrawal of troops and subsequent takeover of Afghanistan by the Taliban—while no surprise to refugees like those I met at the airport—have caused some Americans, at least, to reconsider our recent history. My time in Iran and Afghanistan led me back to policy work in DC, where I met diplomats and military members who continue to puzzle over the challenge of the past two decades. When five-star generals returning from Afghanistan ask me, "What do you think went wrong?" I tell them the story of the feminist horsewomen. I tell them that this all-female army knew every inch of the terrain they were fighting and, more important, knew the Taliban, inside and out.

There are many questions about what went wrong with the US presence in Afghanistan and what is to come now. But in addition to the strategic and tactical analysis that is emerging and will continue to, a twist on the Sun Tzu adage "Know thy enemy" provides another insight. The Americans didn't know their enemy. Worse, they didn't know their friends.

Mina and her women warriors would have been ongoing, steady supporters of the American special forces had they not chosen to align instead with the all-male Northern Alliance. The women living in the caves and smokestacks of the jagged mountains of northern Afghanistan with their sure-footed horses knew more about the ground beneath them, the rhythms of the seasons, and the subtle nuances necessary to overcome an enemy like the Taliban. Had they not proved this by repeatedly defeating the Taliban and holding their part of the country safe from brutality, all while providing safe haven and rejuvenation for women with no place else to go?

Yet still these women remain in the shadows. In the retelling of the now declassified story of the American horse soldiers, including in the film *12 Strong,* the women have been erased. The story told was by men about men.

There is little question that the United States has always known too little about Afghanistan. When they captured prisoners, Arabic translators greeted them at Guantánamo, never mind that Dari and Pashtu are the languages spoken. The focus of the American military was always the weather and the geography, but the people, the ideologies of the Taliban, eluded them and continue to do so.

The women who did know and who remain—my family, past and present—have been finding ways to fight oppression for generations and may still hold a key to bringing peace. If only we might learn from the stories of the Caspian and the women who ride them. Let these female warriors who are battling ISIS in Turkey and Iraq and those who are pushing back the Taliban in Afghanistan show us the way forward: fighting side by side with allies who come in all shapes and sizes, with experience and knowledge unlike anything we have known, because that is, after all, the point. Women allies. Equine allies.

As Louise wrote in 2004, "The story of the Caspian horse is my legacy and has bought me a front row seat to understanding the fighting blood that runs through my veins." It is also the story of how a herd of horses helped transform women into fighters who are defeating enemies that even the most powerful armies in the West haven't been able to combat successfully.

As WE followed Banu from the Turkish-Iranian border into Armenia and then on to Azerbaijan, I kept thinking of my grandmother Maryam and her mother, riding Javan's great-great-grandfather Sohrab, through the same climbing hills and blooming fields. I pictured Louise here too, her brown leather bag sloshing with sperm from her stallions, driving a herd of Turkoman and Caspian horses across the border to ensure that history would live on, no matter how many revolutions the future brought. I could almost hear their voices in the wind, calling to me. And then I thought of a passage from Louise's diary: *There is Persia and there is Iran. One is the soul, the other the heart. And you need both to truly live.*

We ended our ride just north of Baku, the capital of Azerbaijan, in a town called Nardaran that hugged the edge of the Caspian Sea. I climbed down from Javan and stood staring out at the calm water, wishing I could swim all the way to Iran, the cradle of my story. Javan trotted past me into the sea, splashing about and tossing his wet mane proudly. *When I was broken, it was the Caspian that healed me*, my grandmother and aunts had told me. All my life I had thought they meant the sea, but now I know the truth.

Acknowledgments

Tears of joy, laughter, and sorrow nearly drowned my keyboard as I wrote this book. But none of it would have been possible without the support of my friends, family, and editorial team.

Saira Rao was the first person to hear my idea for *Book of Queens*, and it was her infectious enthusiasm for the project that carried me through the whole way. My agent is my soul sister without whom this book would not exist. To Victoria Loustalot who is an editor, mentor, coach, and so much more, words will never be able to express the depth of my gratitude. And my editor, Mollie Weisenfeld, and the entire team at Hachette have been an absolute dream to work with.

My close friends Erin Runions, Riva Kantowitz, Yasmin Michael, Traci Moser, and Kimber McKay kept me laughing when the weight of the story sometimes overwhelmed me. Dick Nodell and Barry Glassner provided key guidance and insights throughout the process. My brothers, Paymohn and Paasha, have always been my biggest fans. They chase away my internal critic when it threatens to take hold of me. My parents, Fereshteh and Mahmood, are a never-ending source of love. And my children, Tara, Shayan, and Raami, are my reason for writing when I want to give up, my inspiration, my support, my biggest joy.

ACKNOWLEDGMENTS

To my grandmother Maryam and to my fairy godmother, Louise, I owe endless debts of gratitude. I know they have reunited with each other and their many Caspian horses in death. My heart swells each time I think of these horsewomen warriors.

And finally, to the horses. Who keep me galloping into the future, while never forgetting my past.

Notes

PROLOGUE

1. The all-female Afghan army that I write about in this book are the ancestors of Afghan army women fighting the Taliban today. More about them can be found at www.voanews.com/a/former-afghan-female -soldier-i-am-so-afraid-under-taliban-/6376154.html.

MARYAM, 1926

1. www.iranchamber.com/calendar/converter/iranian_calendar_converter .php.

2008

1. Mullah Omar was a leader of the Taliban since the late 1970s. More information about him can be found at www.britannica.com /biography/Mohammad-Omar.

Bibliography

Abrahamian, E. *Iran Between Two Revolutions*. Princeton Studies on the Near East. Princeton, NJ: Princeton University Press, 1982.

———. *Khomeinism: Essays on the Islamic Republic*. London: I. B. Tauris, 1993.

———. *Radical Islam: The Iranian Mojahedin*. Society and Culture in the Modern Middle East. London: Tauris, 1988.

Abu-Lughod, L. *Remaking Women: Feminism and Modernity in the Middle East*. Princeton Studies in Culture/Power/History. Princeton, NJ: Princeton University Press, 1998.

———. *Veiled Sentiments: Honor and Poetry in a Bedouin Society*. Rev. ed. Berkeley: University of California Press, 1999.

———. *Writing Women's Worlds: Bedouin Stories*. Berkeley: University of California Press, 1993.

Ahmed, L. *A Border Passage: From Cairo to America—A Woman's Journey*. New York: Penguin Books, 2000.

———. *Women and Gender in Islam: Historical Roots of a Modern Debate*. New Haven, CT: Yale University Press, 1992.

Alavi, N. *We Are Iran: The Persian Blogs*. Brooklyn: Soft Skull Press, 2005.

Allyn, D. *Make Love, Not War: The Sexual Revolution, an Unfettered History*. Boston: Little, Brown, 2000.

Altinay, A. G. *The Myth of the Military-Nation: Militarism, Gender, and Education in Turkey*. New York: Palgrave Macmillan, 2004.

Anderson, B. *Imagined Communities: Reflections on the Origin and Spread of Nationalism*. Rev. ed. London: Verso, 1991.

Asayesh, G. *Saffron Sky: A Life Between Iran and America*. Boston: Beacon Press, 1999.

Azoy, G. Whitney. *Buzkashi: Game and Power in Afghanistan*. New York: Waveland Press, 2002.

Bahrampour, T. *To See and See Again: A Life in Iran and America*. Berkeley: University of California Press, 2000.

Basmenji, K. *Tehran Blues: Youth Culture in Iran*. Tehran: Saqi Books, 2006.

Bird, C. *Neither East nor West: One Woman's Journey Through the Islamic Republic of Iran*. New York: Pocket Books, 2001.

Boyarin, D. *Carnal Israel: Reading Sex in Talmudic Culture*. Berkeley: University of California Press, 1993.

De Bellaigue, C. *In the Rose Garden of the Martyrs: A Memoir of Iran*. New York: HarperCollins, 2005.

Dumas, F. *Funny in Farsi: A Memoir of Growing Up Iranian in America*. New York: Villard, 2003.

Escoffier, J. *Sexual Revolution*. New York: Thunder's Mouth Press, distributed by Publishers Group West, 2003.

Esposito, J. L., and N. J. DeLong-Bas. *Women in Muslim Family Law*. 2nd ed. Contemporary Issues in the Middle East. Syracuse, NY: Syracuse University Press, 2001.

Esposito, J. L., Middle East Institute (Washington, DC), Johns Hopkins University, School of Advanced International Studies, and Royal Institute of International Affairs. *The Iranian Revolution: Its Global Impact*. Miami: Florida International University Press, 1990.

BIBLIOGRAPHY

Esposito, J. L., and R. K. Ramazani. *Iran at the Crossroads*. New York: Palgrave, 2001.

Farrer, J. *Opening Up: Youth Sex Culture and Market Reform in Shanghai*. Chicago: University of Chicago Press, 2002.

Ferdowsi, A. *Shahnameh: The Book of Kings*. Translated by D. Davis and A. Nafisi. New York: Viking Press, 2006.

Firouz, L., and B. Dalton. *Riding Through Revolution*. New York: Advance Global, 2013.

Foucault, M. *The History of Sexuality*. New York: Vintage Books, 1988.

Giddens, A. *The Transformation of Intimacy: Sexuality, Love, and Eroticism in Modern Societies*. Stanford, CA: Stanford University Press, 1993.

Haeri, S. *Law of Desire: Temporary Marriage in Shi'i Iran*. Contemporary Issues in the Middle East. Syracuse, NY: Syracuse University Press, 1989.

———. *No Shame for the Sun: Lives of Professional Pakistani Women*. Gender, Culture, and Politics in the Middle East. Syracuse, NY: Syracuse University Press, 2002.

Hakakian, R. *Journey from the Land of No: A Girlhood Caught in Revolutionary Iran*. New York: Crown, 2004.

Hassan-Kakar, M. *A Political and Diplomatic History of Afghanistan, 1863–1901*. London: Brill, 2006.

Kandiyoti, D. *Gendering the Middle East: Emerging Perspectives*. Gender, Culture, and Politics in the Middle East. Syracuse, NY: Syracuse University Press, 1996.

———. *Major Issues on the Status of Women in Turkey: Approaches and Priorities; Ankara Seminar, January 11–13, 1980*. Ankara: Turkish Social Science Association, 1980.

———. *Women, Islam and the State*. Women in the Political Economy. Houndmills, Basingstoke, Hampshire: Macmillan, 1991.

Keddie, N. R. *Religion and Politics in Iran: Shi'ism from Quietism to Revolution*. New Haven, CT: Yale University Press, 1983.

BIBLIOGRAPHY

———. *Scholars, Saints, and Sufis: Muslim Religious Institutions in the Middle East Since 1500*. Berkeley: University of California Press, 1972.

Keddie, N. R., and B. Baron. *Women in Middle Eastern History: Shifting Boundaries in Sex and Gender*. New Haven, CT: Yale University Press, 1991.

Keddie, N. R., and E. J. Hooglund. *The Iranian Revolution & the Islamic Republic*. New ed. Contemporary Issues in the Middle East. Syracuse, NY: Syracuse University Press, 1986.

Keddie, N. R., and R. P. Matthee. *Iran and the Surrounding World: Interactions in Culture and Cultural Politics*. Seattle: University of Washington Press, 2002.

Keddie, N. R., and Y. Richard. *Modern Iran: Roots and Results of Revolution*. New Haven, CT: Yale University Press, 2003.

———. *Roots of Revolution: An Interpretive History of Modern Iran*. New Haven, CT: Yale University Press, 1981.

Khaldun, I. *The Muqaddimah: An Introduction to History*. Edited by N. J. Dawood. Translated by F. Rosenthal. Princeton, NJ: Princeton University Press, 2015.

Macintyre, B. *The Man Who Would Be King: The First American in Afghanistan*. New York: Farrar, Strauss & Giroux, 2005.

Mernissi, F. *Beyond the Veil: Male-Female Dynamics in Modern Muslim Society*. Rev. ed. Bloomington: Indiana University Press, 1987.

———. *Islam and Democracy: Fear of the Modern World*. Rev. ed. Cambridge, MA: Perseus, 2002.

———. *Women and Islam: An Historical and Theological Inquiry*. New Delhi: Kali for Women, 1993.

———. *Women's Rebellion & Islamic Memory*. London: Zed Books, 1996.

Moaveni, A. *Lipstick Jihad: A Memoir of Growing Up Iranian in America and American in Iran*. New York: PublicAffairs, 2005.

Molavi, A. *The Soul of Iran: A Nation's Journey to Freedom*. New York: W. W. Norton, 2002.

BIBLIOGRAPHY

Nafisi, A. *Reading Lolita in Tehran: A Memoir in Books.* New York: Random House, 2004.

Najmabadi, A. *The Story of the Daughters of Quchan: Gender and National Memory in Iranian History.* Modern Intellectual and Political History of the Middle East. Syracuse, NY: Syracuse University Press, 1998.

———. *Women with Mustaches and Men Without Beards: Gender and Sexual Anxieties of Iranian Modernity.* Berkeley: University of California Press, 2005.

———. *Women's Autobiographies in Contemporary Iran.* Harvard Middle Eastern Monographs, vol. 25. Cambridge, MA: Distributed for the Center for Middle Eastern Studies of Harvard University by Harvard University Press, 1990.

Rashid, A. *Descent into Chaos: Pakistan, Afghanistan and the Threat to Global Security.* New York: Penguin Press, 2009.

Rosaldo, R. *Culture & Truth: The Remaking of Social Analysis.* Rev. ed. Boston: Beacon Press, 1993.

Satrapi, M. *Persepolis: The Story of a Childhood.* New York: Pantheon Books, 2003.

Shahidian, H. *Women in Iran.* Contributions in Women's Studies, no. 197. Westport, CT: Greenwood Press, 2002.

Stanton, D. *12 Strong: The Declassified True Story of the Horse Soldiers.* New York: Scribner, 2017.